D0861987

Assessing the Developing Child Musician

A GUIDE FOR GENERAL MUSIC TEACHERS

Assessing the Developing Child Musician

A

GUIDE

FOR

GENERAL

MUSIC

TEACHERS

GIA Publications, Inc.
Chicago

To my wife, Emmie.

Library of Congress Cataloging-in-Publication Data

Brophy, Timothy S., 1952-
      Assessing the developing child musician : a guide for general music
   teachers / Timothy S. Brophy.
      p. cm.
      Includes bibliographical references and index.
      ISBN 1-57999-090-8 (hardcover)
      1. School music—Instruction and study. 2. Musical ability in children.
   I. Title.

MT1 .B788 2000
780'.71'073—dc21   00-037631

Table of Contents

Acknowledgements

Special thanks to these colleagues who contributed their work to this book:

Carol King – *"A Bunch of Balloons"*

Paul Lehman - *Sample Fourth Grade Music Report*

Ann Okins – *Descriptive scoring guide for vocal pitch accuracy assessment*

Joanne Rutkowski – *The Singing Voice Development Measure*

Nancy Schkurman – *Special seating charts used in the Clark County, Nevada public schools*

Peter Webster – *For sharing his e-mail address and web site with the readers of this book*

Special thanks to my students, past and present, who contributed their work to this book:

Whitney Adsit	Andrea Jernigan
Robert Baddour	Alaina Kunz
Pooja Bhagat	Dan Ying Liu
Leath Bing	David Mann
Hailey Burton	Megan McGlown
Whitney Camp	Rachel McMillan
Joshua Cotton	Sally Morrell
John Dean	Casey O'Rourke
Adrian Doggrell	Alanna Stewart
Becca Foehring	Gail Stratton
Jonathan Friedman	Logan Tate
Douglass Godwin	Jacob Weinstein
Arundahti Gururajan	Kyle Youngblood
Thomas Hamilton	

Introduction

In 1994 the National Association for Music Education (MENC), in conjunction with the Consortium of National Arts Education Associations, cooperated in the publication of the landmark book entitled *National Standards for Arts Education: What Every Young American Should Know and Be Able to Do in the Arts.* This book set out specific content and achievement standards for each of the four artistic disciplines—music, visual arts, dance, and theatre—for pre-kindergarten through twelfth grades, which outline what every American's arts education should include. With the signing of the Goals 2000: Educate America Act by President Bill Clinton that same year, the arts became recognized as a core subject for the first time in the history of American education. The position of the arts in American public education has never been stronger.

In tandem with the growing adoption and implementation of the National Standards for the Arts throughout America's public and private school systems, standards-based reform has reshaped curricular content in all subject disciplines. States and local school districts are implementing new, higher standards for learning across all subject domains. An increasing number of states are incorporating the new and rigorous standards for music into their goals for students, and music curricula are being reviewed and reformulated across the country to help students achieve proficiency in demonstrating those standards. The new state and local standards for the artistic disciplines are being implemented with the expectation and understanding that student progress toward achievement of those standards will be assessed in the classroom and reported to parents.

In 1996 MENC published a book of strategies to help music teachers assess their students' progress toward the National Standards for Music, entitled *Performance Standards for Music Grades PreK-12: Strategies and Benchmarks for Assessing Progress*

Toward the National Standards. This excellent publication not only provides specific assessment strategies, but it has helped many music teachers get started on their way to developing appropriate assessment procedures for their daily classroom use. At the time this book goes to press, MENC is engaged in the "Benchmark Performances in Music" project, which will result in a series of nine books, one for each of the nine National Standards for Music, that will publish benchmark responses to the 1996 Performance Standards publication.

Assessment in general music is complicated by several issues, such as the number of students served by the general music specialist, the nature of musical growth and development, and the number of learning areas addressed by the music curriculum. This book is not meant to be a review of musical tests and measurements (there are fine books on this subject already), but rather a guide for present and future general music teachers who desire to strengthen the classroom assessment component of their programs through the design and implementation of appropriate, meaningful tasks.

This book is specifically designed for general music teachers whose teaching assignments often include hundreds of students from kindergarten through grade eight. The task design elements, implementation and administration procedures, management and data collection suggestions, assessment models and techniques have all arisen from my own music teaching experience and research and have been shown to be effective in the music classroom. Though the student examples presented in the text represent the work of students no older than sixth grade, the assessment models, techniques, and design procedures presented throughout are adaptable to any grade level of general music through the twelfth grade.

There is an old proverb that says, "If you give a person a fish he will have food for one day; if you teach a person to fish he will have food for a lifetime." This book is not a collection of prepared assessment tasks (although there are tasks throughout the book used as examples), nor does it claim to hold answers to every assessment problem or need that may arise. Instead, this book seeks to give pre-service and practicing general music teachers a foundation in classroom music assessment. It also provides techniques and models for classroom-level assessment task and program design, development, and implementation that can be adapted to fit varying music curricula in districts throughout the United States and in other countries.

Chapter 1

Foundations for Assessment in General Music

Across America, music teachers at all levels are finding themselves increasingly responsible for maintaining accurate records of the progress of their students. The extent to which this is happening is not entirely known, but it is clear that the new standards and academic expectations that are the hallmark of the education reform of the late twentieth and early twenty-first centuries require new and more thorough measures of progress record keeping and reporting in all knowledge domains. In general music, the responsibility for a well-planned classroom assessment program falls upon the general music specialist.

This chapter opens by examining some of the philosophical questions whose answers can provide teachers with the reasons and motivation for assessment in the general music classroom. Philosophy serves to explore the fundamental issues that form the foundation for one's motivation for becoming a music teacher and seeks answers to the questions regarding the purpose and function of music education in contemporary society. One's personal philosophy of music education shapes one's every action as a music education professional, including one's attitude toward and implementation of the assessment component of a music program.

Why Assess at All?

Assessment is important to general music teachers because it provides an opportunity to obtain evidence of the musical growth and progress of students. Regular assessments provide data that help to support the musical decisions that teachers make every day, from the selection of special performing groups to the reporting of musical progress to parents. For example, if a teacher is challenged by a parent regarding the decision as to whether or not a third grade child is ready for a special enrichment class like a composer's club, the teacher can provide evidence collected during assessment activities that support the decision that was made. Additionally, when music teachers are armed with assessment data that demonstrate learning and student progress toward attaining educational standards, their programs are much more supportable when districts face budget cuts.

Assessment data can also be used to guide instruction and choice of teaching strategies. If the results of an assessment indicate that students have not achieved what is expected, teachers can use these results to help decide the next course of action. It may become clear that students need more experience with a particular skill or that a new strategy is necessary to help students obtain the skill, concept, or knowledge that is being assessed.

Another reason to assess students in general music is to further validate the music program with parents and students. There is no better advocacy for a music program than consistent assessment and parental reporting procedures. Through a well-structured assessment program, students also gain a sense of their own learning and progress. The general music class should be a place where there is creativity, joy, a high level of displayed musical skill, and *rigorous musical learning*. If students know that musical learning will be assessed and that the results of these assessments will be reported to their parents, the music class will take on a new sense of purpose for the children.

Regular assessment in general music also provides evidence for accountability of student learning. In situations where a music teacher's effectiveness may be called into question, evidence of student learning in the form of assessment data is extremely valuable. A well-designed and -executed assessment component is an asset to any general music curriculum and serves to help further establish the importance of the role of the general music specialist in the school (see Figure 1-1).

Why Assess at All?

- To obtain evidence of musical growth and progress
- To guide instruction and choice of teaching strategies
- To help validate the music program with parents and students
- To provide evidence of accountability for student learning

Figure 1-1.

Defining a Personal Philosophy of Assessment

A personal assessment philosophy is an essential element in the development of a general teaching philosophy. Exploring one's reasons for being a music teacher should inevitably reveal personal reasons and motivations for believing that assessment is important, including why it is important. The depth of one's commitment to music education as a profession is also a fairly reliable predictor of one's commitment to assessment as an important aspect of the music program. One way to develop a personal philosophy of assessment is to honestly answer the following questions (see Figure 1-2):

1. What is important for your students to know and be able to do? Every music teacher, through study and experience, develops a clear idea of the skills and knowledge that students should acquire. The National Standards for Music (MENC, 1994) provide model statements that specifically identify what students need to know and be able to do, and most states and/or local school districts have adopted versions of these. The extent to which a teacher believes in these standards affects that teacher's personal assessment philosophy.

2. How do you know it's important? The extent to which a teacher determines that these skills and knowledge are important also shapes that teacher's assessment philosophy. The reasons why a teacher feels certain skills and knowledge are important is a significant part of that philosophy.

3. How do you find out what students know and are able to do? For many general music teachers, this is often accomplished through teacher observation with no recorded data supporting what is observed. The actual extent to which this occurs in general music is not known, but its practice is primarily due to time constraints and the numbers of students served.

4. Is teacher observation in class enough? While teacher observation in the general music class is a powerful and useful assessment tool, the advent of higher standards for music education requires that a new set of assessment techniques and record keeping strategies be developed to supplement and support teacher observation.

5. Is classroom behavior an appropriate measure of musical progress? In an effort to prevent children from disliking music, general music teachers may sometimes give letter grades based on social and personal factors alone. Countless numbers of high grades are given by well-meaning teachers because students are "really trying" to "do their best" in their music classes. This practice is a reflection of a personal philosophy that places the assessment focus on student attitudes toward the music class and attendance, whether or not that is the teacher's actual belief.

6. Do your personal beliefs about assessment coincide with your assessment practices? Contemporary music programs place many demands upon general music teachers; schedules are full, performance programs are frequent, and time seems to be at a premium. As a result, there often exists a gap between a teacher's personal philosophy of what is important for assessment and that which is perceived as realistically achievable. This disparity between personal beliefs and perceived ability to act upon those beliefs can cause teachers a great deal of frustration. An organized and systematic approach to assessment can help bring beliefs about the importance of assessment and the expression of those beliefs closer together.

7. Is a personal philosophy of assessment even necessary? Yes, it is. Before a teacher can commit fully to an assessment program, it is essential for that teacher to have developed a philosophy of assessment that supports the implementation of such a program. For experienced teachers, the willingness to honestly reexamine and change one's current assessment procedures is a manifestation of a supportive personal philosophy. For beginning teachers, the desire to design and establish a systematic assessment program during the first year of teaching is a sign of the commitment necessary to undertake such an endeavor. These convictions and beliefs can be established by forming a personal philosophy of assessment.

Questions that Shape Personal Assessment Philosophy

- What is important for your students to know and be able to do?

- How do you know it's important?

- How do you find out what students know and are able to do?

- Is teacher observation in class enough?

- Is classroom behavior an appropriate measure of musical progress?

- Do your personal beliefs about assessment coincide with your assessment practices?

- Is a personal philosophy of assessment even necessary?

Figure 1-2.

Assessment and Learning Theory: Constructivism and Objectivism

Much recent progress has been made within the fields of cognitive and educational psychology toward the development of a theory of knowledge acquisition that spans many subject domains. A theory of knowledge acquisition, also known as a *learning theory*, provides an abstract, generalized view of the structure of learning along with a framework for understanding the processes involved in the acquisition of knowledge. An ideal purpose for such a theory is the guidance of instruction within a subject domain in order to facilitate maximum learning. A *meta-theory* is one that includes several more specific theories of learning and serves as a framework for theory building in a specific subject domain.

Within the subject domain of music, teaching can be approached from many educational perspectives. Musical

6

learning is facilitated when teaching aligns with appropriate musical experiences and a student's developmental continuum. Music teaching is unique in its employment of numerous cognitive domains to facilitate the acquisition of musical concepts and skills. General music teachers involve their students in singing, playing, moving, listening, creating, responding, and developing musical creativity through improvisation and composition. The purpose of this section of this chapter is twofold. First, it will briefly present some promising and significant theoretical constructs developed by cognitive and educational psychologists regarding the understanding of how general knowledge is acquired. Second, these constructs will be placed within a metatheoretical view of musical knowledge acquisition as it may occur through general music education.

Knowledge Transfer in Ill-Structured Content Domains

All subjects taught in school present content and skills that are unique to the subject, and one of the primary goals of instruction is to impart this to students. Spiro, Vispoel, Schmitz, Samarapungavan, and Boerger (1987) have described subject content domains as either *well-structured or ill-structured. Ill-structured* domains are those content areas where "there are no rules or principles of sufficient generality to cover most of the cases, nor defining characteristics for determining the actions appropriate for a given case" (p. 184). In this definition, the term *case* is used to mean *an example or application in a particular content domain.* For general music, this means that cases are musical experiences and events that occur as a result of engaging in musical activity. *Well-structured* content domains, on the other hand, are those in which the majority of cases can be explained by general rules or principles. All content areas demonstrate a certain degree of *ill-structuredness*, but some are more well-structured than others are. An example of a well-structured content domain would be arithmetic, where number rules and facts concisely explain the majority of cases, or problems, that occur. A simple case example is that 3 + 3 always equals 6 and 3 x 3 always equals 9 in the number problems that occur within that content area.

Ill-structured domains, however, are not so easily generalized. While every content domain demonstrates a certain degree of *well-structuredness*, some are primarily ill-structured, such as music. In music, "cases" are songs, instrumental pieces, dances, and other exemplars of musical expression that are used to provide an experiential base for the acquisition of musical knowledge. One example of the ill-structuredness of music has to do with rhythm. There is no rule or general principle which states that a quarter note always represents one beat. It is true that a quarter note represents one beat in 2/4, 3/4, or 4/4 meter, but a quarter note represents two beats in 3/8 or 6/8 meter and four beats in 6/16 or 16/16 meter. Another example can be found when one is teaching major and minor mode discrimination. What "rules" apply to the aural discrimination of major and minor? While theoretical explanations can be given for the difference in these modalities, *experience* with the discrimination process is the only way to hear and come to know this difference.

Spiro et al. (1987) argue that content domains that are ill-structured are also *complex*. This means that in order to learn an ill-structured content domain such as music, one must obtain a *multiplicity of perspectives* on musical problem solving through multiple musical experiences. In other words, in music there is no one prototype or analogy sufficient to cover all of the possibilities for potential musical performances or experiences. Therefore, a variety of musical experiences must be provided in order for students to gain a number of *knowledge precedents* that can be applied in new musical situations. In reference to the major-minor mode discrimination concept discussed earlier, multiple experiences with this concept would have to be obtained in order for major-minor mode discrimination to be learned and applied to new situations. In other words, students would need many musical experiences involving major and minor mode discrimination before they could accurately determine the modality of musical works heard in the future.

Cognitive Flexibility, Constructivism, and Situated Cognition

Central to the notion of case-by-case learning in an ill-structured content domain are the ideas of *cognitive flexibility* and *constructivism.* Spiro, Feltovich, Jacobson, and Coulson (1991) define cognitive flexibility as

> *...the ability to represent knowledge from different conceptual and case perspectives and then, when the knowledge must later be used, the ability to construct from those different conceptual and case representations a knowledge ensemble tailored to the needs of the understanding or problem-solving situation at hand.* (p. 24)

Cognitive flexibility develops from the *interconnectedness* of the different knowledge representations obtained from case experiences in an ill-structured, complex content domain and the need to draw upon these interconnections for knowledge application. From the interrelationships among case-related knowledge representations comes the foundation for applying this knowledge to new ill-structured, domain-specific situations. This set of experiences, then, is drawn upon to create an appropriate understanding of the new situation. It is cognitive flexibility that accounts for the processing necessary to apply the relevant portions of this collection of experiences to new situations. Within the domain of music, and specifically in general music experiences, the elements of rhythm, melody, timbre, harmony, form, and expression are presented in their naturally occurring musical complexity. General music teachers respect this complexity by providing students with integrated experiences involving listening, speaking, singing, instrument playing, and moving. Case examples within general music lessons are rich with elaborate musical relationships, thus providing ample opportunity for the development of cognitive flexibility.

When students draw upon previous case knowledge to understand new situations, the newly created knowledge arrangement is said to be "constructed." This *constructivist* view of knowledge is directly opposed to the *objectivist* view, which holds that the world is "completely and correctly structured in terms of entities, properties, and relations" (Duffy & Jonassen, 1991, pp. 7-8). While objectivist theory acknowledges that people have different views and understandings because of different experiences, the goal of objectivist-based learning is to strive for the complete and correct understanding because there exists a clear difference between what is right and what is wrong.

Certain well-structured aspects of music *are* objective. One would not argue, for example, that the second staff line in the treble clef denotes the note g_4 and that any other note name given for that staff line in the treble clef is incorrect. However, the same five lines and four spaces of the staff take on very different representations in other clefs. As shown in Figure 1-3, the second staff line in the bass clef denotes the pitch b_3, not g_4.

**Example of Music as Ill-Structured
Content Domain**

The staff, meaningless without a clef

The staff with the treble clef: each line
and space has a specific meaning

The staff with the bass clef: each line and space
takes on new meaning

Figure 1-3.

The variability in the representation of the lines and spaces that results from the type of clef used is a *prima facie* example of the ill-structuredness of music as a content domain.

In the meta-theoretical view being presented here, the majority of new musical knowledge is constructed from previous knowledge gained from case-by-case, or lesson-by-lesson, experiences. Using the staff example, when one gains experience with clefs other than the treble clef, the ability to know about and to understand other representations for the lines and spaces of the staff becomes clear and, with continued experience, learned. For teachers of general music, musical experiences (playing instruments, singing, moving, listening, and thinking critically) are the *key components* for leading children toward musical understanding and the acquisition of musical knowledge. General music teachers provide an experiential continuum of lessons (cases) from which students obtain the cognitive flexibility to reorganize and reconstruct previous knowledge in new ways to apply to future cases. This enables general music students to apply knowledge gained from previous musical experiences to new musical situations in a flexible manner that reconstructs what they already know into a form that is applicable to the novel experience.

The constructivist view also holds that *meaning* is rooted in experience (Brown, Collins, & Duguid, 1989). That is, in order to be meaningful to the learner, learning must occur as part of an authentically situated cognitive experience. Brown et al. (1989) state that "knowledge is situated, being in part a product of the activity, context, and culture in which it is developed and used" (p. 32). This notion is described as *situated cognition*. Knowledge must be presented in an appropriate context in order to be learned, and learning is a result of knowledge-seeking activity within a meaningful context. With respect to music, this suggests that *meaningful* music learning can only take place when it is embedded in an authentically musical context. Active music making is the heart of the general music curriculum, and active music making is both culturally and contextually situated for optimum musical knowledge acquisition.

Context and Musical Assessment

In complex content domains (Spiro et al., 1987, 1991) such as music, case-by-case learning provides a multiplicity of perspectives from which knowledge can be constructed to account for future situations through cognitive flexibility. Meaningful learning can only be achieved when the learning occurs in the appropriately situated context (Brown et al., 1989). Figure 1-4 presents a graphic representation of these meta-theoretical constructs as they have been outlined here and models their dynamic interrelationship in the domain of music.

How Children Acquire Musical Knowledge

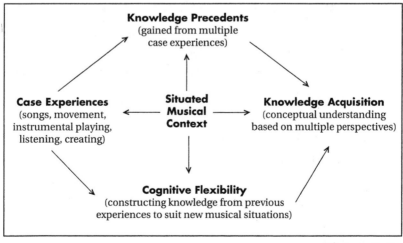

Figure 1-4.

Figure 1-4 also highlights the importance of context to musical learning. In music, context is embedded in the musical experiences planned for the students. Teachers plan lessons around a particular objective, and the musical context of this experience is a natural aspect of the lesson. For example, if a teacher plans to introduce a new song to a class, the context of the lesson would be *singing*. For students, the meaning of the singing experience is embedded in its context, and the experience requires cognition that is unique to singing and vocal performance. Students are required to "think like a singer" while involved in a singing experience, and this cognitive perspective is only available to children during the singing experience.

Therefore, if a teacher wishes to assess a child's singing ability, it is best done *during a singing experience*. This type of assessment requires a context that matches as nearly as possible the learning context and reflects the constructivist view that the new musical situation (such as an assessment task) requires the reconstruction of previously acquired musical knowledge to meet the needs of the situation. This type of assessment context is referred to as *authentic* and simulates conditions under which the learning has taken place.

For purposes of comparison, continue with this example and imagine the assessment of singing from an objectivist point of view. Because objectivism is based on the view that all knowledge is fixed fact and can be acquired in a context-free environment, an assessment of singing would occur in a context-free environment. First, students would come into a classroom, sit at desks, and be taught the facts about singing. The assessment would require them to answer questions about singing without ever singing a note; the answers to these questions would be either right or wrong. This type of assessment seems ineffective because it does not reflect the proper context in which knowledge about singing can be most adequately demonstrated. While an objectivist framework may at times be the proper learning environment for students, this is typically *not* the case within the domain of general music.

Assessment, Measurement, Evaluation, and Reflection

Before this discussion moves on to authentic assessment in music, several definitions must be clarified. The terms *assessment, measurement, evaluation,* and *reflection* are used throughout this book; the definitions that are intended in this book follow.

Assessment is defined as the gathering of information about a student's status relevant to one's academic and musical expectations. This broad definition covers all activities that are employed by a teacher to determine a student's current status with respect to achievement of the state and local district's educational standards and how a student has achieved musically in the past. Assessment results can also serve a diagnostic purpose and help determine where a student *should be* musically at any grade level.

Measurement refers to the use of a systematic methodology to observe musical behaviors in order to represent the magnitude of performance capability, task completion, or concept attainment. This is achieved in a variety of ways, most commonly through the use of a rubric or other scoring or rating system. When assessing a child's improvisation, for example, one might choose to design a scoring system that targets certain behaviors expected in the improvisation process or certain characteristics in the improvised product. As one examines the improviser during an assessment, the score or rating assigned to the improvisation serves as a measurement of the magnitude of task completion when examining the finished product and the performance capability of the improviser when examining the improvisation process.

Evaluation has to do with the comparison of assessment information in relation to a standard or set of pre-established criteria (Saunders, 1996). For example, in the case of the improviser, a certain score or level on the rubric may be evaluated to conclude that the improviser meets the age-appropriate requirements for one of the achievement standards for National Content Standard number 3, "Improvising melodies, variations, and accompaniments." (MENC, 1994, p. 27)

Reflection refers to the systematic review and evaluation of one's previous achievements or accomplishments in order to respond to present needs or questions. This is a metacognitive activity; *metacognition* is defined as the ability to reflect on one's own thinking, learning, and/or development. To engage in reflection, a student must have a sense of the past and the ability to compare it to the present, as well as the ability to apply some sort of judgment as to the relationship between past and present accomplishments. Metacognition is discussed at length in chapter 5.

Authentic Assessment in Music

In response to the increasing implementation of constructivist learning theory in the classroom, new methods of assessment have been formulated that permit teachers to gauge the progress of students while they are involved in knowledge-seeking activity. Meaningful learning through activity in appropriately situated contexts lies at the heart of constructivist learning theory and, consequently, requires properly contexted assessment procedures. These procedures constitute what is referred to as *authentic assessment.*

Because authentic assessment activities are rooted in experience, they are *performance-based* (Darling-Hammond, 1994). Such assessments are conducted while students are involved in a domain-specific learning activity. During a performance-based authentic assessment, the teacher observes student behaviors and collects these observations either on cassette tape or in the form of brief notes or markings that become part of the student's assessment data. Students are informed of what the teacher is "looking for" prior to the start of the assessment. When certain behaviors previously ascertained to demonstrate a particular level of learning are observed, the student is considered to have obtained that level of learning or skill.

It has been claimed that performance-based assessment practices are common to music education and that music educators have been engaged in this type of assessment as part of their regular teaching (Robinson, 1995). However, the accumulation of data necessary for the measurement of progress in music has been difficult due to the numbers of students music educators have under their tutelage.

Authentic assessment occurs when assessment aligns with curriculum, teaching, and a student's developmental trajectory. Authentic assessment has also been deemed to be "intelligence fair," in reference to Gardner's theory of multiple intelligences (Gardner, 1983, 1993), wherein musical intelligence is claimed to be a separate intellectual ability with unique cognitive traits supported by specialized neurological resources in the brain. Authentic assessment reflects a student's learning environment and occurs within a similar environment in which the original learning occurred (see Figure 1-5).

The Authentic Assessment Model

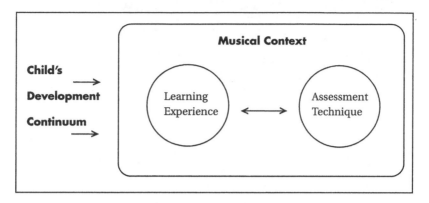

Figure 1-5.

Assessment Response Modes in Music

Because there are three primary modes of authentic artistic expression, there are three corresponding response modes for artistic assessment (NAGB, 1994). The modes of expression are *performing, creating,* and *responding.* For the artistic domain of music, each of these modes places the student in a different musical role, and the context of the role is crucial to the child's understanding of that role.

The role of *performer* places the child within the context of musical interpretation through active music making. In this context, students express and interpret music through singing, instrument playing, movement, and drama. This role is the most common for students at all levels of the music program because of the emphasis on performance and performing groups in contemporary music education in the United States and throughout the world (Lepherd, 1995).

The role of *creator* places the child within the context of musical origination. As a creator of new music or musical arrangements, students explore the roles of composer, improviser, and arranger at a developmentally appropriate level of expertise. In this context, students are given opportunities to demonstrate their accumulated musical knowledge through original musical expressions. The act of *composing* allows children to reflect upon their created music and edit it at will. Conversely, *improvisation* is the spontaneous creation of music within a given musical context (instrumental, vocal, movement, etc.) with no time for reflection or editing of the finished product. Arranging gives students the opportunity to reorganize and reconfigure existing music or musical settings in new and original ways.

The *responding* mode of artistic expression places the child in the role of audience member or consumer of music. It has been claimed that the training of students in this role is not traditionally addressed by most music programs, nor are the roles of composer, improviser, and arranger (Lindeman, 1997). In the role of listener and consumer, students use critical thinking skills and acquired musical knowledge to make reasonable and informed judgments about music and personal values with respect to music. This role is crucial for the development of musically informed and literate citizens.

Authentic assessment techniques attempt to measure the progress of *individual students* in each of these three response modes. This focus on individual development is unique to this type of assessment protocol and precludes "grading" in general music. To give grades in general music that are not based on attendance or effort, one would need to collect numerical scores that somehow represent musical achievement or progress. These scores would then be distributed around a mean and subjected to an arbitrary scale that would rank the students in comparison to each other's progress so that grades—typically "A," "B," "C," etc.— can be assigned. This type of scoring and statistical control of the results is the hallmark of assessments based within objectivist learning theory. These types of assessments are *norm-referenced*, wherein obtained test scores are averaged then compared to the derived mean for the purpose of discriminating among the test takers' individual scores (Boyle & Radocy, 1987).

Constructivist-based authentic assessments simulate real-life situations that are more than fact-based and, therefore, not as easily controlled statistically. Individual progress toward attainment of the National Standards should not be subjected to statistical treatment that results in comparison to a mean because each child progresses through his or her musical developmental trajectory at a unique pace. Assessment of musical progress is best gauged through *criterion-referenced* assessments, wherein individual achievement is measured in relation to specified criteria (Boyle & Radocy, 1987). General developmental trends have been shown to exist in some areas of musical development (Hargreaves, 1986; Hargreaves & Zimmerman, 1992; Shehan-Campbell & Scott-Kassner, 1995; Swanwick & Tillman, 1986; Tillman, 1989), but the exact timing of progression through individual developmental trajectories varies widely among students. Authentic and alternative assessments help music teachers track this individual development in a meaningful and useful manner.

Objectivist-Based Assessment in Music

While the thrust of this book is to help teachers design tasks that are grounded in constructivism, there are times when the general music teacher will find benefit in objectivist-based tests or quizzes, such as when specific content knowledge or skills are being assessed. In situations like this, the content knowledge or skill is isolated in a context-free environment and students are asked to indicate right and wrong responses on a piece of paper. Results or scores are tallied, a mean is determined, and a grading scale is devised.

These assessments can be constructed in clever and age-appropriate ways that remain engaging for children. An example of this type of assessment can be found in Figure 1-6. Carol King, a teacher in the Memphis City Schools in Memphis, Tennessee, designed this test to check her second graders' ability to recognize the notation of performed rhythms. The test is administered by giving each child one of the papers, on which they write their name, the date (always essential when administering any assessment), and the classroom teacher's name. The teacher then performs the rhythms on an unpitched instrument, giving each rhythm a specific number from 1 through 5. When the children hear the rhythm performed, they write the number of the rhythm in the balloon that contains its notation

This type of information can be very helpful to teachers as well as provide hard-copy, nonperformance evidence of certain skills and knowledge. This book, however, does not focus on the design of these types of tasks because there are already books in print that cover this very well, such as Boyle and Radocy's *Measurement and Evaluation of Musical Experiences* (1987). Because this book focuses on constructivist tasks, the reader is not to assume that this is the only approach to musical assessment that is being proferred. Instead, the reader is encouraged to devise meaningful objectivist tests and quizzes when they help to meet the teacher's assessment needs. What is *not* encouraged is the sole use of either type of task; the best information regarding a student's musical progress will be gained from a combination of regular, ongoing assessments.

Objectivist-Based Assessment

Name _____
Date _____
Class _____

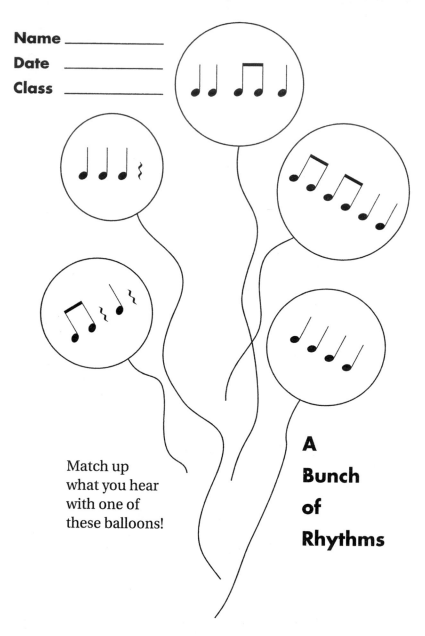

Match up
what you hear
with one of
these balloons!

**A
Bunch
of
Rhythms**

used by permission of Carol King

Figure 1-6.

Alternative Assessment in Music

Alternative assessments can sometimes be very useful tools when measuring the musical progress of general music students. While authentic and alternative assessments are very much alike, there is an important difference between the two for purposes of this book, and the two terms should not be used interchangeably. An *alternative assessment* technique in music is *situated within an authentic context other than that in which the musical learning took place.* One example of alternative assessment in music is writing about music. When writing about music, the authentic context is writing, not music; however, the subject of the writing has to do with music. Students' writings about music can reveal a great deal of knowledge about music if the writing prompt is well developed and focused on what the teacher is wanting to assess. Another alternative assessment example is *concept mapping;* in this assessment the context is drawing, but the assessment value for the music teacher lies in the terms and explanations the student includes in the drawing and how these are connected to show the student's understanding. Both of these techniques are covered extensively in chapter 5.

Preparing for Assessment

Just as teachers must take time to plan thorough and engaging lessons for general music students, similar planning and thought are necessary to develop appropriate musical assessments. Setting up the assessment environment is important, and adequate preparation for implementation of the assessment task is necessary for the success of the assessment experience. These steps, briefly described here and summarized in Figure 1-7, are discussed in more specific detail in chapters 3, 4, and 5.

Preparing for Assessment

- Determine what you want to measure: target a specific behavior or concept.

- Set and know your criteria well in advance: know what you are looking for.

- Prepare rubrics and/or other scoring techniques: think of all the possibilities that might occur.

- Determine your record keeping strategy: how will you keep track, especially if you have hundreds of students?

- Determine your materials for the assessment.

- Inform your students.

Figure 1-7.

First, it is imperative to *determine exactly what is to be measured.* Each assessment must target specific behaviors, knowledge, or concepts that become the focus of the assessment. Examples of musical behaviors include skills such as singing, playing instruments, composing, and improvising. Conceptual assessments target a student's understanding of concepts related to melody, rhythm, harmony, timbre, and form. The more specifically focused the assessment target is at the beginning, the more successful and usable the results will be.

Once you have determined the objective of the assessment, it is then time to *set the criteria for judgment of the assessment results.* Setting the criteria and knowing them well are especially crucial to real-time performance assessments such as those for vocal pitch accuracy and improvisation skills. A good question to ask when setting criteria is, "What specifically is being measured in this task?" or, perhaps more importantly, "What is not?" By thoroughly examining these questions prior to the assessment, you can gain the vital information necessary to judge the assessment results fairly and consistently.

The next step in preparing and implementing an assessment is to *design and prepare the scoring or measurement instrument*. For most musical assessments, this is usually in the form of a rubric, a specialized type of scoring guide that specifically lists levels of performance and specific criteria as indicators of understanding that serve to measure the degree to which the criteria for the assessment are being met.

Once the criteria and measurement instrument have been devised, then it is necessary to *determine a record keeping strategy* for the data collected during the assessment. In many instances, a grade book is a convenient location for this data. A student's file or portfolio can also serve as an important repository for assessment information. These strategies and others will be discussed in later chapters of this book.

The next step in this process is to *determine the materials to be used in the assessment task*. Materials for assessment tasks are in large part determined by the district or state curriculum. For example, if the local district's curriculum guide states that first graders need to sing sol-mi-la as accurately as possible, then your materials for assessment will be songs that contain solos on those pitches as suggested by the curriculum in your district. Many districts are undergoing curricula revision with respect to the new National Standards (Wells, 1997), and these curricula are specific in their requirements for assessment tasks and materials.

The final step in the preparation process is to *inform students of the assessment*. It is appropriate and necessary for you to notify your class of an assessment, including exactly what is being assessed. It is equally appropriate for you to place rubrics or other scoring guides where students can easily view them (usually on the board) so the students are fully informed of what they are expected to do in order to achieve a proficient rating.

Summary

- There are several important reasons for general music teachers to examine their beliefs and to develop a personal philosophy of assessment: assessment data provides evidence of student growth and progress, helps validate the music program with parents and students, provides evidence of effective teaching and learning, and helps guide one's choice of teaching strategies.

- One's commitment to the music education profession is reflected in one's belief in the importance of assessment.

- Because of the ill-structured nature of music as a knowledge domain, students gain musical knowledge through a variety of case experiences. When new musical situations are encountered, these case experiences provide a foundation upon which a new knowledge array is constructed to suit the new musical situation. By applying cognitive flexibility to new musical situations, students demonstrate musical understanding through cognitive strategies uniquely situated to the experience. Assessment that occurs within this framework is called *authentic assessment.*

- Authentic assessments take place within a naturally occurring musical context. There are three assessment response modes in music: (1) *performing,* (2) *creating,* and (3) *responding.* Authentic assessments in music attempt to measure the musical progress of general music students in each of these response modes.

● *Alternative assessments* are those that take place in an authentic context other than that in which the musical learning originally occurred.

● Six steps are recommended for preparing for assessment in the general music classroom: (1) *specific behaviors, concepts, or knowledge must be targeted for measurement;* (2) the *criteria for judging the assessment results must then be carefully thought out and familiarized;* (3) once this is accomplished, *a scoring strategy (such as a rubric) must be determined and developed;* (4) it then becomes necessary for the teacher to *determine a reliable and efficient method of keeping a record of the assessment results;* (5) the *materials for the assessment task must be selected* (the district's general music curriculum is the most common place to find these); and (6) the *students must be informed* that they are being assessed, and the criteria for the assessment must be made clear to them in an age-appropriate manner.

Questions for Clarification

1) Based on the meta-theoretical constructs presented in this chapter, composing a new piece of music is most clearly an example of _____ _____.

2) A lesson in which you teach a song and instrument parts to help students practice musical skills is an example of a

_____ _____.

3) The specialized thinking processes incorporated during a musical experience result in a type of cognition known as

_____ _____.

4) Determining the extent to which musical knowledge has been acquired is one of the goals of musical _____.

5) Content domains for which there are insufficient rules to cover most of the case experiences can be referred to as _____ - _____.

6) Authentic assessment is rooted in experiential learning, and this learning is founded in the meta-theoretical framework called _____.

7) Making portfolios in music is most clearly an example of _____.

8) Asking a student to review writing samples from throughout the school year to determine his/her improvement is an example of _____.

9) Using a rubric for scoring a performance task is most clearly an example of _____.

10) Determining whether a student is emerging, developing, or competent in the attainment of a particular concept is most clearly an example of _____.

11) A pop quiz is an example of assessment based on _____ learning theory.

12) A good source for authentic assessment materials is the local school district's _____ _____.

Questions for Discussion

1) What other reasons can you give for the importance of assessment in general music?

28

2) Take a moment to write down some of the tenets of your personal philosophy of music education. Based on these tenets, discuss your view of the role of assessment in general music and its importance to general music teaching.

3) Discuss the following situations with respect to how they represent constructivist learning theory:

   a) Third graders composing and notating their first original composition;

   b) Fourth graders teaching themselves a simple piece using only the notes B, A, and G; and

   c) Fifth and sixth graders identifying a tonic-dominant harmony change in a familiar piece. → prior knowledge

4) Examine the situations in question 3 from the viewpoint of assessing the learning that has occurred. What might you do?

5) Read the following scenario and discuss the questions below:

A teacher plans and administers an assessment task that involves a fourth grade class in the construction of a two-measure rhythm in 4/4 meter. The teacher has prepared sets of cards that present single quarter notes, pairs of beamed eighth notes, a single quarter rest, and half notes. Each student is given a set of eight of these cards and is told to create a rhythm that (a) uses all of the different note values in the set at least once and (b) has a clear final point. When completed with the task, the students are asked to write the rhythm on a piece of paper, using correct notation, and are told that this will be turned in to the teacher. On the board, the teacher has written the criteria for the rubric and explained to the class what is expected to achieve a proficient rating for the task.

In reference to the above scenario, discuss the following questions:

a) Is this task situated in an authentic context? How did you determine this?

b) What is the assessment response mode?

c) Has this teacher determined how these assessment results will be measured? Evaluated?

d) Does it appear that this teacher has adequately prepared for this assessment?

e) How could this assessment be expanded to include the other response modes?

6) Discuss the advantages and disadvantages of authentic assessment in general music. What do you feel is the best way to gauge musical progress and development of general music students? Why?

Chapter 2

Developing and Managing Assessment Tasks: General Considerations

This chapter examines the important general issues that music teachers must consider when developing and managing assessment tasks that are used in their classrooms. Well-developed tasks require careful thought and planning. The careful consideration of the issues outlined in this chapter can help to ensure that the tasks created for classroom use will yield practical and meaningful results. An understanding of how children develop musically is an important foundation for the development of assessment tasks. This chapter begins with a glimpse at the research pertaining to the nature of cognitive musical growth in children and then presents general issues related to task development and data management.

The Nature of Cognitive Musical Growth in Children: A Glimpse at the Research

The Early Research: Piagetian Stage Theory and Music

From the mid-1960s through the mid-1980s there was a great deal of research activity within the field of music education pertaining to the application of Swiss psychologist Jean Piaget's stage theory of intellectual development and his concept of "conservation" to the elements of music. The four stages of intellectual development proposed by Piaget are (1) sensorimotor, ages zero through two; (2) preoperational, ages two through seven; (3) concrete operational, ages seven through eleven; and (4) formal operational, ages eleven through fifteen (Piaget, 1969a, 1977, 1969b). Early studies of musical development attempted to find musical analogies to the Piagetian notion of conservation and to equate musical development with Piagetian stage theory (Bettison, 1976; Botvin, 1974; Foley, 1975; Jones, 1976; Larsen, 1973; Larsen & Boody, 1971; Nelson, 1984; Norton, 1979, 1980; Perney, 1976; Pflederer, 1964, 1966a, 1966b, 1967; Pflederer & Sechrest, 1968a, 1968b; Serafine, 1979; Zimmerman, 1970; Zimmerman & Sechrest, 1970; Zimmerman & Webster, 1983).

Conservation is defined as the invariance of a particular empirical factor, such as volume, weight, or length, in the child's mind throughout observed changes of state. In Piaget's studies, these observed changes were implemented primarily through the subject's manipulation of certain predetermined variables that altered the stimulus field but not the empirical factor itself (Inhelder & Piaget, 1964; Piaget, 1969a, 1969b, 1977). For example, in his famous conservation of liquid experiment, or conservation of *continuous quantity*, a child was presented with two glasses and asked to pour identical amounts of water into each glass. After the child determined that the two glasses were equal in volume, liquid from one of the glasses was poured into a different-shaped container. The question was posed: Is there still the same amount to drink? Piaget discovered that the responses of the children varied according to age and developmental stage. The attainment of conservation is considered a hallmark of the *concrete operational* period (ages seven through eleven); children who can conserve continuous quantity are considered to have entered this stage of intellectual development.

The tasks designed for the study of *musical* conservation were primarily constructed as listening exercises and did not actively involve the subjects in the experimentation or in the transformation of the material to its altered state, as was the case in Piaget's experiments. For example, Marilyn Pflederer's (1964) landmark pilot study of musical conservation in sixteen five- and eight-year-old children attempted to create musical conservation tasks that were analogous to Piaget's conservation tasks. Pflederer created nine tasks that each presented a musical stimulus (e.g., a familiar song) to the children in her experiments. The stimulus was presented again with some aspect of it changed, or *deformed* (e.g., duration, accompaniment, tone, pitch, rhythm, or key). The test of conservation was to see if the children could recognize the deformed stimulus as simply an altered version of the original, thus "conserving" the original musical element. The results of this pilot study led Pflederer to conclude that stages of musical development that mirrored Piaget's stages of intellectual development might exist.

In the years following this important initial endeavor, subsequent music researchers found it increasingly difficult to "fit" musical development within Piaget's rigid stage theory. Pflederer-Zimmerman's later studies (1968, with Sechrest; 1970; 1983, with Webster) revealed a more linear progression of musical development, with children's abilities to "conserve" musical properties increasing steadily with age rather than in stages. Other conservation studies had mixed results, none of which confirmed an exact correlation to stage-like musical development as implicated by Piagetian theory (Larsen, 1973; Botvin, 1974; Bettison, 1976; Jones, 1976; Perney, 1976; Norton, 1979, 1980). Piagetian research in music education increasingly became the subject of critical analysis as more and more evidence accrued that "stages" *per se* might not exist in musical development (Serafine, 1980).

Bartholomew (1987) suggested that the primary difficulty with attempting to equate Piagetian theory with a theory of musical development rested in the differences between the types of *objects* being manipulated in conservation experiments. Bartholomew reasoned that Piaget's experiments utilized objects with physical properties that children could see and manipulate; musical *objects* as such do not exist. For example, children cannot *hold* a melody in their hands, physically manipulate and alter it, and then make a judgment as to the altered version's relationship to its original *shape*. He concluded that a separate theory was necessary to account for musical development.

Contemporary Views of Musical Cognitive Development

Once it was determined that the existence of true Piagetian conservation in musical development was questionable at best, other psychologists began to examine the accumulated evidence in order to present a more accurate view of musical cognitive development. Howard Gardner (1983, 1993, 1999) has proposed that human intelligence consists of eight autonomous intellectual domains, not just one general competency as previously believed. These intelligence domains are linguistic, musical, logical-mathematical, bodily-kinesthetic, spatial, naturalist, and two forms of personal intelligence—interpersonal and intrapersonal. Of particular interest to music teachers is Gardner's suggestion of a separate musical intelligence that follows its own trajectory of development. If this is indeed the case, it would certainly help to explain the lack of correlation between Piagetian conservation (which, according to Gardner, is a manifestation of logical-mathematical intelligence) and observed musical development.

Sloboda (1985) suggests that the primary thrust of a child's cognitive development in music between the ages of five and ten is one of increasing *reflective awareness*. He defines this as the ability to think about, or *reflect upon*, the structures and patterns that characterize music. Sloboda points out that the ability of five-year-olds to perform their enactive repertoire (e.g., nursery songs) at different tempi implies that a child is aware that the melody remains constant throughout such transformations. However, a child of five does not yet possess the ability to think about the change as a process in itself that has been performed on the music. Several of his studies suggest that as a child develops musically within a culture, this reflective ability and knowledge increases and is expressed in the musical terms of that culture. Sloboda concludes that children experience a linear progression of musical development, with rapid growth of reflective awareness from ages five to ten.

Dowling (1988) argues that certain invariants of melodic and tonal structure often remain implicit in the cognition of music. When listening to certain melodies in one's own culture, one can tell whether or not the melodies are played correctly through implicit knowledge of *pattern* and *tonal invariants*. It is suggested that the development of these culturally dependent, perceptual invariants in children occurs during the first eight years of life. For example, in one of his experiments, Dowling presented three-, four-, five-, and six-year-olds with two melodies, each a version of the same familiar song (e.g., "Mary Had a Little Lamb"). The first version was a tonal derivative in C major, where the intervals remained diatonic but were made larger or smaller within the melody in a manner that maintained the original contour of the melody. The second version was an atonal derivative, created from a scale containing the pitches C-Db-E-F-Gb-Ab-B. The atonal version placed the melodic patterns at analogous points in this scale; thus, the melodic phrase E-D-C-D-E-G-G in C major became E-Db-C-Db-E-Gb-Gb in the atonal version. The children were also asked to sing a familiar song, most often "Happy Birthday," and were rated by twelve independent judges as to how well in tune they sang. The results revealed that those children who were considered the more competent singers, some as early as age three, could respond to the degree of tonality in the melody heard by judging which melody sounded "normal" and which sounded "funny."

Davidson and Scripp (1988) studied the invented musical notations of thirty-nine children for three years and observed significant progress between the ages of five and seven in the cognition of pitch and rhythm. Once yearly, the children were asked to complete a "music book" in which they were to "write the song ('Row, Row, Row Your Boat') down on paper so that someone else who doesn't know the song can sing it back." The results revealed a particularly strong developmental trend toward sophistication in the representation of pitch and rhythm between the ages of six and seven, with pitch emerging as the primary cognitive factor in musical development. They suggested that this trend probably continues as age increases, with pitch increasing in differentiation from language, number, and kinesthetic skills as children get older. Another researcher who studied the invented notations of children, Rena Upitis (1992), found that children could notate melodic contour as early as age five if they were involved in music composition. Upitis suggests that while a predictable order of stages of notational development in children might be identifiable, the *nature* of the development (referring to the amount and type of experience obtained in composition and inventing notation) seems to be more important than the age at which the stage is reached.

Davidson (1994) also examined the songsinging of nine children between the ages of one and six over a period of five years. His findings suggest that there are developmental phases in a child's understanding of "tonal space." He reports that children tend to fit familiar songs into a melodic "contour scheme" that seems to be available to them based on their age. The earliest contour scheme is framed within the interval of a third, and these framing intervals expand through the interval of a sixth by the age of six. None of the children sang the interval of an octave before the age of six. Around the age of six or seven, Davidson suggests that songsinging takes a different developmental direction, in which children redirect their efforts toward couching their understanding of tonal space within the song repertoire of the prevalent culture. These results also corroborate the work of Rutkowski (1990; 1996; 1997, with Miller) with respect to the development and acquisition of the singing voice (there is more on Rutkowski's work in chapter 3).

Bamberger (1991, 1994) describes a difference in the way individuals hear and perceive rhythmic information that appears to be independent of age. Persons who attend to the motivic aspects of a rhythmic event—what Bamberger refers to as the *figural* features of the rhythm—are quite different in their perception from those who attend to the metrical features of the rhythm. *Figural knowledge* is defined as *knowing how*, or having a clear understanding of where and when things happen in a musical event. *Formal knowledge*, defined as *knowing about*, allows the listener a new, alternative perspective based on the metrical aspects of the rhythm. Bamberger suggests that what are perceived as the prominent features of rhythmic musical events depends on what is being attended to during the event.

Serafine (1988) has examined musical development as a unique domain of human cognitive activity. Her definition of music as *cognition*—the development of thought in sound—is supported by the argument that most definitions of music do not account for the fact that much music is "heard" within the mind, in the absence of sound. In other words, the presence of sound is not necessary in order for music to exist; it can and often does exist completely within the realm of thought.

Serafine has attempted to isolate certain *generic processes* present in the cognition of music. These processes are subdivided into two categories: (1) *temporal,* having to do with music's existence in time, and (2) *nontemporal.* She posits that there are two primary temporal cognitive processes:

> **1.** *Succession,* the process having to do with cognitively adding horizontal musical events together to make a musical whole; and
>
> **2.** *Simultaneity,* the operation of synthesizing musical events, or vertically superimposing them on one another, as in the case of hearing a triad.

With regard to the nontemporal processes, four are identified:

> **1.** *Closure,* which is defined as the cessation of musical activity;
>
> **2.** *Transformation,* the process that allows two musical events to be recognized as similar or different, depending on the amount of shared material that exists between the two events;
>
> **3.** *Abstraction,* which allows for a part of a musical event, most often a theme fragment or rhythmic, tonal, or harmonic pattern, to be removed and considered apart from its original context at some other point in the musical whole; and
>
> **4.** *Hierarchic levels,* the process that gives the listener the ability to cognitively assign more or less importance to certain aspects of multiple sound events, which occurs when the mind *separates out* certain focal tones in a piece of music to give the listener a sense of structure based on what is perceived as more or less significant in the music.

Serafine examined the presence of these generic processes in 168 children ages five, six, eight, ten, and eleven. The five- and six-year-olds evidenced none of the identified processes, while the ten- and eleven-year-olds gave evidence of possessing all of the processes. The results suggest that the middle years of childhood, those approximately ranging from ages eight to ten, are periods of rapid growth in music cognition. It is important to note that these are the ages during which most students are in school and involved in a general music education program.

Brophy (1998) conducted a study of one hundred five- and eight-year-olds in which responses to eight playing tasks were observed and analyzed. The playing tasks involved two alto xylophones, one serving as the model instrument and the second as a changed version of the model that presented the visual, aural, and kinesthetic stimulus modalities of the task altered in some way. Subjects were first asked to determine if the two xylophones "sounded the same" and then asked to explain their response. The results indicated that the eight-year-olds were able to incorporate multiple modalities in their responses more often than the five-year-olds, suggesting that this difference in levels of response complexity was the result of a multiple-stimulus processing ability that improves in efficiency with age.

Musical Cognitive Development and Assessment

From this brief overview, certain *general* trends in the musical cognitive development of children ages three through eleven begin to emerge (see Figure 2-1). It appears that the majority of children ages three through seven lack most of the identified musical cognitive traits and processing abilities mentioned here but experience a period of rapid growth in the development of these processes from ages eight through ten. The development of musical cognitive ability appears to be linear and favorably encouraged by musical experience. By age eleven, these processes appear to be generally in operation in most children. The years of greatest growth in the ability to understand and comprehend musical concepts seem to occur during the elementary school years.

Some General Developmental Trends in Musical Cognition in Children Ages 3 through 11

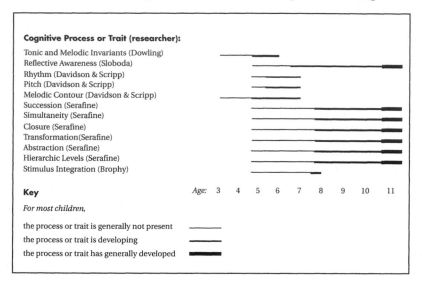

Figure 2-1.

This research informs teachers to the extent that it supports the idea that musical understanding unfolds gradually over time and is not acquired in "stages." The importance of sequenced musical experiences to learning music is underscored by these research findings, and new music curricula are reflecting these results. Because music consists of melody, rhythm, harmony, timbre, and form, the development of understanding of each of these elements is acquired at different rates for individual students.[1]

This has a twofold impact on the development of assessment tasks. First, general music specialists are dealing with *developing* musicians, not finished ones. A single assessment is not going to be a definitive measure for children experiencing such rapid musical growth; a series of assessments must be planned to occur over a period of time. Second, the unique trajectory of musical development for individual children requires that each child be assessed within each area of musical learning in order to follow individual development.

Musical Learning Areas and Assessment Response Modes

One of the most important steps in the development of assessment tasks is the determination of the musical learning area within which the task falls. A *learning area* in music is a categorical designation based on the nature of the musical behaviors that are inherent in both the learning and assessment contexts. A learning area is defined by the musical behaviors that are embedded within a particular learning activity.

The creation of an assessment task requires a clear understanding of what is being assessed by the task, and the situation of a task within a particular learning area determines a great deal about how the task is performed. There are five primary learning areas in general music (see Figure 2-2). These areas and their corresponding assessment response modes can be described as follows.

In most school systems, the local school district's music curriculum describes and categorizes what musical content is to be learned and when it should be taught; the musical behaviors that teachers can observe and assess at the classroom level categorize a learning area. Achievement standards, such as those included in the National Standards for the Arts, are excellent specific statements that describe musical knowledge as it should be demonstrated in the fourth, eighth, or twelfth grades. The learning areas presented here are organized in more general terms that can be applied across varying curricula and across all of the grades taught by the general music teacher.

Musical Learning Areas and Suggested Assessment Response Modes

Assessment Response Mode	Performing	Creating	Responding
Learning Area:			
I. Musical Skills			
singing	X	X	
playing instruments	X	X	
improvising	X	X	
composing	X	X	
arranging	X	X	
2. Literacy			
sight-reading	X		
notating music		X	X
3. History and Literature			
musical form	X	X	X
musical styles	X	X	X
historical periods	X		X
identifying specific composers/works	X		X
4. Analysis and Preferences			
musical structures	X	X	X
timbre	X	X	X
criteria building		X	X
evaluating performances/products			X
presenting logical arguments			X
5. Related Arts and Humanities			
describing relationships between music and culture			X
making connections between music and other arts, and disciplines outside the arts			X

Figure 2-2.

1. *Musical Skills—singing, playing instruments, composing, improvising, and arranging.* This learning area includes all musical performance skills as expressed both in the classroom and in large performing groups such as choirs and instrumental ensembles. Because these skills are an important part of every general music program, they need to be assessed regularly. Musical skill assessments are conducted in the performance response mode during musical performances. While these are among the most challenging assessments because they occur in real time, they are also among the most authentic. Improvising, composing a new piece, or arranging a familiar song or story is also a *creative* musical act, and while a child's creative ability may not be assessed (creativity is discussed in depth in chapter 4), the *product* of the creative act (the musical composition, arrangement, or improvisation) can provide many indicators of musical progress. Therefore, improvising, composing, and arranging tasks are designed within both the performance and creating assessment response modes.

2. *Literacy—reading and writing music.* This learning area includes sight-reading and musical notation. Musical notation is assessed within the responding mode as a product of the act of composition or arranging. Sight-reading is a performance activity, and is assessed within the performance assessment response mode.

3. *History and Literature—appreciation and listening.* This area includes identifying types and styles of music, general historical periods, composers, and specific musical works. In this learning area, the primary assessment mode is responding; discussion, writing, and dramatic speech are effective assessment tools.

4. *Analysis and Preference—evaluating music and reactions to music.* This learning area includes describing the use of musical elements in selected works and the process of building criteria for evaluating musical works and performances. This learning area is unique in that children are required to look inward and to reflect upon their accumulated knowledge about music and/or their personal preferences toward music in order to evaluate and make judgments about music. The assessment of criteria building involves the creating assessment response mode in an alternative way, insofar as the

43

criteria must be generated and developed by the students. Musical evaluation and critical reactions to music require the responding assessment response mode, most often through having students write while listening.

5. *Related Arts and Humanities—understanding culture, society, music's relationship with other art forms, and music's relationship to disciplines outside the arts.* This broad learning area includes developing an understanding of world musics and their functions within their indigenous societies, as well as the ability to recognize and make connections between music, dance, drama, and visual art and disciplines outside of the arts. Assessment in this learning area is also conducted in the responding mode through discussions, writings, and integrated projects.

This categorization of musical learning areas reveals that three of the five are assessed primarily through children's *responses* to music. General music programs have traditionally concentrated on performance skills and, to some degree, creating skills in music. The opportunity for children to become musical respondents and to have their writings, discussions, evaluations, and preferences emphasized as an equally important part of the general music program is largely a result of the new National Standards.

Classroom Environment Issues Related to Assessment

- Selection of appropriate materials
- Scope of the assessment task and time allotted for completion of the assessment task
- Student behavior and conduct
- Teacher involvement

Figure 2-3.

The Classroom Assessment Environment

The assessment environment is crucial to the success of any assessment task. The music teacher must do everything possible to ensure that the classroom environment maximizes the productivity of the students during the assessment (see Figure 2-3). Some of the important issues for teachers to consider are as follows:

1. *Selection of appropriate materials*—The overview of children's cognitive musical development at the beginning of this chapter describes how children change in their ability to process and understand musical information over the period of years they spend in general music. This has a direct impact on assessment, particularly in the area of materials selected for use during assessment tasks. Materials include some of the following: (a) songs and instrumental pieces for performance assessments; (b) choice of media and specific guidelines for developmentally appropriate compositions; (c) choice of formal structures to facilitate improvisation; (d) literature, songs, and instrumental pieces for arranging; (e) musical works for listening and evaluation; and (f) critical writing prompts. The curriculum, because it is the general source for learning materials, is an excellent source of materials for assessment. The best materials for assessment are those that are developmentally appropriate for a child's age and grade level, involve the child in a musical learning activity, and clearly display the targeted behavior being assessed. Appropriate materials facilitate assessment implementation.

2. *The scope of the assessment task and the time allotted for the completion of the task*—When developing a task, consider the length of the class period (typically thirty to sixty minutes) and gauge what can reasonably be completed within that time frame. Teachers with shorter time periods may choose to span larger assessments over a period of several lessons. For example, a teacher assessing first graders on their ability to sing sol-mi on the pitches g_4 and e_4 in the context of a singing game may be able to successfully complete that assessment within a thirty-minute period. However, that

45

same teacher will need to allow several lessons for her fifth grade students to create and notate a four-measure piece for the recorder. When deciding the scope of the tasks to be employed, consider the following: (a) the attention span of the class; (b) for creative tasks, time to experiment and play; (c) for responding tasks, the writing level of the class and the children's available vocabulary; and (d) for performing tasks, the age-appropriate skill levels. Because many music teachers only see students once per week, the time allowed for the completion of the task should comfortably fit within a class period whenever possible. Tasks that span a series of lessons are best accomplished with older children, preferably no earlier than grade three.

3. *Student behavior and conduct*—This is a crucial issue in general music assessment, particularly with respect to authentic and alternative assessment tasks. If a music teacher does not have an adequately controlled and positive classroom atmosphere, the results of an authentic assessment can be compromised. Children involved in assessment tasks must be motivated to do their best work, and this motivation usually is a result of a combination of engaging activities, appropriate and interesting materials, and the teacher having set high musical expectations throughout the academic year. When faced with a class that is particularly difficult to control due to extramusical factors, a teacher can choose to devise an assessment task and administer it as a trial (piloting assessment tasks is discussed in chapter 7). The degree to which the trial is successful can serve to help the teacher decide whether or not to keep the task, redesign the task, or discard it and start over. All students will respond favorably to a well-designed and -executed assessment strategy.

4. *The level of teacher involvement*—Because authentic assessment situations so closely approximate the learning environment, the role of the teacher during an assessment must be considered carefully. A well-developed assessment task is one in which the learning and assessment contexts simulate each other closely, with the crucial exception of the teacher's involvement. Through their lessons, teachers strive to impart knowledge and facilitate learning through a variety of teaching strategies. The teacher's role in the context of the lesson is to support, answer questions, demonstrate skills, and encourage a high level of musicianship. However, during an assessment the teacher must allow the students to demonstrate skills and knowledge *on their own;* the teacher becomes an observer. A positive and encouraging demeanor on the part of the teacher has a tremendous effect on the students involved in authentic assessment tasks, but this is where the similarity to the facilitator role ends. The only questions that teachers should answer from students during assessment tasks are those pertaining to the procedures of the task; content- or skill-related questions cannot be answered.

Measurement Issues: Ensuring Usable Results

In addition to the environmental issues discussed above, certain issues pertaining to the measurement of musical behaviors must be considered when developing assessment tasks. Whereas environmental issues pertain to extramusical factors in the classroom that the teacher may or may not be able to fully control, concerns about measurement pertain to the task and its administration. These issues relate directly to the design and construction of the assessment task and help to ensure that the results obtained will remain relevant to what the teacher needs and expects (see Figure 2-4).

Validity

An assessment task is considered valid to the extent that it measures what it is supposed to measure. There are several types of validity that can be determined, but for the overall purposes of the general music teacher, *content validity* is the primary concern. (For an excellent discussion of content and other types of validity,

I refer the reader to Boyle and Radocy, 1987.) For example, if a teacher wants to assess students' acquisition of their singing voices, then an appropriate song must be chosen that will allow the teacher to judge this; an entirely different song would be necessary to measure vocal pitch accuracy on two specific pitches. The extent to which the content of an assessment facilitates the demonstration of its targeted skill or knowledge is the primary measure of the assessment task's content validity.

Measurement Issues in General Music Assessment

- **Validity**–how well the task measures what it is supposed to measure

- **Reliability**–the consistency with which the task measures what it is supposed to measure

- **Determination** of the possible outcomes

- **Design** of tasks that fit curriculum and assessment needs

- **Process** or product–what to measure

Figure 2-4.

The content validity of any assessment task is determined qualitatively by the judgment and common sense of the classroom teacher. Validity is strengthened when the assessment and learning contexts match as closely as possible. Another way to determine validity is to examine task results to determine that the results are revealing what the teacher has taught. If the results obtained from an assessment task do not demonstrate its targeted skill or knowledge, then the task needs to be reexamined and redesigned. If questions arise regarding the validity of a particular task, another music teacher can be asked to examine the task. The input of colleagues, if it is available, can be an invaluable asset to any teacher with respect to validity determination.

The key to content validity lies in the selection of appropriate materials (see earlier section, "The Classroom Assessment Environment"). The overview of children's cognitive musical development at the beginning of this chapter describes what research tells us about how children change in their ability to process and understand musical information. This has a direct impact on assessment, particularly the selection of materials used in specific tasks.

As mentioned earlier, it is extremely important in an authentic or alternative assessment context to have well-developed and clear criteria for judgment of the results. The misapplication of a rubric or single-criterion scoring guide can threaten the validity of an assessment, as well as its reliability, the subject of the next section of this chapter.

Reliability

An assessment task is reliable to the extent that it *consistently* measures what it is supposed to measure. There are several types of reliability appropriate in various testing situations. (Again, I refer the reader to Boyle and Radocy, 1987, for an excellent overview of reliability.) For general music teachers, the primary reliability issue lies in one's ability to judge assessment results across a large student population in a consistent and objective manner. Every assessment task that a teacher designs also includes a multiple- or single-criterion scoring guide (design guidelines are presented later in this chapter). The teacher's diligence in the objective application of the scoring guide to the results of an assessment task determines the extent to which the task can be considered to be reliable.

The key word in reliability for general music teachers is *objectivity*. Because music teachers grow to know their students over the period of years those children attend school (in elementary school, as many as six or seven years; in middle and high school, three to five or more years), it becomes very easy to allow extra-musical factors to enter into judgment decisions. For example, if a child is not singing on pitch, a teacher who knows this child well may want to compromise a bit on the judgment of pitch accuracy based on what the teacher knows about the child (he or she may be experiencing the divorce of parents, living with persons other than his or her parents, etc.). This type of compromise of the scoring criteria renders the results of that child's assessment unusable and calls into question the reliability of the entire assessment. Teachers must *learn to become objective observers of musical behaviors* in order to achieve success with an assessment program.

Determination of the Possible Response Outcomes

A *variable* is defined as any aspect of a situation that can vary, or have more than one possible outcome. Variability is an extremely important issue in all testing and in research, and individuals involved in these endeavors attempt to identify, control, and account for as many of the variables as possible prior to testing or conducting research studies. For the general music teacher, the primary concern is to anticipate the effects of the variables present in assessment tasks on the results obtained and to plan how to deal with them.

Authentic musical assessment tasks, by nature of their similarity to real-life situations, contain numerous variables and potential confounding factors that are uncontrollable because of the authenticity of the task. One way that general music teachers can help plan for this variability is to consider and attempt to predict all of the possible response outcomes that might occur during an assessment that might affect the assessment results. In other words, when designing a task the teacher should ask: What if...happens during the assessment? How will I handle this in my judgment of the results? This important process is essential to both the validity and reliability of the task, and as much time as possible should be devoted to determining these variables.

Referring to the vocal pitch accuracy example once again, if a teacher is setting out to determine whether or not the students in a second grade class can sing on pitch the notes g_4 and e_4 (the interval sol-mi in C major) in a particular song, then a number of possible outcomes need to be planned for in advance. This is a single-criterion assessment, the easiest type to score; the child is either "on" or "off" pitch, or so it seems. What if the child sings the proper pitches but the incorrect words or melody? What if the child sings the sol-mi interval but on different pitches other than g_4 and e_4? What if the child begins on the pitches g_4 and e_4 but then wavers to a new set of pitches during the assessment? Authentic assessments, even those that are scored as a single-criterion assessment, can become quite complex in the variability of the results. Because this type of assessment is conducted in the performance assessment response mode, the teacher has very little (if any) time to make judgments regarding these questions while the assessment is in progress. Deciding in advance how these situations will be scored can prevent a great deal of frustration on the part of the teacher as well as maintain the integrity of the task.

As shown in the previous example, single-criterion scoring can become complicated in an authentic assessment situation. Multiple-criterion, or *rubric,* scoring can present even more challenges. Chances are there will be many students who do not meet each single criterion for the rating of *proficient* on any given task, resulting in different criteria being met at different levels of achievement. Therefore, the teacher needs to determine ahead of time how *combinations* of different levels of achievement within one task will be evaluated. In this situation, the questions the teacher anticipates should be along these lines: If the rubric contains four criteria, each scored using four levels of achievement, what happens if a student meets two of the criteria at level 3 and two of the criteria at level 2? What will the overall level be? There are a number of combinations of this type that can occur during an assessment. The ultimate judgment lies with the teacher, and a mere "averaging" of the numbers representing different levels is not sufficient. If a student is rated on a four-criteria rubric (with each criterion scored using four levels of achievement) as level 1 on one of the criteria and level 3 on the remaining three criteria, the teacher may decide to determine that the student has reached an overall level 3, or proficient, rating. Resolving such scoring difficulties can be facilitated by examining the results of other assessments and the student's musical skills and knowledge as demonstrated *outside* of the assessment experience. While the teacher maintains the ultimate job of deciding whether or not a student has reached a particular overall rating, the decision made needs to be supportable, especially if the decision is challenged.

Design of Tasks that Fit Curriculum and Assessment Needs

One of the misconceptions about authentic and alternative assessment in music stems from the similarity between the learning and assessment environments. This misunderstanding concerns whether or not every activity undertaken in the class can be considered an "assessment." This is certainly not the case; everything that is done in the music class is not an assessment. This becomes particularly true in the construction of portfolios (covered in chapter 6), when deciding what to place in the portfolio is of paramount importance.

To ensure that tasks reflect the curriculum and what has been taught in the music class, they must be founded in the same content and skills. The curriculum should be rather specific as to what should be taught and when it should be mastered, and the skills necessary to demonstrate this musical knowledge should be part of the everyday lessons that music teachers prepare for their students. Assessment tasks should be carefully planned into the curriculum sequence and they should directly reflect the curriculum content. The materials for an assessment can certainly come directly from the recommended curriculum materials, and when used appropriately in an assessment context, they provide the perfect bridge between assessment and curriculum.

When it becomes necessary to design assessment tasks that employ extracurricular materials, the teacher needs to be especially careful that the task still fits the needs of the curriculum. Aligning assessment with the curriculum is essential, so care must be taken to choose materials that are similar to those suggested by the curriculum. Aligning assessment tasks with the teacher's assessment needs is also important. Teachers need to know and be able to check the progress of their students in all of the facets of musical learning. Assessments that do not meet either the curriculum or the teacher's assessment needs are a waste of time and should not be undertaken.

Process or Product: What Is the Focus?

Because music is an art form, there are two distinct aspects of music making. The first is *process,* having to do with the processes and procedures that involve the child in active musical performance or creation. The second is *product,* the end result of music making or writing.

The *process* of music making is temporal in nature, rendering it the most challenging to observe and assess. Because classroom musical performances exist only during the time they are in process, they cannot be easily captured for later observation. The presence of audio- or videotaping equipment in the classroom threatens the authenticity of performance or creative process assessments; one potential confounding effect is the reaction of the children to the video camera or tape recorder. Furthermore, the schedules of most general music teachers and the availability of the proper equipment often do not permit the capturing of musical performances on audio- or videocassette for later assessment.

When a teacher decides to assess a performance skill such as singing or playing instruments, it becomes imperative that the *focus* of the assessment remains on the performance skills *only*. For example, the teacher who is examining instrumental technique (e.g., hand position on the soprano recorder, mallet technique, etc.) may observe that a child who is performing a musical piece on a classroom instrument is also performing the incorrect notes. Because this was not the focus of the assessment, it is recommended that for the purposes of that particular assessment the student's technical skills *only* be examined. A later assessment may focus on the correctness or incorrectness of the notes performed. This does not, however, prevent the teacher from making a brief written comment about any observed note-playing difficulty for later use, if time permits. Additionally, the teacher may observe that the incorrectness of the notes may have stemmed from the quality of the student's instrumental technique. The same holds true for assessments of the creative musical process; it is imperative that the focus of the assessment remains consistent.

Musical *products* are what remain at the conclusion of the music making or writing process. If a musical product is the focus of the assessment task, the teacher must be prepared in advance for the type of product expected and the medium in which it will be presented. For example, the end result of a composition assessment will be a created musical work, which can be presented in one of three ways: in performance, in notation, or both. While the performance context of a composition assessment is the same for both process and product, the focus of the assessment in each instance is quite different. A product assessment of a *performed composition* is perhaps the most challenging of all authentic assessments; the teacher must be well prepared in order to listen to a performance of a newly created student composition and judge it for product characteristics such as phrasing, melodic motion, or sense of closure. This is especially true when assessing the products of musical improvisation.

The assessment of *compositional products* is made easier for the teacher when the creation of a written copy of the composition is part of the assessment task. The written copy can be used to support the teacher's observation of the performed product. All types of performances can be recorded on audio- or videotape for later product assessment (as mentioned earlier with respect to process), with the understanding that the recording process can jeopardize the authentic quality of the musical products for some students.

How Much Time Should Be Allotted for Assessment?

Another important issue for general music teachers has to do with the amount of time involved in the administration of the tasks and the usefulness or value of the results obtained. For example, a music curriculum may state that a child should be able to sing expressively. The curriculum should elaborate on exactly what parameters of expression should be expected, as well as provide specific examples of what those parameters are. In this curriculum, children in the fourth grade may be expected to demonstrate contrasting "piano" and "forte" in a given song where these dynamics are part of the song's interpretation. If this skill is critical to the curriculum, the music teacher may assess these behaviors during a performance that targets multiple curricular components, one of which could be use of dynamic contrast. On the other hand, if the skill is not critical to the curriculum, a music teacher may be forced to decide that his or her limited time with the children could be better spent assessing other behaviors. However, this decision should not preclude teaching "piano" and "forte" or providing students experience with these dynamics. In an ideal situation, a music teacher would have enough lesson time to regularly track progress in each of the performance task target areas, but in reality, choices must often be made. To help avoid frustration over what should be assessed, each teacher must develop a hierarchy of assessable components based on the following considerations:

1. *Its importance within the overall curriculum* (this is often decided at the district level, especially if the component is placed on a district- or state-level assessment);
2. *The number of minutes allotted for music instruction per week*; and
3. *The value of the results to the overall assessment scheme.*

Assessment and Children with Special Needs

Many general music specialists are finding that children with special needs are a regular part of their teaching responsibilities. In some situations, the music specialist sees the special needs class as a self-contained unit; in other situations, the children are included in non-special needs classes for their music instruction (this practice is called *mainstreaming*). In both instances, musical assessments can be conducted with success, with certain additional considerations.

In most instances, special needs children are under the supervision of a classroom teacher who specializes in instructing children with cognitive or physical impairments. These specialists are required to create for each child an *Individual Education Plan,* often referred to as an I.E.P. Other methods may be employed by individual school districts, but the primary purpose of the I.E.P. remains the same. The I.E.P. spells out the special services that the child will receive in order to help him or her progress at the fastest and most rewarding rate possible given the impairments the child possesses.

Because these children appear in the music class and receive instruction from the general music teacher, it is important that the music teacher be informed of the requirements of the I.E.P. The music teacher most likely will have to seek this information on his or her own, and the easiest and most direct method of accomplishing this is to schedule a brief conference with the special needs teacher. All persons responsible for the instruction of a particular child have the right to view that child's records, and taking the time to review the records of the children in special needs classes can be extremely valuable for lesson and assessment planning.

The type and purpose of musical assessment with special needs children will depend upon several factors. First, the requirements of the I.E.P. must be considered. Second, social factors play an important role. In this instance, children who are being included in a regular classroom for music instruction need to participate in all of the assessments that the teacher plans. The special needs child should never be denied the opportunity to participate in any assessment task; however, the results of the task will need to be viewed with respect to that child's cognitive or physical impairments. For example, the assessment of a quadriplegic child's ability to keep a steady beat can be accomplished through head or eye movements, or singing. Informed and sensitive music specialists can, with good planning and proper strategies, obtain a good deal of useful musical progress information about children with special needs.

Integrated Projects

As children reach upper grade levels (fifth grade and higher), they usually become capable of undertaking more complex musical assessment tasks. These tasks are designed to assess more than one skill or behavior and are called *integrated projects*. Such tasks can also integrate more than one musical learning area within the same task. These can be highly effective assessments and extremely engaging for the children as long as the following considerations are made.

Integrated projects are generally conducted and completed over a period of two or more lessons. It is important to determine at the outset of the project how much time will be allowed in class to complete the project. Certain projects may require work outside of the class, and this should be anticipated. Additionally, these projects sometimes require more than one person for their successful completion. How to divide the class into small groups is something the teacher must predetermine.

These types of projects should sensibly integrate skills and knowledge from at least two of the musical learning areas and can involve knowledge from domains outside of music. A common integrated project is one in which a child first composes and notates a piece, and then performs it, combining musical skills (playing or singing and composition) and literacy (notation). A sample composition project and its rubric are presented in Figure 2-5. Another example of a project is to ask a group of children to musically illustrate and perform a story, again combining several musical skills: instrument playing, singing, improvising, and arranging. Arranging projects can be further expanded to include analysis and preference by requiring the group to write down their reasons for creating their arrangement.

Sample Composition Project

Sixth Grade Compostion Project

Name_____   **Teacher**_____

Requirements

You and a partner (or partners–up to three people per group) will compose a piece that contains a tonic-dominant-tonic (I-V-I) harmony change. The piece can be for an instrument of your choosing and must have an accompaniment. You may use the accompaniment provided or compose one of your own. The following requirements must be met for your piece to be complete:

1. The piece can be in 3/4 or 4/4 meter. Other meters can be used with special permission.

2. The piece must be in the C major diatonic scale. Other scales must be pre-approved.

3. The rhythm must employ at least ♩ , ♪ , and ♪ notes, and their corresponding rests when necessary.

4. You may use ○ and ♩ notes and rests if your final rhythm using these values is approved. The rhythm and melody should reach a final point at the end of the piece.

5. You and your partner(s) must *each* write and turn in a neat, complete, and correctly notated score that uses a grand staff to show the melody and accompaniment. This must be handwritten first and, when approved, can be notated on the computer.

6. The piece must be at least four measures in length.

7. You and your partner(s) must be able to perform the piece with accuracy and expression.

8. You will keep a log of your progress each week and turn in your log each week.

Schedule and Due Date

You will have four weeks to complete this project. Here's the schedule:

Week 1 Choose your partner(s); compose and notate your rhythm; get the rhythm approved; decide your instrumentation; begin a draft copy of the melody

Week 2 Finalize the melody draft copy; begin transcribing the final copy

Week 3 Complete notation of the piece; practice for performances in Week 4

Week 4 Decide performance assessment criteria; practice and perform pieces. You will assess your own work as well as the other performances. You will then turn in your completed project, including your score and your performance assessments.

Note: This project assumes one one–hour class per week.   **Figure 2-5. (front)**

Sample Composition Project Rubric

Rubric for Finished Compositions

1. The piece is in an approved meter and scale.

> **2** = yes
> **1** = no

2. The composition presents a I-V-I harmony change that is correctly employed.

> **2** = yes
> **1** = no

3. The rhythm employs at least ♩ , ♪, and ♪ notes, and their corresponding rests when necessary.

> **2** = yes
> **1** = no

4. The piece comes to a musically satisfying conclusion.

> **2** = yes
> **1** = no

5. The score is neat, complete, and correctly notated.

> **4** = notation is perfect and the score is neat
> **3** = notation is mostly correct and the score is neat
> **2** = notation is inconsistent and the score is messy
> **1** = notation is mostly incorrect and sloppy, and the score is messy

6. The piece is an appropriate length.

> **3** = the piece is longer than four measures and remains musically interesting
> **2** = the piece is four measures in length
> **1** = the piece is less than four measures in length or incomplete

7. Progress logs are turned in each week.

> **3** = logs are accurate, complete, and neatly written
> **2** = logs are mostly complete and readable
> **1** = log is incomplete and messy

8. You and your partner(s) must be able to perform the piece with accuracy and expression.

> **2** = the piece is performed as written with accuracy and expression
> **1** = the piece is not peformed as written

Figure 2-5. (back)

Integrated projects that employ musical knowledge and knowledge domains outside of music include the design of musical interviews or radio plays (see Figure 2-6). When children design these types of projects, they must employ their language arts skills, and the music teacher needs to be prepared to assess those skills as part of the total assessment of the project. Another project that integrates musical knowledge, visual arts, and logical-mathematical skills is the game-building project (see Figure 2-7). For this project, teams of students work toward the design of a board game that is visually pleasing, logically designed with clear rules for play, requires factual knowledge about music in order to win, and employs language arts skills with respect to the writing of a log of the team's progress. The assessment of these types of projects is covered in chapter 5.

Such projects must be assessed using rubrics designed for each aspect of the results obtained, taking into account the potential effects of the additional learning areas. For example, in the previous story arranging example, the criteria that comprise the rubric for instrument playing technique will need to be general enough to accommodate a variety of instruments and flexible enough to account for unusual playing techniques that the children may employ to create sound effects necessary for their arrangement. Additionally, the rubrics should be presented to students at the outset so that they may work toward meeting the criteria as the project develops. (Figure 5-8 presents a sample rubric for the game-building project; Figure 5-9 presents a rubric for the radio play project.)

When designed with specific assessment goals in mind, the integrated project is one of the most authentic assessments available to the general music teacher. It yields a wealth of musical progress information and allows students to demonstrate their accumulated musical knowledge in an engaging and challenging format.

Sample Radio Play Project

Sixth Grade Music Project

Name_____   Teacher_____

Goal

The purpose of this project is for teams of 5-6 students to write and produce
15-minute radio programs that are brief music lessons on one topic. Selected
lessons will be recorded and sent to our local public radio for consideration
for broadcast. This project should produce a series of music lessons
that can be broadcast over a period of weeks in the late winter/early spring.
The target audience for these programs is children ages 8-10
(approx. grades 3-5).

Approximate Schedule and Time Frame

Week 1	Introduction; select teams, team leaders, and topics; begin research of topic
Week 2	Continue/complete research
Week 3	Complete research; begin writing; develop characters and sound effects
Week 4	Continue writing and development of characters/ sound effects; begin rehearsing and timing the lesson
Week 5	Rehearse; fine-tune; time the lesson
Week 6	ASSESSMENT AND SELECTION OF LESSONS TO BE RECORDED
Week 7	Final rehearsals
Week 8	To be scheduled—trips to recording studio

Weekly Grading Criteria

Progress toward each week's goal will be monitored. Special evaluation forms
will be provided each week to the team leader. These will be turned in at the
end of each lesson and will present evidence of the work completed in each period.

Final Evaluation

Each team is expected to produce a radio program that meets the goals
of the project. It is expected that all projects will meet these minimum
requirements and therefore be graded as "S" for satisfactory. To receive
an "E," the project must demonstrate exceptional clarity of topic, excellent choices of materials, and a creative, engaging, musical presentation.

Selection for Recording

This will be done by a panel of observers (teachers) who will listen to the
programs and score them. The highest scores will be those that are recorded and sent for broadcast consideration.

Note: This project assumes one one–
hour class per week.

Figure 2-6.

Sample Game-Building Project

Game-Building Project

Name_____   Teacher_____

Starting Date_____

Requirements

For this project, you and your group will design and build a board game
that is interesting, fun to play, and teaches at least ten facts (more are OK!)
about music harmony, music reading, music symbols, music history
(composers), instruments, instrument playing, or musical works. Here's
what your game project must include:

1. A clear set of rules that are easy to follow;
2. A hand-made game board and set of pieces
   (cards, spinner, moving artifacts, etc.) for
   playing the game;
3. An original title;
4. A log of the steps you took to create your game
   (these will be turned in at the end of each class
   by the group leader); and
5. A final presentation and demonstration of your
   game to the class.

Grading

This project will be judged by the class and the teacher using the rubric on
the back of this sheet. You will be responsible for turning in your group's
log at the end of each class and for participating in the final presentation.
The assessment of the finished game board, pieces, rules, and title will
be counted for each member of the group. *This will be your primary
grade for this grading period.*

Schedule and Due Date

Here's the schedule for this project:

Week 1   Choose your groups; determine the ten or more facts that your
            game will teach; begin a sketch of the design, determine the
            type of game and game pieces you will produce; each group
            will turn in a log listing these items

Week 2   Finalize the game design and rules; begin creating the board and
            pieces; turn in log

Week 3   Finish the board and pieces; play the game in your group; turn
            in log

Week 4   Set assessment criteria; give presentations; turn in final game,
            pieces, and logs (including this sheet!), as well as assessments
            of your own game and the other presentations

Figure 2-7.

The Musical Aptitude Profile

In addition to teacher-designed assessments, a teacher may choose to administer a commercially available standardized music test, the *Musical Aptitude Profile*, or one of its shorter versions, the *Primary Measures of Music Audiation* or the *Intermediate Measures of Music Audiation*. While authentic and alternative assessments are designed to measure individual musical progress in relation to the curriculum and standards of a particular school system, standardized music tests provide information with respect to how an individual student compares to the population at large with regard to certain musical abilities or skills. The standardization process usually includes trial testing with large numbers of students across the nation so that the test items can be scrutinized statistically to determine their reliability, validity, and effectiveness at discriminating levels of a particular musical ability or skill among test takers.

While standardized music tests can provide valuable information for general music teachers, the primary drawbacks include the expense and time involved in conducting the tests. The remainder of this section provides a description of the *Musical Aptitude Profile*. Teachers who desire more information on this and other tests can consult the *Mental Measurements Yearbook* (in print or online), published by Buros Company, or the test manuals.

Edwin Gordon (1978, 1984) has developed a sequential learning theory that is based on the development of audiation, a type of internal representation of music related to memory. Gordon claims that audiation "takes place when one hears music silently, that is, when the sound is not physically present" (1984, p. 11). According to his theory, audiation develops until age nine, when it stabilizes and does not change throughout the rest of one's life. Gordon's concept of audiation is the fundamental construct underlying his *Musical Aptitude Profile*.

makes up musical aptitude.

Gordon (1987) describes musical aptitude as a product of both environment and inherited potential. Even though varying degrees of musical aptitude exist among the population, he claims that all normal persons possess some level of musical aptitude. His test measures the most basic aspects of musical aptitude: "musical expression, aural perception, and kinesthetic musical feeling" (Gordon, 1965, p. 1). He claims that the test provides objective information regarding aptitude but that it must be combined with other factors to enhance its relative worth as an assessment of *overall* musical aptitude. He states:

> *Test scores, when considered without regard for human judgment and extra-musical factors, are of limited usefulness in the assessment of basic musical aptitude and the prediction of success in musical endeavors.* (Gordon, 1987, p. 2)

Gordon presents five purposes for his test. The first is to encourage musically talented students to participate in music performance organizations such as choir and band. Second, he claims that the results are useful for adapting music instruction to meet the individual needs and abilities of students with varying degrees of musical ability. Third, the test can be used to formulate educational plans in music and guide students with higher aptitude toward appropriate musical endeavors. Another purpose of his test is that it makes it possible to evaluate the musical aptitude of groups of students, a desirable feature in school systems where testing time and administration costs must be held down. A final advantage of this test is that it can provide parents with objective information about their child's musical abilities so that they do not hold inflated views of their child's musicianship.

The test is presented in three sections: (1) *Tonal Imagery,* (2) *Rhythmic Imagery,* and (3) *Musical Sensitivity.* The general procedures for the presentation of the material in the *Tonal and*

Rhythmic Imagery sections are as follows. First, students are presented with a "musical question" phrase and a "musical answer" phrase. The musical answer manipulates the musical question phrase in some fashion or repeats the question exactly. The test takers then mark their answer sheets as to whether or not the musical question and the musical answer are the same (S), different (D), or they don't know (?). Their answer sheets are encoded accordingly. The *Musical Sensitivity* section is a musical preference test in three parts (phrasing, balance, and style), and the procedures for presenting the test material are slightly different. The test takers are presented with two renditions of the same selection and asked to decide which makes better "musical sense." They mark their answer sheets accordingly.

1. *Tonal Imagery*—This section of the test is administered in two parts. In "Part I: Melody," students are presented with two melodies and asked to determine if the musical answer is the same as the musical question, even though the musical answer contains "extra notes." In "Part II: Harmony," the musical question is a two-part melody, and the musical answer is a version of the musical question with only the lower part altered (or not altered).

2. *Rhythmic Imagery*—This section is also administered in two parts. In "Part I: Tempo," the ending of the musical answer is faster, slower, or exactly the same as the musical question. In "Part II: Meter," the musical answer is sometimes presented in a different meter than the musical question.

3. *Musical Sensitivity (Preference)*—The last section of the test is administered in three parts. For "Part I: Phrasing," students decide which of two renditions of a musical phrase is performed with better musical expression. In "Part II: Balance," the second rendition has a different ending; the test takers must decide which ending is better, both melodically and rhythmically, for the selection. In the final section, "Part III: Style," the same selection is performed twice at different tempi. The test takers must decide which one is best.

Gordon considered several important factors in the construction of his test. First, he felt that test takers should not have to be familiar with technical or historical musical facts. While appropriate for a test of musical achievement, Gordon determined that such information was not necessary to determine aptitude. He also attempted to construct the test so that a high degree of musical memory would not interfere with the results. To minimize recognition factors, music on the test was composed specifically for the test. The selections are performed by professional musicians (two violinists and a cellist) and recorded with the highest technical quality available to ensure the best reproduction of sound. Gordon also believed that test takers should enjoy the tests, so a variety of music is used to help keep the test takers interested. He also designed the test to be suitable for a wide range of ages, with item difficulty varying through the test to further stimulate student interest. He also considered that the type of response should not be so complex as to introduce abilities extraneous to musical judgment; hence, a simple "fill in the dot" answer sheet was devised. He also felt that students should not be forced to respond when unprepared to make a choice. Hence, "in doubt" responses are allowed on the answer sheet.

This test was first marketed in 1965 after six years of development. The *Musical Aptitude Profile* was designed to test stabilized musical aptitude. Since its publication, four tests of developmental musical aptitude have been developed and published by Gordon: (1) *Primary Measures of Music Audiation (PMMA)*, 1979; (2) *Intermediate Measures of Music Audiation (IMMA)*, 1982; (3) *Advanced Measures of Music Audiation*, 1989; and (4) *Audie: A Game for Understanding and Analyzing Your Child's Music Potential*, also in 1989.

Designing Single- and Multiple-Criterion Scoring Guides

To review, a *criterion-referenced* assessment is one in which a student's performance on an assessment task is judged by comparing the student's performance to one or more specific criteria. For each criterion, there is a range of levels, expressed in numbers or word descriptors, that covers the expected range of achievement. There are two primary types of scoring guides: the *single-criterion guide* and the *multiple-criterion guide*. The assessment criterion or criteria expressed in these guides can be developed to display two or more levels of achievement.

Scoring guides that indicate more than two levels of achievement per criterion are known as *rubrics*. Rubrics encompass one criterion with three or more levels of achievement for judgment, or two or more criteria with two or more levels of achievement. In a rubric, each higher achievement level indicates a corresponding higher degree of criterion demonstration. Single-criterion rubrics are designed to indicate levels of achievement with respect to one specific criterion and are the simplest to employ in a performance situation. Rubrics that involve multiple criteria and multiple levels are the most complex scoring guides and can be unwieldy in real-time performance assessments but valuable in other assessment contexts. Each level of a rubric is usually assigned a *descriptor* (a word or phrase that describes achievement at that level) that indicates to some degree the magnitude of the criteria demonstration. A general model is presented in Figure 2-8. (More specific rubrics and scoring strategies are presented in later chapters.) While rubrics can present from two to as many as six or more levels of achievement, most rubrics have four achievement levels that can be generalized as follows.

Level 1. Achievement at this level can be described in words like *novice* or *beginner*. At this level, results indicate that the knowledge or proficiency that was the target of the assessment has not been demonstrated in any manner that would indicate that it has been acquired. A good rule of thumb to follow when designing this level is to employ the words "does not" when describing the outcome of the assessment. For example, in an assessment of the ability to notate melodies on the staff in the treble clef, one might include "does not make the treble clef correctly" or "does not correctly place the meter signature at the beginning of the melody" in the rubric description of Level 1 performance if these are notation skills that the assessment is targeting.

Level 2. Students at this level can be described as *apprentice, developing,* or *progressing.* At this level, student performance indicates only partial acquisition of the targeted knowledge or skill. Criteria at this level are best described in terms such as "occasionally," "sometimes," "sporadically," or "inconsistently." It is also possible to express this level in general quantities, such as "less than half of the time." For example, if one is examining a child's instrumental technique (such as the proper use of mallets with barred percussion instruments or proper striking of a hand drum), one might include statements like "uses alternating mallet technique inconsistently" or "strikes the drum with the proper stroke less than half of the time" in the rubric to describe Level 2 achievement if these are targeted behaviors for the assessment.

Level 3. Students at this level are classified as being *proficient* or *competent* with the targeted knowledge or skill. This is the level of the rubric that teachers seek to have their students attain. Indications of this achievement level are described in terms like "consistently," "definitely," and "most of the time." For example, in an assessment of a child's melodic composition, the rubric might include statements such as "consistently creates melodies in easily discernible phrases" or "consistently varies melodic direction" if these are criteria that the assessment seeks to measure.

It is also important to note that at this achievement level a teacher must make a determination with respect to the extent to which the term "consistently" will be interpreted to mean "always." With children, it is very limiting to use terms such as "always" or "never" when constructing rubrics because they leave no room for subjectivity of judgment by the teacher. For instance, in terms of the above example regarding phrasing characteristics of a child's melodic composition, if a child composes a melody that expresses easily discernible phrases most of the time throughout the piece, then it is perfectly appropriate to ascribe Level 3 to the child's work if the teacher feels that this aspect of compositional skill has been acquired. For most children, this is the desired level of achievement.

Level 4. At this level, students are described as *distinguished, outstanding,* or *extraordinary.* This level is reserved for those few students who express skill or knowledge beyond what is expected or anticipated for proficiency. Criteria for this level can be described with words such as "exceptional," "remarkable," and "advanced." Children who study music outside of school or who have naturally higher levels of motivation, skill, or musical ability are most likely to fall into this category due to their generally higher level of expertise or musical knowledge. An example of a Level 4 achievement would be the third grade student who is participating in a guided composition assessment (a technique described later in this book) and is expected to create and notate a four-measure melody in the treble clef in C-pentatonic in 4/4 meter for a barred percussion instrument. Instead, this student composes a twelve-measure piece for the piano in treble and bass clef in 3/4 meter and notates and performs it perfectly. Most teachers have a few students like this, and these are the *only* students who should be designated as having acquired Level 4.

Formulating a Rubric

Most often, there are four levels of achievement or ability (can be three to five or more). These can be generally categorized as follows:

Level 1 *novice, beginner*
The level of performance or outcome is not indicative of the targeted behavior or concept.

Level 2 *apprentice, developing, progressing*
The level of performance or outcome is inconsistently or sporadically indicative of the targeted behavior or concept.

Level 3 *proficient, competent*
The level of performance or outcome is consistently or definitely indicative of the targeted behavior or concept.

Level 4 *distinguished, outstanding, extraordinary*
The level of performance is remarkable and exceptional with respect to the targeted behavior or concept.

Figure 2-8.

The Keys to Keeping Track: Compatible Rubrics and Record Keeping Strategies

It is vital for music educators to design rubrics for classroom use that are compatible with simple and efficient data collection procedures. The overall goal is twofold: *effective assessment* with *efficient record keeping*. For general music teachers, this is a primary concern because of the large number of students served.

This section provides a description of each of the types of scoring guides that classroom music teachers may want to employ along with a classroom-tested example. These are summarized in Figure 2-9.

Rubric Types and Suggested Data Collection Techniques

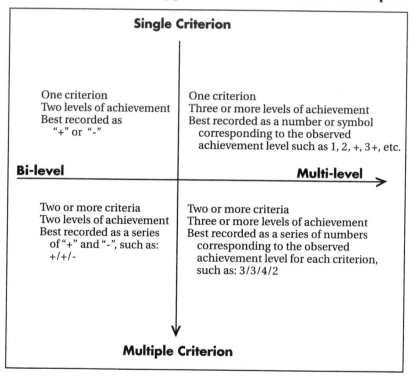

Single Criterion

One criterion
Two levels of achievement
Best recorded as
"+" or "-"

One criterion
Three or more levels of achievement
Best recorded as a number or symbol
corresponding to the observed
achievement level such as 1, 2, +, 3+, etc.

Bi-level   **Multi-level** →

Two or more criteria
Two levels of achievement
Best recorded as a series
of "+" and "-", such as:
+/+/-

Two or more criteria
Three or more levels of achievement
Best recorded as a series of numbers
corresponding to the observed
achievement level for each criterion,
such as: 3/3/4/2

Multiple Criterion

Figure 2-9.

The *bi-level, single-criterion* scoring guide is used when a teacher targets a single proficiency and determines that the proficiency is either *demonstrated* or *not demonstrated*. Therefore, there are only two levels of achievement: *attained* or *not attained*. This is the easiest to implement in real-time performance assessment situations and the most practical for general music teachers. In this type of scoring guide, the teacher notes the two levels of achievement or performance, usually marked as a "+" or a "-." For example, when a third grade class is playing a do-re-mi singing game for the assessment of their vocal pitch accuracy on D, E, and F#, as each solo is performed the teacher encodes on the data collection sheet a "+" if the child is on pitch and a "-" if the child is off pitch. While this type of scoring guide may appear to be the simplest to understand and employ, the complexities of real-time performance situations may present variables that will cause some difficulty with judgment. If one invests the appropriate amount of time and thought in setting a clear description of the criterion, however, this can be avoided.

The *multi-level, single-criterion* rubric is employed when a teacher wishes to assess one criterion but desires to record more than just whether or not the criterion was *attained* or *not attained.* With practice and efficient design, this can be used quite effectively. This type of rubric permits a single criterion to be assessed on three or more levels of achievement. Once the criterion is selected, the teacher must then identify and create symbols to represent the different information or levels of achievement that are anticipated. These symbols can be arrows, lines, numbers, or any marking of the teacher's choosing. During the assessment, appropriate markings are notated on the data collection form in the most sensible manner. This type of rubric can also help the teacher record meaningful descriptive data. For example, when recording vocal pitch accuracy data, as described in the previous paragraph, the teacher may want to also note the starting pitch of the inaccurate children as above or below the targeted pitch with an arrow pointing up (↑)or down (↓); this adds descriptive information to the assessment data. Children's voices that waver— sometimes on pitch, sometimes off pitch—can be indicated with a wavy line (⇥). This adds a third level to the assessment; children can be on pitch, off pitch, or waver in their pitch. In some instances, this information may be helpful to the teacher, especially when dealing with the assessment of young voices that are developing.

The *bi-level, multiple-criterion* rubric is used when a teacher is assessing two or more criteria as either *attained* or *not attained*. This can be useful for a teacher who needs information about several facets of a child's demonstrated knowledge. For example, when a fourth grade class has learned a piece for the Orff instruments, the teacher may wish to assess both the accuracy of the piece (criterion #1) and the child's ability to alternate the mallets (criterion #2, mallet technique). To record this data, the teacher marks a "+" or "-" for each criterion, with a "/" in between. The order of the markings follows the order in which the criteria are assessed. In this example, the child who plays the piece accurately and alternates mallets receives a "+/+" marking; if the child played the piece accurately but did not demonstrate proper mallet technique, the child receives a "+/-," and so on. This type of scoring increases in complexity as more criteria are added and simultaneously assessed. When employing multiple-criterion rubrics, data recording requires a great deal of skill on the part of the teacher, as well as a performance of sufficient length to permit accurate assessment.

The *multi-level, multiple-criterion* scoring guide involves the judgment of more than one criterion, where at least one criterion has more than two levels of possible achievement. This is the most difficult type of scoring guide to use effectively in performance. In the general music classroom, student performances are generally short in duration; therefore, this type of rubric requires a great deal of judgment in very little time. These scoring guides can be very useful, though, in the examination of complex musical products such as notated composition scores and written responses.

Figure 2-10 presents a multi-level, multiple-criterion scoring guide that was developed to assess children's improvisations. The guide is written in two forms: Form 1 follows a *level-by-level* design and Form 2 follows a *criterion-by-criterion* design. The level-by-level design is unwieldy when judging several criteria in a performance or product because it limits a judgment about all criteria to only one of the multiple levels. The level-by-level design does not allow for a judgment to be made regarding different levels of achievement for the different criteria; in the example shown in Figure 2-10, there is no way to adequately mark a student who, for example, exceeds on one of the criteria, meets proficiency on two criteria, and does not meet the other two criteria. The criterion-by-criterion design, on the other hand, allows the criteria to be rated individually and at levels appropriate for the individual criterion. The criterion-by-criterion design is recommended for classroom use, but the level-by-level design may be preferred in certain situations. The final choice of the most appropriate and useful design for a specific task is at the teacher's discretion.

If using the level-by-level design, the multi-level, multiple-criterion assessment data can be recorded as a number corresponding to the level of achievement. When employing the criterion-by-criterion design, information is best recorded as a series of numbers that correspond with the level of achievement demonstrated, with a slash marking (/) between each number. The order of the numbers should correspond to the order in which the criteria were judged, and this order of marking should be consistent among the students being assessed. An example of the marking scheme for the multi-level, multiple-criterion rubric shown in Figure 2-10 would be 3/3/1/2/2 for a student who maintained a consistent, steady beat and tempo but did not create an original rhythm or end on tonic, and whose mallet technique was inconsistent.

Two Versions of a Multi-Level, Multiple-Criterion Rubric

The goal of this assessment was for the children to create an improvisation in C-pentatonic that was rhythmically original and ended on the tonic pitch.

Form 1—Level-by-Level Design

Level 1 —steady beat largely absent; tempo unsteady; mallet technique does not alternate; does not end on the tonic pitch; rhythm is not original

Level 2 —steady beat/tempo wavers at times; mallet technique is inconsistent; may or may not end on the tonic; rhythm shows some originality

Level 3 —steady beat and tempo maintained throughout; mallet technique is correct; ends on tonic pitch; rhythm is original and uses a variety of durations

Level 4 —technique is exceptional (e.g., use of three mallets); rhythm involves complex subdivisions of the beat as well as contrasting longer values; ends on tonic pitch

Form 2—Criterion-by-Criterion Design

1) Steady Beat

1 = largely absent
2 = wavers
3 = maintained throughout

2) Tempo

1 = unsteady throughout
2 = inconsistent
3 = maintained throughout

3) Rhythm

1 = unoriginal
2 = rhythm shows some originality
3 = original and uses a variety of durations
4 = complex subdivisions of the beat as well as contrasting longer values

4) Ends on Tonic

1 = yes
2 = no (bi-level)

5) Mallet Technique

1 = does not alternate
2 = alternates inconsistently
3 = correct mallet technique
4 = exceptional mallet technique (e.g., use of three mallets)

Figure 2-10.

Data Collection Forms

An important step in preparation for the management of assessment results is the design of an appropriate and efficient data collection form. There are two primary formats for general music teachers to use when collecting data: the standard grade book and the self-designed seating chart.

When using the *grade book* as a data collection form, the music teacher must carefully list each student in each class in the grade book in an order that makes data collection easiest. For most teachers, an alphabetical listing is the most efficient format, written in pencil so that names and places can be changed if necessary. Grade books also provide a numbered listing of the students in each class. For teachers who do not know the names of all of their students, performance assessments can be facilitated if the students wear numbers during the assessment that coincide with their numbers in the grade book.

For some teachers, a specially designed seating chart works best. These seating charts have spaces for the children's names, and attached to these designated name spaces are boxes or blocks that are used to record assessment information. These charts serve the dual purpose of organizing the music classroom and providing space for data collection. When grades are needed for report cards, information for each child can be easily found and evaluated. Figures 2-11 through 2-13 (used by permission, Nancy Schkurman, Clark County School District, Las Vegas, Nevada) and Figure 2-14 provide examples of teacher-made seating charts for music classrooms in rows, circles, and cooperative groups.

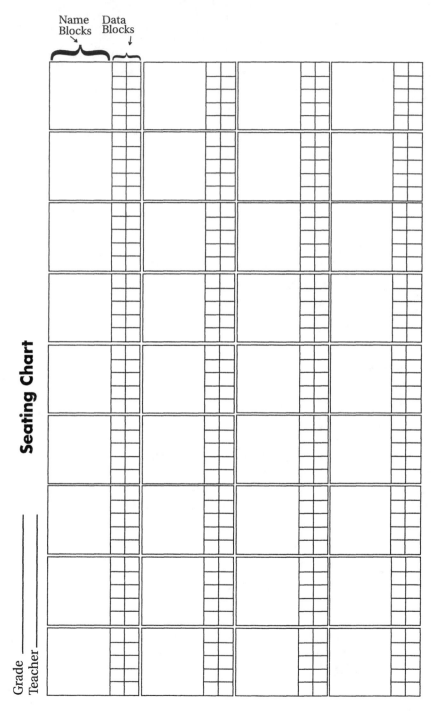

Seating Chart

Name Blocks   Data Blocks

Grade
Teacher

Figure 2-11.

Circular Seating Chart

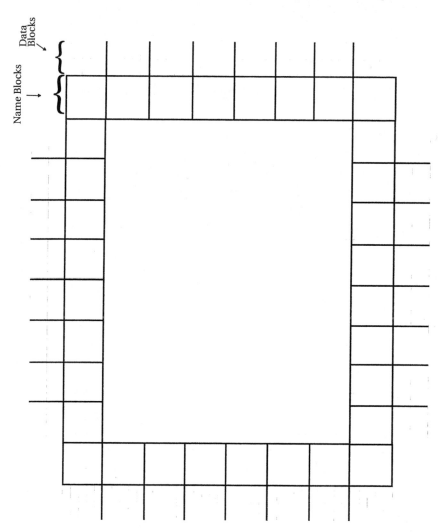

Figure 2-12.

Cooperative Grouping Seating Chart

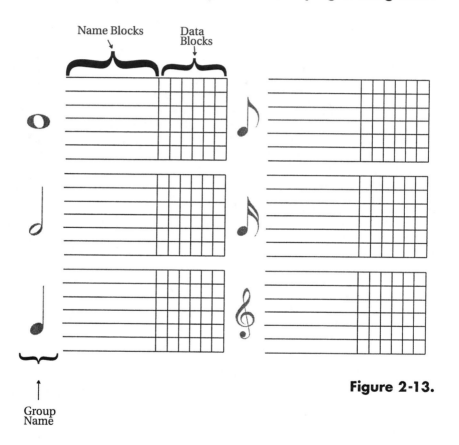

Figure 2-13.

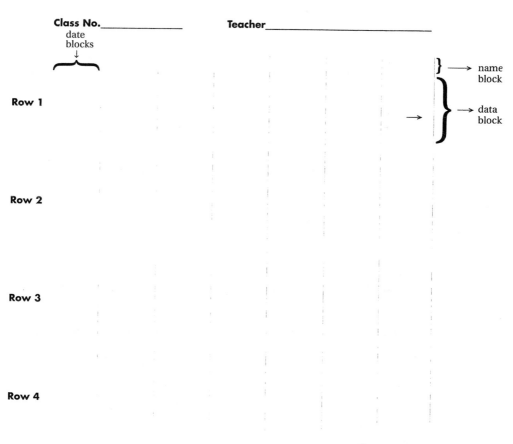

Music Seating Chart

Class No._____   Teacher_____

date
blocks

Row 1

Row 2

Row 3

Row 4

name block

data block

Figure 2-14.

Summary

- There are five primary learning areas in music: (1) *musical skills,* (2) *literacy,* (3) *history and literature,* (4) *analysis and preference,* and (5) *related arts and humanities.* Each learning area elicits particular musical behaviors that determine its appropriate assessment response mode.

- When developing assessment tasks for use in the general music classroom, teachers must take into consideration certain environmental and measurement issues.

- To ensure the proper implementation of a teacher-designed task, the teacher must: (1) *select appropriate materials,* (2) *determine the scope of the task and the amount of time that will be allotted to complete the task,* (3) *determine the parameters of student behavior and conduct that will be acceptable without affecting the task results,* and (4) *assume the role of observer during the assessment.*

- Measurement issues that the teacher must take into account when devising tasks include (1) *validity,* (2) *reliability,* (3) *determination of the possible response outcomes,* (4) *assurance that the tasks meet the assessment needs of the teacher and the curriculum,* and (5) *the process or product focus of the task.*

- Children with special needs can successfully participate in musical assessments as long as the teacher has an idea of the nature of the child's disabilities and consults with the child's special education teacher about the relevant provisions in the child's Individual Education Plan.

- Once a task is devised, an appropriate rubric or scoring guide must be developed to facilitate the measurement of task achievement. There are four basic types of scoring guides: (1) *bi-level, single-criterion;* (2) *bi-level, multiple-criterion;* (3) *multi-level, single-criterion;* and (4) *multi-level, multiple-criterion.*

- Data collection during assessment is also facilitated by a well-designed format, whether it be a *standard grade book* or a *specially designed seating chart.*

- Although the purpose of this book is to guide teachers in the construction of their own authentic and alternative assessment tasks, there are certain standardized music tests that teachers may choose to administer to their classes that can provide important musical data.

- Integrated projects are another important type of authentic assessment design that integrates two or more musical learning areas into one task and permits multiple behaviors and skills to be assessed.

Questions for Clarification

1) A musical learning area is defined by the nature of the _____ _____ embedded within a particular learning activity.

2) Determining the media and the specific student guidelines for developmentally appropriate compositions is an example of the _____ _____ _____ _____.

3) The role of the music teacher during an assessment task is that of an objective _____.

4) The extent to which an assessment task measures what it is intended to measure is referred to as its _____.

5) The consistency with which a task measures what it is intended to measure is referred to as its _____.

6) If a music teacher alters the pre-established scoring procedure for one or two students for extramusical factors, the _____ of the task is jeopardized.

7) One of the primary concerns of general music teachers who are preparing assessment tasks is to anticipate as much of the response _____ as possible.

8) When devising a task, a music teacher must first decide if the musical _____ or _____ will be the focus.

9) Children with _____ _____ should never be denied the opportunity to participate in an authentic or alternative assessment task.

10) In addition to regular classroom assessments, a music teacher may choose to administer a _____ _____ _____ to his or her classes if it will provide information that is relevant to his or her needs.

11) A task that involves multiple learning areas and assesses multiple musical skills and behaviors is an _____ _____.

12) Determining whether a student performs an original rhythm correctly or incorrectly is an example of a _____-criterion assessment.

13) A multi-level, single-criterion, or bi-level, multiple-criterion, or multi-level, multiple-criterion scoring guide is a _____.

Questions for Discussion

1) Develop a task for each of the musical learning areas that can be scored based on a bi-level, single-criterion scoring guide. Discuss the possible confounding elements in the task and the variability of responses that can be anticipated. Is your task better assessed with more than two levels?

2) Choose one of the musical learning areas and develop a task for that learning area that can be scored using a multi-level, multiple-criterion scoring guide. Discuss how you would handle situations where the criteria are met at different levels of the rubric.

3) Should improvisation be included in the "musical skills" learning area? Why or why not?

4) How do you feel about the influence of student behavior and conduct during an assessment on the results of the assessment? Is this an important issue for you?

5) Discuss the role of teacher as instructor and as objective observer. Is it important to change roles during an assessment exercise?

6) How important is validity to the development of an assessment task? How important is the reliability of the task? Discuss the teacher's part in controlling the validity and reliability of assessment tasks.

7) Can you think of a scenario where you might develop an assessment task that does not meet the curriculum or your assessment needs? What would it be?

8) Why is it important to determine the process or product focus of an assessment task in advance?

9) How do you feel about the use of standardized musical tests as part of an overall assessment program?

10) How do you feel about including special needs children in assessment tasks? What considerations would you make before, during, and after the task administration?

11) Develop a project that integrates at least two of the musical learning areas and then do the following: determine the skills, behaviors, or concepts to be assessed; create the scoring guides; anticipate the variability in the responses and how you will deal with them; determine the process/product focus of the project.

12) Develop a project that integrates at least two of the musical learning areas and one or more knowledge domains outside of music (language arts, science, mathematics, social studies, or other arts) and then do the following: determine the skills, behaviors, or concepts to be assessed; create the scoring guides; anticipate the variability in the responses and how you will deal with them; determine the process/product focus of the project.

---

[1] An excellent source of developmental sequences for the elements of music is chapters 4-10 of *Music in Childhood* (1995), by Patricia Shehan-Campbell and Carol Scott-Kassner.

Chapter 3

Assessing the Performing Child Musician

Chapters three, four, and five of this book apply what has been presented in the first two chapters to the development of assessment tasks within specific response modes. This chapter will discuss the development, purpose, and use of assessments of musical performance skills.

Related National Standards

The National Standards for Arts Education (MENC, 1994) list specific musical knowledge and skills that should be expected of students at the preK, fourth, eighth, and twelfth grade levels in American public schools. Each content standard is subdivided into specific achievement standards for each of four grade level groups: preK, K-4, 5-8, and 9-12. This chapter deals with the development of tasks that assess musical performance, and there are two National Standards that deal specifically with content and achievement in this area. National Content Standard number 1 has to do with "singing, alone and with others, a varied repertoire of music," and National Content Standard number 2 pertains to "performing on instruments, alone and with others, a varied repertoire of music." Some performance assessment tasks may include a sight-reading component, and these types of tasks also address Content Standard number 5, which has to do with "reading and notating music." (MENC, 1994, pp. 26-27)

These musical behaviors are expressed within the Musical Skills and Literacy learning areas, and elicit responses in the performance assessment response mode, the mode that most nearly simulates authentic musical performance. Because movement is an important part of the general music program, and movement is also used to demonstrate certain basic skills and concepts (particularly with young children), assessments involving movement are also discussed in this chapter. In this book, movement for assessment purposes is defined to include movements that provide students a nonverbal means of expressing musical knowledge through simple physical action; this does *not* include movements that are necessary components of technique (e.g., hand positions, fingering movements, etc.) or movements related to learning activities (unless the movement is integral to the assessment task).

Determining What Is Important to Assess

The first step in developing assessment tasks for performance skills is to break down these skills into components that can be assessed accurately and comfortably by the classroom music teacher. There are several sources for these *assessable components* (see Figure 3-1), namely: (1) the National Music Standards for content and achievement, (2) state content and achievement standards for music, (3) the school district's adopted music series, (4) the curriculum, and (5) the school district's standards and/or performance indicators. A *performance indicator* is a specific statement that describes a performance that indicates the acquisition of required knowledge and/or skill. Performance indicators are one of the best sources for assessable components because they have been designed to identify the specific musical behaviors that the district has deemed to be an important indication that a student has obtained a specific level of musical knowledge. In the absence of specific performance indicators, the curriculum is the next best place to find these components, although it may be necessary for the teacher to formulate these on his or her own if the curriculum does not specifically address assessment. In situations like this, the National Standards provide an excellent framework for identifying specific assessable musical behaviors.

Sources for Assessable Components

- Local district standards/performance indicators
- Local district curriculum
- National Standards
- State standards
- Adopted music series

Figure 3-1.

Task Target Areas

To review, a teacher who is developing an assessment task should first determine exactly *what* is to be assessed; these are the *task targets*. These targets can be classified into categories, which are called *task target areas;* the assessable components for each task target area are the specific behaviors, skills, or products that will be assessed. Task target areas are the general types of behaviors or products the task is designed to assess. Assessments designed for particular task target areas focus upon either the *process(es)* employed during task completion or the *product* resulting from the assessment exercise, depending upon the expected outcome of the assessment task. With respect to the performing child musician, there are six primary task target areas: (1) *enabling competencies,* (2) *fundamental aural discriminations,* (3) *performance technique,* (4) *musical skill development,* (5) *musical qualities, and* (6) *musical skill achievement.* These six areas are demonstrated through one or more of three performance media: movement (both locomotor and non-locomotor), use of the voice (singing and speaking), and instruments.

Enabling competencies are the basic skills that underlie and facilitate musical performance. There are four primary enabling competencies: (1) *beat competency,* referring to a child's ability to demonstrate the underlying pulse of musical works; (2) *imitation/echo competency,* referring to a child's ability to exactly reproduce given melodic and rhythmic patterns; (3) *following/ mirroring,* having to do with a child's ability to follow the teacher's motions or actions during a musical experience; and (4) *kinesthetic musical response,* referring to a child's ability to meaningfully express aesthetic qualities (or other appropriate task targets) through movement. These competencies are demonstrated during a performance activity, which means the teacher must focus on process for assessment.

Fundamental aural discriminations should be regularly assessed through performance demonstration, particularly in the elementary grades when these are a primary focus of the curriculum and are developing most rapidly within the students. These fundamental discriminations facilitate or underlie musical performance and thinking, and serve as the prerequisites for higher-level musical understanding. A child's understanding of a musical concept depends upon the acquisition of one or more of these fundamental aural discriminations. Furthermore, these discriminations are interdependent (that is, success with one discrimination may also depend upon a level of skill with another discrimination), and identifying these for assessment should be undertaken with this in mind. These discriminations are both taught and assessed in the form of opposites such as high/low, loud/soft, etc. These discriminations and their related musical concepts are listed in Figure 3-2.

Fundamental Aural Discriminations and Their Related Concepts

Fundamental Aural Discrimination(s)	Related Musical Concept(s)
High/low	Pitch, melody
Long/short	Rhythm
Beginning/ending	Form
Stop/start	Form
Fast/slow	Tempo
Loud/soft	Expressive qualities
Like/different	Harmony Timbre Form

Figure 3-2.

Performance technique and *musical skill development* must be assessed during music making activity, requiring the teacher to focus upon the music making processes embedded within the task. For child singers, the assessment of performance technique targets breath control, formulation of vowels and consonants (when words are involved, this is referred to as *diction*), and posture. For instrumental performance, the targets are hand and/or instrument positioning, fingering, and mallet or striking technique. When assessing musical skill development, the task should target a specific developmentally appropriate aspect of a musical skill and check for its acquisition. For developing child voices, these assessment targets include pitch accuracy and singing range; for developing instrumentalists, this includes pitch accuracy (for instruments where this is appropriate), security, dexterity, and fluency with specific notes and fingerings that are requisite to learning more complex fingerings. This can also include mallet/striker coordination (dexterity) and fluency. For both singers and instrumentalists, skill development assessment also includes both rhythmic accuracy and developmentally appropriate sight-reading.

When examining musical qualities or musical skill achievement, the outcome being assessed is a product of the music making experience, requiring the teacher to focus upon the product of the assessment task. Task targets for the assessment of the musical qualities of an instrumental or vocal performance include timbre, tone quality, expressive characteristics (such as use of dynamics and appropriate phrasing), and interpretation. The assessment of musical skill achievement targets the level of musical complexity in which a child can comfortably perform. In general music, vocal and instrumental skill achievement assessments primarily seek to determine whether or not a child can perform a separate, independent part while others perform contrasting parts (see Figure 3-3). If the curriculum specifies that certain musical works must be sung or performed at a certain grade level, this area can be extended to include these requirements. Figure 3-3 summarizes the components that can be assessed during musical performance.

Certain components are appropriate for both individual and group assessment tasks. Some imply group performance, such as the ability to perform an independent part while others perform different parts. The teacher must predetermine this aspect of the assessment context so that the performance *task* matches as nearly as possible the performance *learning environment*.

Assessment Models and Techniques

Chapters 3 through 6 of this book will present assessment models and techniques that can be adapted to assess specific musical skills, knowledge, and concepts. For this book, a *model* is a broad, general framework within which the music teacher can build specific assessment strategies that employ a variety of materials and approaches that suit the needs of the curriculum.

Components for Performance Assessment

Task Target Areas/ Components	Performance Demonstration Medium		
	Movement	Voice	Instrument
Enabling Competencies			
Steady beat	x	x	x
Imitation/echo	x	x	x
Following/mirroring	x		
Kinesthetic musical response	x		
Fundamental Aural Discriminations			
High/low	x	x	x
Loud/soft	x	x	x
Fast/slow	x	x	x
Stopping/starting	x	x	x
Long/short	x	x	x
Beginning/ending	x	x	x
Like/different	x	x	x
Technique			
Breath control/support		x	x
Voice placement		x	
Posture	x	x	x
Diction		x	
Hand position			x
Instrument position			x
Fingering			x
Dexterity			x
Mallet technique	x		x
Striking technique	x		x
Musical Qualities			
Timbre/tone quality		x	x
Tone quality		x	x
Dynamics		x	x
Phrasing	x	x	x
Interpretation	x	x	x
Technical Musical Skill Development			
Pitch accuracy		x	x
Rhythmic accuracy		x	x
Sight-reading		x	x
Vocal range		x	
Voice acquisition		x	
Dexterity		x	x
Skill Achievement			
Specific solo pieces		x	x
Specific dances	x		
Ostinati	x	x	x
Partner songs		x	
Rounds/canons	x	x	x
Simple accompaniments	x	x	x
Scales		x	x

Figure 3-3.

A *technique* is more specific and more limited in scope than a model, requiring the use of a specific procedure or context to obtain assessment data. A technique can be varied, though, to suit the teacher's assessment needs or pedagogical perspective.

Each technique is discussed using specific terms as *task design parameters*. *Component definition* has to do with determining age-appropriate performance level expectations for the selected performance assessment component(s). The *focus* of an assessment is either process or product, depending on the specified assessment target. The type of activity involved in a task determines the assessment *tool* that the teacher will use; for performance assessments, the tools will primarily be observation and listening. The assessment *context* refers to the general type of material or performance condition that is best for observing or generating the assessment target. Specific scoring guides and record keeping strategies, covered in general in chapter 2, are also suggested.

Assessing Enabling Competencies

The four identified enabling competencies serve as individual assessable components, defined by the task's level of difficulty and the materials used. All of the competencies are assessable through movement, and this is the recommended medium for young children. Steady beat and imitation/echo competencies can also be demonstrated both instrumentally and vocally. The primary tools for assessing these competencies are observation and listening; the focus is process. The general procedure for assessing these competencies is to:

1. Define the acceptable level of the competency (the target criterion),

2. Determine the musical materials and context to be used, and

3. Observe each child's level of competency as it is demonstrated.

A bi-level, single-criterion scoring guide is recommended for record keeping with all of the enabling competencies because a competency is either *demonstrated* (+) or *not demonstrated* (–) during an assessment. A third achievement level – "developing" or "inconsistent" – may or may not be useful for assessing enabling competencies; this is at the discretion of the teacher. The contexts for the assessment of enabling competencies are many and varied.

Beat Competency

Beat competency can be assessed during nearly every musical activity because most music performed or studied in the general music classroom has an embedded steady pulse (with the notable exception of certain twentieth century styles, e.g., aleatoric music). When assessing young children, beat can be shown in many playful ways through movement – patting the lap, tapping the head, touching the floor with the hands, or engaging in finger-plays while singing a familiar song, playing a familiar game (such as the name game shown in Figure 3-4), or listening to a familiar piece. However, this technique is not the most efficient perform-ance demonstration for record keeping purposes; in this play context, not only is the teacher usually the leader of the activity, but the teacher must also carefully observe and later recall who is on or off the beat for record keeping purposes.

There are two models for beat competency assessment that facilitate more efficient record keeping. The first is the *Icon Model*, wherein children point to beat icons on a page or chart while singing a song or listening. This model is very effective with children in the early grades. Figure 3-5 shows a sample page from a beat book that is part of the Clark County (Las Vegas, Nevada) music curriculum. In this example, the pie icons are related to the subject of the poem "Pie, Pie, Bake the Pie." When using this as an assessment, the teacher judges beat competency while the

Name Game Technique

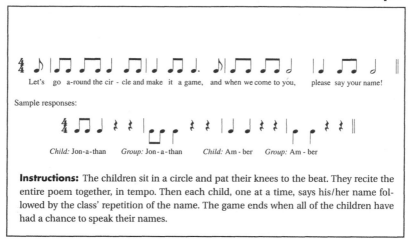

Instructions: The children sit in a circle and pat their knees to the beat. They recite the entire poem together, in tempo. Then each child, one at a time, says his/her name followed by the class' repetition of the name. The game ends when all of the children have had a chance to speak their names.

Figure 3-4.

children sing or speak the poem and point to the pie icons with their fingers. In general, when employing the Icon Model for assessment, the beat icons should be designed to fit the words of the song (e.g., hearts, pails, horses, etc.) and should be sufficiently large enough and evenly spaced to facilitate clear observation of the finger movements.

When using a chart for assessment purposes, it is recommended to have individual children "lead" the pointing of the beats, allowing the teacher to assess beat competency individually as the child is leading. When doing this, the teacher should be prepared with several charts of different songs and poems of the same length so that the material is varied to hold the interest of the children during the assessment.

Another effective model for beat assessment with older elementary students (generally grades three, four and, in some situations, five) is the *"Making a Machine" Model*. This model permits the teacher to view each child's beat competency individually. In this exercise, the children form a large circle, and the teacher begins a steady beat on a drum or other unpitched instrument (temple blocks, wood block, or piccolo blocks are particularly effective). The children are then called or musically signaled (with a specific sound, such as a triangle or bell) to enter the circle one at a time and become a "part" in a "machine." To do this, each child creates a movement that can be repeated easily (e.g., moving the hands in and out, bending the arm at the elbow). The child then joins the other children in the center, maintaining the movement, and finding a place to fit that movement into the existing "parts" (the other children) of the machine. The children are added one at a time until the entire class is moving together. The game ends when the teacher gradually slows down the beat until it ceases, stopping the machine.

Assessing Beat Competency: The Icon Model

♩ ♪ ♩ ♪
Pie   Pie

♩ ♩ ♩ ♪
Bake the pie

♩ ♩ ♩ ♩
Ap-ple, cher-ry

♩ ♩ ♩ ♪
Pump-kin pie

Figure 3-5.

If the teacher is leading this activity and performing the steady beat for the class, the teacher must observe carefully and attempt to recall those students who do not keep the beat throughout the exercise for later grade book marking. Data recording for this exercise is facilitated when a beat-competent student is given the task of keeping the beat, allowing the teacher to record data for each child as he/she enters the machine and either demonstrates or does not demonstrate the steady beat. The machine can be introduced with a song or a poem, and can conclude that way also; this is at the teacher's discretion. There are two types of "machines" that can be created: one in which the children (the "parts") do not touch and one in which they may touch lightly. The teacher's discretion is advised as to which machine is most appropriate for the class.

For older students (grades four, five, and above), a familiar song, instrumental piece, or ostinato performance performed at an appropriate, steady tempo is a comfortable context in which to assess steady beat. In each of these contexts, the teacher records assessment results during the exercise. That is, while the child is performing the song or piece, the teacher records a "+" or "−" to indicate whether or not the child is maintaining the steady beat throughout the performance; the third level of "inconsistent" might also be useful in some situations and could be indicated with a checkmark (√).

Imitation/Echo Competency

The assessment of *imitation/echo competency* is best done within the context of an echo game or rhythmic "mini-canon" (Wuytack, 1994). One specific technique is the rhythmic echo game "Riddle Ree" (see Figure 3-6), where the teacher begins with an opening phrase and leads the class in age-appropriate rhythmic patterns by performing them first and having the children echo them. The rhythmic patterns can be as simple or as complex as the teacher wishes to assess, and may employ unpitched instruments or body percussion. This technique can be extended to echoing patterns on melodic instruments also, with the teacher singing a melodic pattern and the children echoing it on a classroom melody instrument. Older children enjoy the challenge of a mini-canon; with this technique, the children do not echo the teacher's rhythmic patterns until a specified number of beats (e.g., two, three, four, etc.) after the teacher begins (also see Figure 3-6).

In each of these contexts, the teacher carefully observes the students' performances and judges them accordingly. If this is a critical component to the curriculum, and the teacher is leading the echo assessment task, then the teacher's observation needs to focus upon those students who are not echoing correctly and, therefore, not meeting the criterion. In this case, these students must be memorized during the assessment and recorded after the event. With older children, it is possible to turn over the leadership of such assessment activities to a student (such as having a child lead a mini-canon), facilitating record keeping. Echo/imitation competency can also be assessed through echoing vocal and instrumental rhythmic or melodic patterns (see Figure 3-6).

Following/Mirroring

The assessment of *following/mirroring* is accomplished in a similar manner to the assessment of echo/imitation. Such an assessment might progress like this: during the playing of a familiar musical work, the teacher begins a series of movements and the children follow and recreate the movements as they are being performed. This differs from imitation/echo in that the movement response is immediate.

Again, if the teacher is leading the exercise, he/she must focus upon the students carefully, mentally note the students who are not able to follow or mirror, and record the results when the exercise is over. When students become familiar with this type of exercise, a student may be used to lead the exercise to facilitate record keeping.

Assessing Imitation/Echo Competency:
Sample Techniques

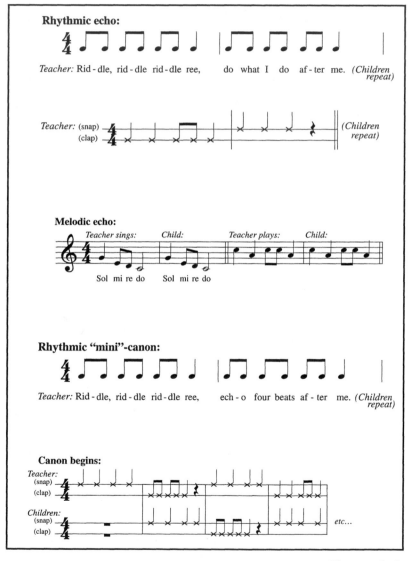

Figure 3-6.

Kinesthetic Musical Response

Kinesthetic musical response is assessed during exercises where students are given an opportunity to respond through movement to a musical work. In this context, response has to do with the matching of creative or guided movement in a purposeful way to an identified characteristic in the music (such as the beat, specific rhythm pattern, timbre, etc.), or to the overall effect of a piece. For example, guided locomotor movements include walking or running (and run-walking) to the beat, waltz-walking (when getting a feeling for beats in groups of three), skipping, galloping, and so forth. Creative movements include activities where children may be asked to create a new type of walk or step to a particular piece, a new dance, a new combination of known steps, etc.

Non-locomotor movements are also commonly used in general music; students may be given a particular space in which to move their bodies, arms, and hands only (not their feet) in response to music. For example, younger students may be asked to express the feeling of the music from "The Swan" or "Turtles" from Saint-Saens *Carnival of the Animals* while standing or sitting in one position. Older students may be asked to draw phrase arcs in the air with their hands or scarves to show their understanding of the phrase structures within a song.

Movement is a valuable tool in general music for teaching, strengthening musical concepts, and facilitating musical expression. The purpose of this type of assessment is to determine if students can be kinesthetically responsive to music, not to make judgments regarding the *quality* of the response. Again, this is best judged with a bi-level, single-criterion scoring guide. The assessment of *appropriateness* and *suitability* of movement response will be discussed in chapter 4.

Assessing Fundamental Aural Discriminations

Figure 3-2 lists the fundamental aural discriminations presented in general music and their related musical concepts. Component definition for these has to do with determining the materials and context used for the assessment. The teacher's primary tools for these assessments are observation and listening. These discriminations are most appropriately assessed during a performance activity, requiring that the teacher focus upon the process during assessment, not the product. (There is more about the assessment of concepts later in this chapter and in chapter 5.) All of these can be demonstrated through movement or through vocal or instrumental performance. Judgment is most efficient with a bi-level, single-criterion scoring guide, indicating *demonstration* of the discrimination with a "+" and *non-demonstration* with a "–."

These discriminations can also be assessed through paper-and-pencil tests. In such tests, the teacher provides examples of the discriminations as "questions" and the students respond by circling or writing a correct answer. Since the purpose of this book is to provide teachers with techniques and models for assessments that are as efficient and authentic as possible, examples of these objectivist-based tests will not be provided; I refer the reader to Boyle & Radocy (1987) for more information on test and quiz design. However, these can certainly be created and used at the teacher's discretion (refer to chapter 1, Figure 1-6, for an example).

The following examples do not represent an exhaustive list of possible techniques (such a compilation would be beyond the scope of this book) but are provided to guide the teacher toward similar lessons or exercises that are already part of the curriculum or are suggested in the district's adopted series books. Additionally, each of these techniques should be done for several trials before an assessment is conducted.

Each of these discriminations can be demonstrated through movement, voice, or instruments. Because these fundamental discriminations are generally taught in the early grades, the context for most of these assessments is playful or game-like. However, these assessments still yield valuable data on the early musical development of children.

1. *High/low*—High and low are the fundamental aural discriminations for pitch and underlie concepts related to *melody*. When assessing high and low pitch with young children (kindergarten through second grade, possibly third), it is appropriate to use movement as the demonstration medium. One technique is to have the children stand around the room and close their eyes, with the instruction to move their hands up when they hear a high pitch and down when they hear a low pitch. The teacher then provides pitches (or clusters of pitches, chords, etc.) on a melodic instrument of choice, often a piano or keyboard. This exercise can be extended for the middle range also by having the children hold their hands straight out in front of them when they hear pitches in this range. Results can be recorded briefly between selected pitch examples when the teacher instructs the class to "freeze."

Young children may also demonstrate this discrimination with their speaking voices, when asked to speak a poem in a "low voice" or a "high voice," with their "regular voice" serving as the middle range reference point.

For older children, highest and lowest pitches can be identified in songs by asking them to identify the word or phrase in the song where the highest and/or lowest pitch occurs.

When performing instrumental pieces, children can be instructed to "stop playing on the highest pitch" or to "stop playing on the lowest pitch." Both approaches will provide clear results for simple record keeping.

2. *Long/short*—Long and short are the fundamental aural discriminations for duration and underlie concepts related to *rhythm*. One assessment technique for young children is to instruct the children that they will be hearing some long and short sounds, and they are to hold up one finger if they hear a long sound and make a fist if they hear a short sound. The teacher then asks the children to close their eyes, then performs a series of three or four long or short durations on an unpitched or melodic instrument. In this type of assessment, it is important that two or more identical durations be initially presented so that the children have a frame of reference within which to determine whether a sound is long or short; these are relative terms.

As students get older and can make comparisons between sounds, this can be assessed through verbal descriptions of pitch or rhythmic patterns in terms of their relative durations. For example, a teacher may clap a pattern such as ♩♩♪♪♩ and ask a child to describe it in terms of long and short durations, resulting in the response "long, long, short, short, long." This technique can also be done in reverse: the teacher speaks the durations and the child responds rhythmically by performing a rhythm that matches the spoken version.

Another technique is simply to have the children perform a familiar piece or song "with all durations very short" or "with all durations very long." This can be accomplished with both younger and older students, and will provide clear assessment results.

3. *Stop/start; beginning/ending*—Young children need to develop the sense that music has both a starting point and an ending point. This is the fundamental discrimination that underlies the concept of *musical form* and facilitates awareness of musical structures. This discrimination is most efficiently assessed through movement exercises.

One technique is the "talking drum," where the teacher plays certain musical cues on a hand drum that "tell" the children specific things to do. For example, the sound of ♩♩ on the drum may signal "stand up"; the pattern ♪♪♩ may signal "ready stop." A steady progression of quarter notes becomes a signal to walk in place, with the "ready stop" signal coming at any time. The walking may be part of a story (such as a walk to school, which could be expanded to include skipping over sidewalk cracks, jumping over puddles, etc.) or within a context of the teacher's choice. The assessment of starting and stopping would require that the teacher stay in one place, focus on a few students at a time, and record results immediately following the exercise indicating which children were able to stop and start. This technique, however, must be examined and administered carefully because the teacher must be sure that the child who does *not* stop understands the musical cue for stopping; otherwise this assessment is not valid.

This technique can be easily extended to a melodic instrument; instead of playing the drum, the teacher simply plays a melody on an instrument or improvises at the keyboard, with the instructions to walk or step when the melody begins and to stop when it stops.

It is recommended that these exercises be completed while stepping in place so that the children may close their eyes and not be influenced by the movements of others. If the teacher decides to assess this discrimination during an exercise where the children can see each other (such as the walk to school context mentioned earlier), assessment results must be interpreted with this influence in mind.

4. *Fast/slow*—A child's ability to discriminate between fast and slow underlies the concept of *tempo* in music. These two distinctions are relative; that is, music is fast or slow in relation to something that is given or known. Therefore, assessments of this discrimination require that this point of reference be part of the task. For example, one technique is to have the children sit and close their eyes while the teacher plays a steady beat on an unpitched instrument. The children should be invited to pat the beat silently in their laps to match the beat being played (similar to a beat competency assessment); this will be the reference point. After about twelve or sixteen beats, the teacher suddenly changes the speed of the beat. The children are to hold up one finger if the tempo is slower than the original or a fist if it is faster. This "fast/slow" game requires that the teacher observe carefully during the changes, a few students at a time, and record results between rounds of the game.

Another way to assess individual fast/slow discrimination is to play the "Can you fool the puppet" game, where children are gathered together with the teacher and a favorite puppet. (Many general music teachers use puppets as teaching tools with young children.) In this playful context, the children are asked (prior to getting out their puppet friend) to think of a way to sing a favorite song either faster or slower than usual, with the purpose of "fooling" the puppet when it comes out "to hear the children sing." During the assessment, each child sings the chosen song; the teacher informs the child that the puppet was fooled and asks the child to describe whether or not the song was performed faster or slower than it should have been. Results from this exercise are valid only if the child is fluent in the use of the terms "fast" and "slow," so ample experience with these terms is necessary prior to the assessment being conducted.

5. *Loud/soft*—The ability to discriminate between loud and soft in music is central to a child's understanding of dynamics and underlies the concept of *musical qualities* or *expressiveness*. This aural discrimination is efficiently demonstrated through performance in a number of contexts, including the "Can you fool the puppet game" described in the previous paragraph for demonstration of fast and slow. In this case, the game is played by having the children perform a familiar song "louder" or "softer" than usual in an effort to fool the puppet. The child then describes whether or not the song was louder or softer and is assessed accordingly. Instruments may also be used for this game, as long as the child is well instructed in the proper playing techniques that produce both loud and soft sounds. The same precaution regarding terminology must be advised here: the children must possess an understanding of the words "loud" and "soft" in relation to music in order to make the assessment valid and reliable. Children must experience this terminology extensively prior to using this technique.

Children can also demonstrate this discrimination through movement. One technique involves having children stand in their own space and close their eyes, then step softly in place when they hear a soft drum beat and step firmly when they hear a louder drum beat. This technique can also be extended to the use of a melodic instrument, preferably the piano, where the teacher can present the class with brief musical selections that are clear examples of contrasting dynamics. In this instance, the teacher would observe a few students at a time, record results, and begin another round of playing.

6. *Like/different*—The fundamental aural discrimination of like and different underlies the concepts of *harmony, timbre,* and *form* in music. Discriminating differences in timbre facilitates a child's understanding of various instrumental and vocal sounds; discriminating differences in chords facilitates a child's understanding of chord changes and relationships; and the ability to discriminate differences between melodies, themes, and larger sections of musical works facilitates the understanding of form.

It is recommended to assess *timbre* discrimination through a simple and direct listening exercise. This technique has many forms of implementation, but one that is efficient for record keeping involves having the children sit quietly with eyes closed, listen to two different timbres or sounds, and indicate if they are *alike* by raising a hand or *different* by silently clasping both hands in front. For example, young children may be learning about the difference between instrumental and vocal sounds; the teacher who is assessing this would prepare a series of sound pairs using instruments in the room and the teacher's voice, perform them for the class, and observe and record results for a few children at a time at the end of each pair. This can be extended to differences between men's and women's voices; wood, metal, or skin instruments (drums); and orchestral timbres. It is important to remember that this assessment is only examining a child's ability to discriminate like and different sounds; the identification of specific instrumental timbres by name is a different assessment altogether.

The ability to discriminate between different *harmonies* can be assessed in a similar manner to timbre differences. The following technique is especially effective with older children, who may be learning about chords and chord changes. The children sit quietly with their hands on their knees and close their eyes. The teacher plays a tonic triad (using this term if this is part of the curriculum) several times, instructing the children to silently clasp their hands in front of them when they hear this sound. The teacher then plays a series of dominant triads and instructs the children to return their hands to their knees when they hear this sound. The task is to play a series of tonic and dominant triads, changing at infrequent intervals, with the children demonstrating their ability to discriminate the two harmonies through their hand movements. When assessing this understanding, the teacher observes a few students at a time and then records results before continuing.

The assessment of the ability to discriminate like and different *sections* (and their respective themes) in a musical work can be accomplished through a straightforward technique which involves the children in identifying differences in themes or sections through signals or movements. For example, if sectional works such as Kodaly's *Viennese Musical Clock* or Mozart's *Rondo Alla Turca* are being studied, children could be instructed to raise their hands (with their eyes closed) while the main theme is playing and to lower them when it is not. Record keeping is facilitated by the fact that recorded music is being used for the task; the teacher is free to observe students for the length of the work. One objectivist-based technique is particularly effective with upper elementary students who are familiar with the standard practice of assigning letter names (e.g., A, B, C, etc.) to sections of a musical work. In this procedure, the students are first familiarized with the main theme or section of a work, generally assigned the letter "A." They are then asked to write down the form of the work while they are listening to it. This can then be assessed as either *correct* or *incorrect*, providing straightforward data. When assessing students at this level, it is always best to choose clear examples of forms (sectional or developmental). These examples can be found in the curriculum or the district's adopted series books.

Assessing Musical Concepts

The assessment of fundamental aural discriminations, or any musical concept, is one of a music teacher's greatest challenges. Webster's dictionary defines a concept as "a mentally perceived image; an idea or thought." General music teachers strive to help their students obtain musical concepts related to the elements of music—rhythm, melody, harmony, timbre, and form. The expected sequence of concept introduction and attainment is generally provided by the school district's curriculum. General music textbook series' teacher's editions also present a concept sequence around which the series has been developed. An excellent overview of concepts and their place in general music teaching can be found in Shehan-Campbell and Scott-Kassner's *Music in Childhood* (1995, pp. 163-170). Shehan-Campbell and Scott-Kassner (1995) state that "ultimately, concept teaching aims to help children transfer or generalize their knowledge and apply it to new works of music" (p. 163). The acquisition of musical concepts is essential to a child's attainment of independent, accomplished musicianship, the ultimate goal of a high-quality, sequential music education.

Because concept teaching is so important to the general music curriculum, it is equally important to assess concept attainment. However, because concepts are mental constructs, a number of assessment complications arise. For many children, the use of appropriate terminology to express musical thoughts and ideas is problematic (Bettison, 1976; Hair, 1977, 1981, 1987; Pflederer & Sechrest, 1968b; Serafine, 1980). Children do not often possess the vocabulary to express what they know in musical terms. Demonstrations of conceptual understanding through musical activities (such as those described for the assessment of enabling competencies and fundamental aural discriminations) can provide evidence of procedural knowledge, which is certainly an important manifestation of a child's conceptual musical understanding. An example of this is the six-year-old who can readily demonstrate the concept of high and low pitch, either by singing high and low sounds or by reaching up when listening to high music and down when listening to low music, but who cannot verbally express this concept. Bridging the gap between what a child can think musically and what the child can outwardly express for assessment purposes is the primary difficulty teachers face when assessing concept acquisition.

The assessment of concept acquisition, therefore, is best approached through *multiple* assessments in more than one response mode. Referred to as *triangulation* (Dr. Scott Shuler, personal communication, July 1, 1999), a series of assessments within each of the three assessment response modes is the most thorough procedure for assessing a student's concept acquisition. Through an ensemble of tasks designed to assess specific, targeted behaviors, a teacher can obtain a reasonably good view of a child's understanding of the concepts and fundamental aural discriminations underlying the targeted behaviors. The performance response mode offers teachers an opportunity to view conceptual understanding within the context of music making. This response mode is a window to a child's *procedural understanding* of a particular concept; that is, the child demonstrates understanding of the concept through the process of performing. For example, when sixth grade students are studying the harmonic concept of tonic-dominant relationships, the performance assessment mode can be employed by devising a task that requires them to perform a piece with a tonic-dominant relationship. The ability to perform and identify a tonic-dominant harmony change in a piece for classroom instruments is one avenue for a teacher to use when determining a child's understanding of this concept. Additional supporting assessments within the creating and responding modes, such as the composition and notation of a short piece with a harmony change, are necessary to provide the teacher a more thorough view of the attainment of this concept (more on these modes is coming in later chapters). Once a teacher has acquired assessment data in the appropriate response modes, a more thorough determination of the child's conceptual understanding can be made.

Certain conceptual understandings within the elements of melody and rhythm are particularly suited for performance assessment. Teachers who have their students compose and notate original rhythms and melodies (a creating/responding assessment response mode) should require that their students perform the composed works to verify that they not only know how to notate music but how to read and interpret the notation they have created. An example of this occurs when a teacher assigns a fourth grade class the task of creating a four-measure rhythm and writing it down in standard musical notation. To complete the assessment task, the teacher should have the children perform the rhythm by clapping it or playing it on unpitched percussion instruments. A child who can create and notate a rhythm or melody but who cannot *perform* that creation has not acquired the complete conceptual understanding necessary to accomplish this important musical objective.

Performance response mode tasks of conceptual understanding are particularly valuable for use with younger children (generally kindergarten through third grade) who have not yet acquired the adequate writing or verbal/vocabulary skills necessary for successful completion of a task that might be facilitated by a written or spoken response. Young children can demonstrate their understandings of important musical concepts through activities that allow the concept to be clearly demonstrated. For example, a teacher who wants to assess a younger child's understanding of melodic contour or direction can obtain important information by administering a task in which hand movements are used to "draw the melody in the air." In tasks like this, the teacher must collect the data for the children in the same manner as discussed earlier, using a "+" or "—" to indicate whether or not the child has successfully completed the demonstration (refer to "Assessing Fundamental Aural Discriminations"). Additionally, some concepts are inseparably linked to performance and knowledge of the concept can only be demonstrated in performance contexts. For example, acquisition of the steady beat is best shown through moving in some way, playing an instrument, or singing to a prescribed tempo. The concept of steady beat cannot be adequately described through writing or discussion.

Overall, the performance assessment response mode provides an important vehicle for gathering assessment information regarding a child's concept acquisition. Performance task results, when triangulated with the results from creating and/or responding assessment tasks, can provide a broad view of a child's conceptual understanding from multiple perspectives and in a variety of appropriate contexts.

Assessing Performance Technique

The assessable components for performance technique include the following:

1. *Breath control/support* – referring to the ability to control and support breathing for both instrumental and vocal performance;

2. *Voice placement* – having to do with the placement of the voice in the head or chest when singing;

112

3. *Posture* – referring to the proper positioning of the body for musical performance;

4. *Diction* – having to do with the articulation of consonants and vowels when singing;

5. *Hand position* – having to do with the position of the hands when playing instruments;

6. *Instrument position* – referring to the proper positioning of an instrument that is being held for performance (e.g., recorder, guitar, autoharp, etc.);

7. *Fingering* – having to do with the specific placement of the fingers to produce appropriate pitches or patterns on wind or keyboard instruments;

8. *Dexterity* – referring to the quickness or fluency of (a) the fingerings or hands during a performance on a specific instrument or (b) with voice during rapid or melismatic passages;

9. *Mallet technique* – having to do with the specific positions and appropriate alternations of mallets while performing on melodic percussion instruments; and

10. *Striker technique* – referring to the specific positions and appropriate use of strikers that are used to play unpitched percussion instruments (see Figure 3-3).

Components one and eight refer to both *instrumental* and *vocal* technique; the second, third, and fourth components refer specifically to *vocal* technique; and the remaining components have to do specifically with *instrumental* technique.

To appropriately define the assessable components for technique, the teacher must carefully determine what demonstrated technical level is adequate and developmentally appropriate for the age of the student being assessed. The primary assessment tool is observation. The basic procedure for assessing technique is as follows: (1) *define the level of acceptable technique* (the target criterion), (2) *determine the appropriate musical context,* and (3) *check for the demonstration of the criterion technique.* It is best to assess children's technique with a bi-level, single-criterion scoring guide; they either demonstrate the technique or they don't.

When assessing the *vocal technique of individual children,* the context should be a familiar song, a singing game that contains solos, or a song/story with solo parts. It is very important that the teacher remain true to the criterion being assessed; for example, if a fourth grade class is playing "Johnny Cuckoo" (found in Erdei, 1974), and the teacher is examining breath control, then breath control should be all that is examined during that particular round of the game. Diction or posture can be assessed during another round. If a teacher feels competent to assess more than one of these technical areas at a time, the assessment of each technique should employ a bi-level, multiple-criterion scoring guide. Two or more judgments can be made during one performance if the per-formance is long enough and the teacher has developed the skill to correctly judge each criterion reliably. In this instance, the teacher would observe each technique during the performance and assess it as being either demonstrated or not demonstrated; multiple levels of achievement would be too cumbersome in this context and are not recommended.

If a teacher chooses to assess *vocal technique during a group song,* the context should be a song familiar to the entire class. While some technical assessment can be made during group singing, the value of these judgments is compromised by the teacher's focus on the group and not the individual child. Assessing the technique of individuals during group singing is possible and the results can be of use to the teacher, but the results can also be somewhat confounded if the teacher moves about the group to hear separate students. This activity can be distracting both to the teacher and to the group being led by the teacher.

There is also little or no opportunity to accurately record assessment results during group assessment of technique.

Assessment of *instrumental technique* is best completed within the context of a familiar piece or exercise, preferably with the child performing as a soloist. Again, the teacher's primary assessment tool is observation, and a bi-level, single-criterion approach to scoring is recommended. For example, if a teacher wishes to assess mallet technique during the playing of a class-room melodic percussion piece, then the child should be given the opportunity to perform the piece individually for the class. The piece should be familiar so that the child's mallet technique is not compromised by a lack of knowledge of the piece. The two levels of judgment should have to do with whether or not the child demonstrates correct mallet technique, and that is all. Other errors that might occur may be noted if they do not interfere with the teacher's concentration on mallet technique. If a teacher feels comfortable with conducting bi-level, multiple-criterion assess-ments for instrumental technique, it can certainly be done, but this must be carefully thought out and planned for in advance.

The same precautions apply to group instrumental assessment as to the group assessment of vocal technique. Focusing on individual assessment during group activity is distracting to the teacher and to the students. Individual assessment is recommended for the components of instrumental technique.

Technical Musical Skill Development

The assessable components for technical musical skill development include:

1. *Pitch accuracy* – referring to a child's ability to produce pitches either vocally or instrumentally (using wind or string instruments) that are accurate and in tune;

115

2. *Rhythmic accuracy* – referring to a student's ability to produce accurate rhythms on instruments or with the voice;

3. *Sight-reading* – referring to a student's ability to sing or play age-appropriate rhythms or melodies accurately at first reading;

4. *Vocal range* – referring to a child's comfortable range for singing;

5. *Voice acquisition* – having to do with a child's developmentally appropriate acquisition of control of the singing voice; and

6. *Dexterity* – in this instance having to do with the developmentally appropriate level of fluency for the singing voice and instrumental playing, as demonstrated through performance of specific pieces (see Figure 3-3).

In this list of components, pitch accuracy, rhythmic accuracy, sight-reading, and dexterity refer to both the development of *instrumental* and *vocal* skill; vocal range and voice acquisition have to do with the development of *vocal* skill.

The development of musical skill is of primary importance to general music teachers, and this area is one that requires regular assessment as children grow through the general grades. Tracking the development of a child's *vocal pitch accuracy* and *vocal range* provides music teachers important clues with respect to the child's acquisition of his or her singing voice. Monitoring the development of *instrumental skill* provides direct information that helps teachers plan strategies and sequence activities that maximize acquired skill levels as well as prepare the students for subsequent skill development. The monitoring of rhythmic accuracy provides the teacher information with respect to a child's rhythmic development and understanding. Periodic assessment of sight-reading provides the teacher with diagnostic information that can be employed in the development of further instruction in this skill.

Vocal Pitch Accuracy: A Glimpse at the Research

Vocal pitch accuracy has to do with the ability of a child to match a specific pitch with the singing voice. Because of the prevalence of singing as a fundamental activity in general music education, music education researchers have rather extensively studied its development. The following is a brief overview of some of the results obtained by these researchers and the techniques researchers employ to measure vocal pitch accuracy.

Numerous factors have been demonstrated to have an influence on the vocal pitch accuracy of general students. Researchers have shown that accuracy improves as children get older (Geringer, 1983; Goetze, 1985/1986; Gould, 1969; Green, 1990, 1994; Mizener, 1993; Stauffer, 1985/1986; Yarbrough, Green, Benson, & Bowers, 1991). Differences in vocal pitch accuracy between boys and girls have been examined, and the effects of gender have been mixed. Some researchers have found that girls sing more accurately than boys (Goetze, 1985/1986; Goetze & Horii, 1989; Jordan-DeCarbo, 1982), while others found no significant difference between the genders (Apfelstadt, 1984; Cooper, 1993/1994; Moore, 1994; Smale, 1987/1988). Girls have also been shown to respond more accurately to higher pitch tones, whereas boys were more accurate when responding to lower tones (Price, Yarbrough, Jones, & Moore, 1994).

The type of vocal model that the child simulates may also have an effect on the ability to match pitch. In some instances, children have sung more accurately when echoing a female voice (Sims, Moore, & Kuhn, 1982; Small & McCachern, 1983; Yarbrough et al., 1991). Others have found that children sing more accurately with a child vocal model (Green, 1990), or that the child's own voice is the best model (Gratton, 1989/1992). The vibrato of the vocal model can also be a factor, and children have demonstrated superior accuracy when presented with a voice without vibrato (Yarbrough, Bowers, & Benson, 1992).

Melodic and/or harmonic accompaniment has been shown to have a significant effect on the vocal pitch accuracy of first through third grade children, with harmonic accompaniment appearing to be more beneficial for older children (Stauffer, 1985/1986). Atterbury and Silcox (1993) supported this finding when they found that harmonic accompaniment showed no significant effect on the singing ability of kindergarten students after a year of instruction. The effect of attitude on vocal pitch accuracy has also been explored. Mizener (1993) found that the attitudes of third through sixth graders regarding singing were not correlated to assessed singing skill or the children's perception of their own singing skill.

When studied by researchers, the assessment of vocal pitch accuracy has been approached from two directions. One objective method researchers have employed is the computer analysis of the subjects' recorded voices (Cooper, 1992/1993; Green, 1990; Moore, 1994; Price et al., 1994; Sterling, 1984/1985; Welch, Howard, & Rush, 1989; Yarbrough et al., 1992, 1991). The second, more subjective approach is human judgment based on test results or pre-determined rating scales (Atterbury & Silcox, 1993; Green, 1994; Mizener, 1993; Moore, 1994; Rutkowski, 1990; Smale, 1987/1988). The procedure for determining vocal pitch accuracy and identifying inaccurate singers involves individual testing of children. Subjects have been tested under varying conditions, sometimes individually (Green, 1990; Moore, 1994; Price et al., 1994; Rutkowski, 1990; Welch, 1994), and sometimes in small groups (Green, 1994; Welch et al., 1989). The singing material used in these studies also varies, from familiar songs (Atterbury & Silcox, 1993; Goetze, 1985/1986; Green, 1994; Mizener, 1993; Rutkowski, 1990; Sterling, 1984/1985) to motives sung with neutral syllables such as "la" and "loo" (Moore, 1994; Price et al., 1994; Smale, 1987/1988; Welch et al., 1989; Yarbrough et al., 1992).

The use of technological means to assess vocal pitch accuracy has been found to be time-consuming. In reference to their efforts to analyze 216 subject responses using digital loops, Price et al. (1994) comment that:

> ...it took an average of 20-30 minutes to analyze the six stimulus and six response intervals for each subject; this does not include the time required to go to school, make recordings, and convert the analog data into digital form. (p. 282)

In a separate study, Goetze et al. (1990) noted that "accurate acoustic analysis, made possible by the oscilloscope and stroboscope, may be more exacting than necessary for evaluation of singing melodies because these devices provide more precise measurements than the judgments teachers can make in the classroom" (p. 30).

One study has examined authentic measures of vocal pitch accuracy. Brophy (1997) sought to determine whether children's singing games were valid and reliable for use in authentic assessment of vocal pitch accuracy on sol-mi (a_5-f#$_4$, respectively) and do-re-mi (f_4-g_4-a_5, respectively). Two singing games were chosen to test vocal pitch accuracy of sol and mi, and two singing games were chosen to test vocal pitch accuracy of do, re, and mi. The sol-mi games were "Doggie, Doggie, Where's Your Bone?" and "Aunt Dinah." "Aunt Dinah" (found in Steen, 1992) is a call-and-response game in which the lead child sings first and is then echoed by the class; all solos in this game contain only the pitches sol-mi. "Doggie, Doggie, Where's Your Bone?" (traditional) is a question-and-answer game, with the lead child in the middle of a circle singing answers to questions sung by the class in the circle. The first solo incorporates the pitches sol-mi; however, the second solo includes the note la as part of its melody. The la (b_5) was not assessed for pitch accuracy in this study.

The do-re-mi games were "The Closet Key" and "Charlie Over the Ocean" (found in Erdei, 1974). The "Closet Key" game involves only the pitches do-re-mi (f_4-g_4-a_5), sung first by the group and echoed as a solo by the child who has "found" the key. "Charlie Over the Ocean" is an echo game, with the lead child singing first, echoed by the class. The majority of "Charlie Over the Ocean" remains strictly on do-re-mi; however, the second phrase incorporates low sol (c_4, middle C) one time. The low sol was not assessed in this study. Because of the authenticity of the singing material used in these assessments, the presence of additional pitches other than those being assessed (the sol in "Doggie, Doggie" and the low sol in "Charlie Over the Ocean") was assumed to be a contextual necessity, and the melodies were not artificially altered to eliminate them.

Brophy (1997) assessed the vocal pitch accuracy of 236 children in grades one through three as they performed the solos while participating in the games in the classroom. Accuracy on sol-mi was checked for 134 children, and 102 children were assessed for do-re-mi accuracy. Each child was assessed twice for each criterion song. The results revealed that the selected games are reliable and valid indicators of pitch accuracy on the targeted pitches.

This research informs teachers to the extent that it helps to clarify the nature of the development of vocal pitch accuracy in general music students. The developing nature of the child voice is underscored by the differing results of the research studies presented here; there is a large amount of variability in the findings, a sign that this trait is unstable across the general school population. This is not surprising to music teachers who regularly observe students in their own schools at varying levels of vocal pitch accuracy development. The examination of the vocal pitch accuracy assessment methods employed by researchers reveals that music teachers need methods for assessment that are easy to employ, valid, and reliable.

Vocal Pitch Accuracy Assessment

One of the simplest and most accessible techniques available to general music teachers for the tracking of vocal pitch accuracy development is the singing game with an embedded solo. Component definition for vocal pitch accuracy requires the teacher to predetermine target pitches for assessment. Most singing games of this type contain solos that are limited in range, possess only a few pitches, and are several measures in length, making them ideal for assessing the vocal pitch accuracy of individual children in group classroom settings. A game becomes an assessment when the teacher simply announces that he or she will be listening for the accuracy of the singing and that everyone in the class needs to sing his or her very best during the game, and that a record of the student's accuracy will be kept.

Even though the results of Brophy's (1997) study of authentic assessment of vocal pitch accuracy show that four particular singing games can be reliable and valid for this purpose, it cannot be assumed that every singing game that features solos on targeted pitches is equally reliable or valid. The reliability of the task is dependent upon the consistency with which a teacher applies the criterion for judgment. The validity of the task is dependent upon whether or not the game successfully isolates the targeted pitches in a solo for enough time to allow an accuracy judgment to be made. The results of vocal pitch accuracy assessments are scored with a bi-level, single-criterion guide; the children are either "on" or "off" pitch.

An example of a singing game that is appropriate for first and second grade students is "I Hear a Bird in a Tree" (Figure 3-7). This game clearly targets the pattern sol-mi as a solo, and it can be performed at various pitch levels to detect accuracy. The game moves quickly, and an entire class can be finished within twenty-five to thirty minutes.

Individual vocal pitch accuracy can be assessed during group singing to a degree; this can be effective with older children who may be more reticent about singing alone. The context for such an assessment would be a familiar song that contains pitches that the curriculum targets as appropriate for the child's grade level.

"I Hear a Bird in a Tree"

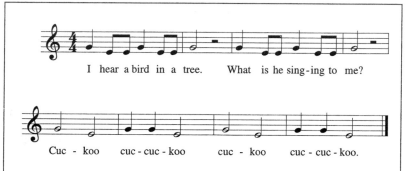

I hear a bird in a tree.   What is he sing-ing to me?

Cuc - koo   cuc - cuc - koo   cuc - koo   cuc - cuc - koo.

To play the game:

All of the children but one scatter about the room, close their eyes, and shape their bodies into "trees." The remaining child becomes a "bird." While the "trees" sing the group section of the song, the "bird" silently "flies" around the room and by the end of the group section has "landed" behind one of the "trees." The soloist then sings the "Cuckoo" part, and the rest of the children must indicate they know where the "bird"/soloist is by listening and pointing toward the soloist. When all of the "trees" have "found" the "bird," the game resumes with the "tree" child becoming the next "bird." The former "bird" sits on the floor as a "bush." The children who are the "bushes" still play the game, but from a sitting position, and the new "bird" never lands on a "bush."

Figure 3-7.

The group should perform the criterion song in a standing position, and the students who have been told that they are being assessed for their vocal pitch accuracy should be spaced far enough apart so the teacher can walk among the students while they are singing. Some teachers incorporate this in their regular teaching practice, making this set-up quite comfortable for the children during the assessment. While moving about the room, the teacher listens carefully to each voice in order to judge its pitch accuracy. This approach is not as effective as listening to individual voices during solos (the same difficulties occur as do when the teacher wishes to conduct a group assessment of technique, discussed previously), but it can yield important information for the teacher, especially when he or she is trying to locate an off-pitch singer.

Acquisition of the Singing Voice: Range

Another developmental skill component that can be assessed is the child's ability to use the singing voice. A child's ability to control and correctly use the voice has been shown to be important "as a separate but requisite behavior to the ability to sing with accurate intonation" (Rutkowski, 1990, p. 93). Rutkowski (1990, 1996) has constructed the *Singing Voice Development Measure (SVDM)*, a nine-point rating scale for classifying developing singers based on the range of their singing voices (see Figure 3-8). Each higher level on the scale represents an increasing level of control over the singing voice as demonstrated by the range in which the child is able to reproduce criterion phrases.

Levinowitz et al. (1997) examined the reliability of the SVDM as employed by general music teachers in grades one through six. In this study, five of the six researchers were general music teachers, and they used their own students (approximately 200 total) as subjects.

123

Singing Voice Development Measure

1   **Pre-Singer** does not sing but chants the song text.

1.5   **Inconsistent Speaking Range Singer** sometimes chants, sometimes sustains tones and exhibits some sensitivity to pitch but remains in the speaking voice range (usually A^2 to a^4).

2   **Speaking Range Singer** sustains tones and exhibits some sensitivity to pitch but remains in the speaking voice range (usually C^3 to c^4).

2.5   **Inconsistent Limited Range Singer** wavers between speaking and singing voice and uses a limited range when in singing voice (usually F^3 to f^4).

3   **Limited Range Singer** exhibits consistent use of limited singing range (usually D^3 to d^4).

3.5   **Inconsistent Initial Range Singer** sometimes only exhibits use of limited singing range, but other times exhibits use of initial singing range (usually A^3 to a^5).

4   **Initial Range Singer** exhibits consistent use of initial singing range (usually B^3-flat to b^5-flat).

4.5   **Inconsistent Singer** sometimes only exhibits use of initial singing range, but other times exhibits use of extended singing range (sings beyond the register lift: B^3-flat and above).

5   **Singer** exhibits use of consistent extended singing range (sings beyond the register lift: B^3-flat and above).

reprinted by permission

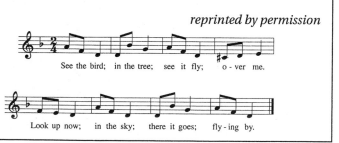

See the bird; in the tree; see it fly; o - ver me.

Look up now; in the sky; there it goes; fly - ing by.

Figure 3-8.

The criterion songs "Row, Row, Row Your Boat" (a major-mode song) and "In the Sea" (a minor-mode song) were taught over a period of one month. The students then performed the songs as solos, and these performances were recorded and judged using the SVDM. The SVDM was found to be most reliable for grades one through five, with a drop in the reliability of the measure for the grade six performances. Furthermore, the results indicated that the children's singing voice acquisition did not significantly improve across grades one through six, calling into question the developmental nature of this trait. These researchers also discovered a significant difference in SVDM ratings based on the modality of the criterion song. These teachers recommend the SVDM for classroom use.

Rutkowski and Miller (1997) are tracking the singing voice development of a group of twenty-eight children through their elementary school years. So far the results indicate that general music instruction has a significant and positive effect on the acquisition of the singing voice. At the present time, the SVDM is being prepared for commercial availability (J. Rutkowski, personal communication, June 11, 1999). While the research is unclear with respect to the developmental nature of children's acquisition of their singing voices, the SVDM appears to be a promising assessment protocol for general music teachers. The practicality of the test must be determined by the individual teacher and will depend on the amount of time that the teacher can set aside for the individual testing involved.

Instrumental Skill

Many general music teachers employ melodic and percussion instruments in their teaching, and periodic checks of performance skill are useful. The assessment of instrumental skill in the general music class is best conducted during a performance using the instruments of interest. The primary assessment tool for the teacher is observation, and instrumental skill assessments should be judged using a single-criterion scoring guide. The context for this can be an accompaniment to a piece or song, or an instrumental piece written for use with children. Most general music students study an instrument as part of their regular work—recorder, guitar, keyboard, autoharp, etc.—and playing skills can be assessed when they have acquired a basic repertoire of pieces. The teacher and/or the curriculum determine this basic repertoire. For example, if a sixth grade class has studied the note Bb on the recorder and the curriculum states that this must be learned, then the teacher can assess this by having each student perform a recorder solo of a piece that involves Bb. This type of assessment is quite straightforward.

As is the case with singing, the most reliable assessment method is to judge skill development during a solo performance on an instrument. In the case of classroom instrumental ensembles (such as those employed by teachers of Orff-Schulwerk), group performances can provide a rich and engaging context for instrumental skill demonstration. However, the reliability of individual skill assessment is compromised when the teacher is unable to focus fully upon the performer. Quickness, dexterity, and security are some of the skills to be examined as children perform on instruments. These skills, when used as assessment criteria, require careful consideration during task development with respect to the level of expertise that should be reasonably expected.

Assessing Rhythmic Accuracy

The assessment of accurate rhythmic performance is most directly achieved by having students learn and perform a simple rhythmic piece for body percussion or unpitched instruments. These can include simple rhymes accompanied by verbal ostinati (such as "The Grand Old Duke of York," found in the Orff/Keetman *Music for Children, Volume 1,* Margaret Murray edition, published by Schott), or short pieces for unpitched instruments (found in numerous publications for Orff classrooms, such as S.W. McRae's 1992 book, *Playtime,* published by Memphis Musicraft Publications).

Another straightforward approach is to assess rhythmic accuracy during the performance of a song or instrumental piece that is being assessed for other components as well (e.g., technical or musical quality components). This can also be assessed in situations where there is a specific additional rhythmic part to a song or instrumental arrangement (these can be found in most series' books as well as in other publications of children's music). Rhythmic accuracy is judged in a similar manner to pitch accuracy: the performance is either rhythmically *accurate* (recorded as a "+") or rhythmically *inaccurate* (recorded as a "–"). The addition of a third level, such as *sometimes accurate,* is not useful in most rhythmic accuracy assessments; it is often most helpful for the teacher to record a rhythmic performance only as either *accurate* or *inaccurate.* This determination, however, remains at the discretion of the teacher.

Assessing Sight-Reading

The extent to which sight-reading is assessed in general music is directly related to its importance to the overall curriculum (review chapter 2, pp. 55-56). The assessment of sight-reading skill requires the assessment of both pitch and rhythmic accuracy during a student's initial reading of a short rhythm or melody written in standard musical notation. What makes sight-reading different from the assessment of pitch and rhythmic accuracy alone is the inclusion of reading notation as a part of the performance process.

The assessment of sight-reading is done individually during a sight-reading exercise. To prepare for such an exercise, the teacher must first design several (a suggested minimum is five sets) short, three-item sets of simple rhythms or melodies (this could also include harmonic progressions if the students are trained to perform these on harmonic instruments) that are age-appropriate and at least three levels of difficulty. These levels of difficulty are related to notation reading; however, in a sight-reading exercise the reading of notation is inseparable from the pitch and/or rhythmic accuracy components of performance, so the assessment of sight-reading levels is also an assessment of levels of pitch and rhythmic accuracy. The three levels of difficulty recommended are *easy* (below the expected level of skill demonstration), *average* (what each student is expected to be able to sight-read), and *difficult* (requiring a level of skill beyond what is expected). These levels of difficulty are not revealed to the student; on the written copy given to students, the exercises are numbered and not classified as to level of difficulty. It is recommended that each student perform the three sight-reading exercises in order of difficulty, performing the easy one first (labeled as "exercise number 1"), the average one second (labeled as "exercise number 2"), and the difficult exercise third (labeled as "exercise number 3").

The next step for the teacher is the determination of a performance medium that is comfortable for the student. This should be either the voice or an instrument with which students have obtained enough technical proficiency to perform the exercise without being impeded by lack of skill, and with which they have had sight-reading experience in class. For example, if students have learned to play barred percussion instruments, are technically proficient with these instruments, and have had experience sight-reading short melodies on these instruments, the sight-reading assessment exercises can be performed on these familiar instruments with a minimum of interference from lack of familiarity with or performance skill on the instrument.

Finally, the teacher will also have to predetermine the recommended tempo for the sight-reading exercise and how the student's chosen tempo affects his or her assessment of sight-reading skill. For example, the teacher must determine if a student's choice of a slower tempo than recommended is indicative of a lower degree of sight-reading skill, an indication of lack of adequate skill with the performance medium, or a combination of both.

Figure 3-9 shows an example of a fifth grade recorder sight-reading task. The three levels of the task are designed to become progressively more difficult with respect to the notation, pitches, and rhythms involved.

At the beginning of a sight-reading assessment task, the teacher should inform the class that each student will be asked to "try his or her best" to "perform at first sight" a set of rhythms or melodies, and that they will be assessed on the degree of accuracy or inaccuracy of their performance. Students should then be called upon one at a time (volunteers can certainly go first!) to perform. Following the selection of a student performer, the teacher should hand the student a sheet of paper that presents the three exercises for sight-reading in standard notation. As the student performs the exercises as a soloist, the teacher assesses the performances. Of course, as is the case with all performance events in general music (but especially with sight-reading tasks), the class should express its appreciation of each student's efforts with brief applause at the end of each performance. Once the task is completed, the teacher should collect the exercise sheet from the student for later use with another student.

In this type of assessment, a multiple level approach to scoring is recommended. It is important for the general music teacher to

**Sample Fifth Grade Recorder
Sight-Reading Exercise and Scoring Guide**

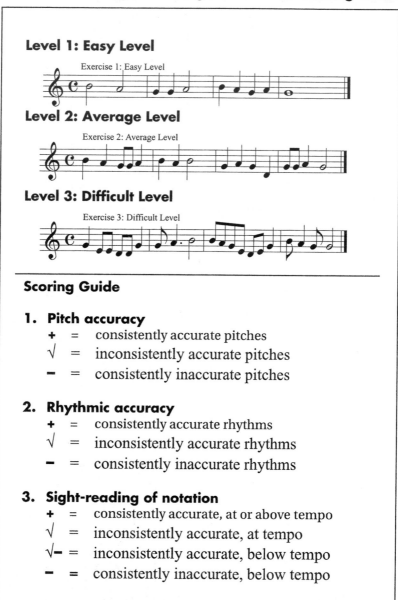

Level 1: Easy Level

Level 2: Average Level

Level 3: Difficult Level

Scoring Guide

1. **Pitch accuracy**
   + = consistently accurate pitches
   √ = inconsistently accurate pitches
   − = consistently inaccurate pitches

2. **Rhythmic accuracy**
   + = consistently accurate rhythms
   √ = inconsistently accurate rhythms
   − = consistently inaccurate rhythms

3. **Sight-reading of notation**
   + = consistently accurate, at or above tempo
   √ = inconsistently accurate, at tempo
   √− = inconsistently accurate, below tempo
   − = consistently inaccurate, below tempo

Figure 3-9.

determine at the outset what levels of achievement will be recorded. While bi-level scoring can be done (in which the performances are judged as being *accurate* or *inaccurate*), it can be useful for the teacher to record additional levels such as *accurate most of the time* (which could be indicated by a checkmark or a marking of the teacher's choice). This is a different number of levels than recommended for the assessment of pitch or rhythmic accuracy alone. This type of assessment is also multiple-criterion, which requires that the teacher be able to assess pitch and/or rhythmic accuracy along with the ability to read notation. Figure 3-9 also presents a sample scoring guide for the sight-reading task presented there. This scoring guide employs three levels of achievement for pitch and rhythmic accuracy and four levels for sight-reading, and the teacher would encode three markings for each of the three sight-reading exercises for each student. For example, if a student performed the easy exercise accurately at the given tempo (tempo determination is at the discretion of the teacher), the teacher would encode "+/+/+" on the data collection instrument for that exercise. If the student performed the average exercise a little below the tempo with accurate pitches but with some errors in rhythmic accuracy, the teacher would encode "+/√/√—" on the data collection instrument. If this student was unable to perform the difficult exercise accurately at the suggested tempo, the teacher would record "—/—/— ."

Assessing Musical Qualities

The assessable components for musical qualities include the following:

1. *Timbre/tone quality* – referring to the quality of the instrumental or vocal sound produced by the student;

131

2. *Dynamics* – having to do with the expressive use of contrasting levels of volume;

3. *Phrasing* – referring to the performance of sensible, musical phrases that enhance the interpretation of the music; and

4. *Interpretation* – having to do with a child's reproduction of an existing work in a manner that is consistent with the intentions of the composer while exhibiting sound musical judgment, expression, and skill in performance (see Figure 3-3).

All general music teachers strive to have their students become expressive musicians, and most general music curricula contain a component related to this aspect of musical skill demonstration. Clearly, expressive musicians are needed and valued, and musical expression is one of the distinguishing characteristics that separates the art of music from mere noise or unorganized sounds.

For both vocal and instrumental developing musicians, the expressive qualities of music are the same. Timbre, tone quality, use of dynamics, phrasing, and interpretation are important features of musical performances. The extent to which child musicians apply these features to their performances is based on three primary factors: (1) the extent to which they have experienced and feel comfortable with these features, (2) their motivation to incorporate these features into a performance, and (3) the performance material and the child's judgment of the appropriateness of the application of these features. Expression in music is a very personal event for any performer, and the child musician is no different.

Assessment of musical qualities is largely a subjective determination. Component definition of musical qualities requires that the teacher pinpoint what is appropriate and within reasonable expectation. The teacher is responsible for determining exactly what constitutes adequate or good tone quality and/or timbre, as well as the parameters for expression of dynamics, phrasing, and interpretation.

The primary tool that the teacher employs in the assessment of musical qualities is a sensitive, well-developed musical ear. The ability to listen to a performance and judge its musical qualities requires the teacher to call upon his or her own musicianship as a guide. This type of assessment is most efficiently scored with a bi-level, single-criterion scoring guide, with the judgment as to whether or not the expressive quality is present. In the case of timbre and tone quality, the two judgments are *adequate* and *inadequate.* When judging dynamics and phrasing, the two levels can be *present* and not *present.*

The judgment of interpretation can be recorded as *musical* and *nonmusical,* or *appropriate* and *not appropriate,* but judging interpretation becomes problematic unless very specific assessment criteria are clearly defined for the students. For example, in an assessment of a child's musical arrangement of a story, the teacher may wish to deem the interpretation of the story and the matching of sounds to the story either *appropriate* or *not appropriate.* However, it is very important that what is not appropriate be clearly defined *prior* to the assessment. Also, if a teacher believes that a child has chosen an "incorrect" sound to represent a story character or sound effect, then it is best to question the child about the choice of instrumentation rather than assess it as *not appropriate.* I once observed a teacher who had very strict ideas about which instruments best represented particular sounds. She had her class arrange a story, and the story contained a scene where the characters are running through some tall grass. The teacher "expected" that the proper sound effect (for the sound of grass swishing against clothing) could be achieved either by rubbing the hands together back and forth or by scraping rhythm sticks together. Instead, the child used the sound of the tambourine, quite to the surprise of the teacher. When questioned, the child explained that this instrument was chosen because the characters had coins in their pockets, and the sound of the coins jingling was the sound of the tambourine, and the sound of the coins was louder than the sound of the grass against their clothing. This was a well-supported, creative choice, and the interpretation was certainly appropriate.

Musical Skill Achievement

The assessable components for musical skill achievement include the following:

1. *Specific solo pieces* – referring to specific works that the curriculum states every child should learn and perform;

2. *Specific dances* – having to do with specific dances that are included in the music curriculum;

3. *Ostinati* – referring to a student's ability to perform repeated melodic or rhythmic patterns during a song or instrumental ensemble;

4. *Partner songs* – having to do with a student's performance of a partner song while a more commonly known melody is being sung;

5. *Rounds/canons* – referring to a child's ability to hold his/her part in a round or canon of appropriate difficulty;

6. *Simple accompaniments* – having to do with a child's ability to perform specific accompaniment patterns (e.g., in the case of Orff Schulwerk, performance of the crossover bordun in third grade); and

7. *Scales* – referring to a child's ability to prepare, play, or recite the tones of a particular developmentally appropriate scale (e.g., third grade, pentatonic; fourth grade, hexatonic; etc.) (see Figure 3-3).

Component definition of musical skill achievement requires the teacher to carefully determine the level of musical complexity within which a child should remain independent. When assessing musical skill achievement, the teacher should focus on the performance product. Observation and careful listening are the primary assessment tools, and the performance product should be assessed using a bi-level, single-criterion scoring guide.

Some curricula may require that certain specific instrumental works or songs be memorized for performance by a certain grade level. In this case, the student is assessed on whether or not he or she performs the work from memory with accurate words, rhythmic and/or pitch accuracy, phrasing, performance technique, or whatever components the curriculum requires. This judgment can only be made at the conclusion of the child's performance. The primary assessment context should be solo performance; individual assessment during group performance is not recommended.

The assessment of the ability to play or sing contrasting parts, scales, and simple accompaniments can be completed in small group performances. The ability to sing rounds, ostinati, and partner songs can be achieved either in duos or trios, during which the teacher listens closely to the two or three voices for their melodic and rhythmic independence from one another. While the musical context should be a familiar song, the extramusical context can be a game or friendly competition. For instance, after a class has learned to sing several two-part pieces, the class can divide into small "teams" of two or three, with the goal of each group to sing the criterion pieces for the class as well as possible. If structured properly so that there are no "winners" or "losers," the teacher can assess the independent part-singing abilities of students in an authentic and engaging manner. This type of activity is particularly effective with older students and easily extends to pieces, scales, and accompaniments for classroom percussion, wind, string, and keyboard instruments.

A special case occurs with respect to the Orff instrumentarium. For teachers of Orff-Schulwerk, the assessment of the ability to perform contrasting instrumental parts is best accomplished during classroom instrumental ensembles. The Orff ensemble involves children in the performance of numerous contrasting ostinati and accompaniment figures. Teachers assessing student skill achievement in this context should focus on one instrumental part at a time (which may be performed by several children at once) and have the criterion for assessment memorized for immediate judgment. This may require that the performance be repeated several times.

The assessment of specific dances is straightforward and simple. Once students know the steps to the dance, they are instructed that they are being assessed on their accuracy in performing the dance. The dance is then started, and the teacher observes the students in pairs (in the case of partner dances) or individually (in the case of line, circle, or other group dances). A bi-level, single-criterion scoring guide is recommended for efficient record keeping, with "+" indicating a *correct* performance of the dance and "−" indicating an *incorrect* performance.

Keeping Track

The assessment of the performing child musician most often requires the use of bi-level, single-criterion scoring guides and yields data that inform the teacher as to whether the child does or does not demonstrate or meet the criterion. Keeping track of the results of single-criterion assessments involves having a list of the children's names prepared in advance, usually in the form of the music teacher's grade book or specially designed data collection form (refer to chapter 2).

For most assessments, the plus symbol "+" can be used to indicate meeting the criterion, such as being "on pitch" or having "good" breath control. The minus symbol "–" can be used to indicate that the criterion was not demonstrated during the assessment. Both of these markings are quick and easy to make while a performance is in progress. Additional descriptive information can be captured if it has relevance to the teacher, but the teacher must predetermine to the best of his or her ability exactly what this information will be (as discussed in chapter 2). When this is completed, a specific set of symbols can be created to indicate this additional information. For example, during a vocal pitch accuracy assessment of two notes, perhaps g_4 and e_4 in a sol-mi singing game, a teacher may wish to record whether or not the off-pitch singers started above or below the pitches. In this instance, the teacher may choose to place arrows next to the minus sign corresponding to the beginning pitch location.

Ann Okins (1997), a practicing music specialist, provides an excellent example of a multi-level, single-criterion scoring guide that has been designed to include descriptive aspects of a vocal pitch accuracy assessment. As the child is singing, she assesses each individual pitch that is sung, resulting in a series of pluses for correctly intoned pitches and minuses for incorrectly matched pitches. Her system also allows her to gather information regarding the quality of the interval the child sings (whether or not, for example, the child sings the minor third sol-mi). If the child begins the solo on a pitch lower than the given one, a number "2" is assigned, followed by a minus sign because the first pitch is incorrect. If this child sings a correct interval from the lower starting pitch, an additional plus sign is added. If a child begins the solo on a pitch higher than the given one, the number "3" is assigned and the same procedure of plus and minus is employed. If all of the pitches are incorrect, a series of minus signs with arrows indicating the direction of the incorrect pitch from the original is used (see Figure 3-10).

Because today's music teachers serve so many students, it is often not possible to learn all of the children's names. One way to facilitate assessment when you don't know all of your students' names is to organize your grade book or data collection form in alphabetical order. Most grade books are also numbered; and if a specially designed seating chart/data collection form is used, these can also include numbers for the students. If the students wear specially made number cards (with the numbers on both sides) that match the grade book or the data collection form, the teacher can keep track by number as the assessment unfolds.

Okins' (1997)* Multi-Level, Single-Criterion Scoring Guide for Vocal Pitch Accuracy Assessment

Key

+	(plus sign)	=	correctly intoned pitch
−	(minus sign)	=	incorrectly intoned pitch

During the vocal solo, the following is encoded:

++	=	correctly intoned solo with two pitches (i.e., sol, mi)
+++	=	correctly intoned solo with three pitches (i.e., sol, mi, la)
2−+	=	starting pitch too low, interval correct
3−+	=	starting pitch too high, interval correct

If all of the pitches are incorrect in the solo, the following is encoded:

− ↑	=	incorrect pitch, higher than correct pitch
− ↓	=	incorrect pitch, lower than correct pitch

used by permission

Figure 3-10.

Another method to employ when unsure about all of the children's names is a seating arrangement, using numbered chairs or individual carpets. Not all general music teachers use chairs in their classrooms; thus, seating arrangements can vary widely. Teachers who have classrooms with carpeted floors can arrange students on the floor according to alphabetical order either in rows or in circles. In classrooms where there is no carpet, rectangular carpet samples, which can be obtained at most flooring dealers at little or no cost, can be used. If carpet samples (often called carpet "squares") are used, a number can be written in permanent marker in the upper corner of each sample and the children can be seated according to their assigned numbers.

The teacher's full attention to the performance in progress facilitates keeping track of assessment results during musical performances. Careful consideration must be given to record keeping if a teacher is going to accompany children's performances at the piano, guitar, or other instrument. For the most part, solo and group performances should be unaccompanied if they are being assessed. If desired, an exception can be made in the case of singing games. In this context, the teacher may choose to accompany the group sections of the game in order to keep the class in the proper key area. If accompaniments are included, the teacher still needs to be able to immediately note the assessment results, requiring a quick change between accompanying and writing during the game. Figure 3-11 summarizes the design task parameters for assessing the performing child musician.

Summary

- The first step in designing a task in the performance response mode is to carefully define an assessable performance component from one of six task target areas: (1) *enabling skills,* (2) *fundamental aural discriminations,* (3) *technique,* (4) *musical qualities,* (5) *musical skill development,* and (6) *musical skill achievement.*

- The second step is to carefully choose the assessment context and materials to maximize the validity of the task.

Task Design Parameters: Assessing the Performing Child

Parameter: Task Target Area:	Component Definition	Assessment Focus	Assessment Tool	Assessment Context	Scoring Guide	Record Keeping Strategy
Enabling Competencies	define the acceptable level of competency demonstration	process	observation/ listening	play or game	single-criterion (bi-level)	grade book, seating chart, class list; + or –
Fundamental Aural Discriminations	determine what is age appropriate	process	observation/ listening	play or game; familiar song or piece; standard repertoire	single-criterion (bi-level)	+ or –
Technique	carefully determine what is to be considered adequate	process	observation/ listening	familiar song or piece	single-criterion/ multiple-criterion (bi-level)	+ or –
Expressive Qualities	pinpoint what is appropriate and within reasonable expectation	product	observation/ listening	song or piece with embedded; but unambiguous expressive variety	single-criterion (bi-level)	+ or –
Skill Development	predetermine target pitches for singing/ dexterity levels for instrument playing	process	observation/ listening	singing games with embedded solos/ instrumental solos/ criterion songs	single-criterion (bi-level)	+ or –
Skill Achievement	determine level of complexity for musical independence	product	observation/ listening	criterion songs and pieces/small group performances/for Orff-Schulwerk, class ensembles	single-criterion (bi-level)	+ or –

Figure 3-11.

- The final step in preparing a performance response mode task is the determination of a practical and meaningful record keeping strategy. A simple "+" and "−" system is recommended, with "+" indicating that the criterion was met and "−" indicating that it was not.

- Performance response mode assessments are designed to provide assessment data with respect to a targeted musical behavior while a child is engaged in musical performance.

- Once an assessable component is selected and defined, it must be decided whether the musical process or product will be the focus of the task.

- For performance response mode assessments, the primary assessment tools available to the teacher are close observation and careful listening.

- A bi-level, single-criterion scoring guide is recommended for all performance response mode tasks, but bi-level, multiple-criterion assessments could be employed once the teacher is comfortable with this. The multi-level, single-criterion scoring guide may include descriptive symbols that can be quickly noted during a performance to provide additional information about the performance.

- Performance response mode assessment data can provide information that enhances a teacher's understanding of a child's concept attainment.

- The extent of a child's conceptual knowledge is most adequately judged from multiple assessment perspectives. Performance data should be combined with results from creating and responding assessment tasks in order to demonstrate a child's conceptual understanding in a variety of musical contexts and situations.

Questions for Clarification

1)   When designing a performance response mode assessment task, the teacher should first determine and define an _____ _____ that can be the target of the task.

2)   Enabling skills, fundamental aural discriminations, technique, musical qualities, musical skill development, and musical skill achievement are the six _____ _____ _____ for performance response mode assessment in the general music classroom.

3)   The primary assessment tools available to general music teachers when judging general musical performance tasks are _____ and _____.

4)   The best technique for scoring musical performance tasks in general music is the _____ - _____ _____ _____, which can be modified to include descriptive information.

5)   Keeping track of performance assessment data can be most easily accomplished through the use of a _____ sign to indicate criterion achievement and a _____ sign to indicate that the criterion was not observed.

6)   Performance assessment data can be used to provide supporting information regarding a child's _____ acquisition.

7) Assessing a child's conceptual understanding in music is best achieved through _____ assessment perspectives.

Questions for Discussion

1) If your local school district has prepared assessment performance indicators, obtain a copy of these and discuss which of them are suitable for assessment during musical performance. If district-level indicators are not available, examine the scope and sequence of one grade of a music series text for assessable performance components and discuss your findings.

2) Of the six assessment target areas appropriate for assessment during musical performance, discuss the areas you feel are most important in general music and why. Are they all equally important, or can you establish a hierarchy of importance for assessment? Support your answer.

3) Discuss how technology might help in assessing musical performances. Do you think that the presence of technological apparatus in the general music classroom threatens the authenticity of assessment tasks? Why or why not?

4) Discuss various ways of keeping track of assessment data obtained during children's musical performances. Which method do you think is most effective?

5) Can you think of a situation where you might want to use a multi-level, multiple-criterion scoring guide to judge a classroom performance? If so, describe the situation and the criteria you would include in the rubric. If you do not feel that you would use a multi-level, multiple-criterion scoring guide for general music classroom performances, would you ever use a bi-level, multiple-criterion scoring guide? Support your answer.

6) Discuss what you believe is the most important information that the assessment of a child's musical performances could yield with respect to that child's acquisition of the following concepts:

a) A kindergartner's understanding of high and low, slow and fast;

b) A third grader's concept of sol-mi;

c) A fifth grader's understanding of two-part singing;

d) A second grader's concept of the subdivided beat; and

e) A sixth grader's understanding of triads.

Assessment Practice

Select one of the six task target areas for performance response mode assessment, then complete the following steps to devise a task:

1) Choose a grade level that you currently teach or will teach in the future.

2) Carefully define an assessable component.

3) Determine a target behavior appropriate for the component.

4) Describe the focus and context of the assessment task.

5) Compile at least five examples of appropriate materials.

6) Devise a scoring strategy.

7) Determine a record keeping strategy.

Next, choose one of the materials you have collected and teach the selection to one of your general music classes or to the other members of the class taking this course. Then inform the class that you are going to assess them on the targeted behavior you have chosen, and describe how you will be judging them. Administer the task, collect your data, and discuss the following:

1) The validity of your task;

2) Your reliability in judging the performances;

3) Your ability to stay focused on the targeted behavior; and

4) The value of your results as assessment information.

Chapter 4

Assessing the Creating Child Musician

This chapter focuses on purpose, use, and design of assessment tasks that are founded within the creating assessment response mode. In general music, children involved in creative assessment activities generate one of three musical products: (1) a *composition,* (2) an *improvisation,* or (3) *an arrangement.* While these are all newly created musical works, the processes and materials required to create them are different. When composing, the child creates new music with the intent to revise the musical product to suit his or her needs or wishes. Improvisation is very different from composition in that the improviser spontaneously generates new music without intent to revise; what the child creates remains unchanged. Arranging music involves creating a new musical presentation of an existing musical work and, for the purposes of this book, also includes development of musical settings for existing literary works, a process that may involve composition, improvisation, or both.

This chapter opens with a review of the National Content Standards related to creative musical products, followed by a brief discussion of some of the research pertaining to musical creativity and its measurement. Following this, appropriate models for the assessment of musical compositions and improvisations will be introduced, along with brief examinations of some of the research into children's compositions and improvisations.

Related National Standards

There are two National Standards that deal specifically with content and achievement embedded within the creating artistic process. National Content Standard number 3 has to do with "improvising melodies, variations, and accompaniments," and National Content Standard number 4 states that general music students should engage in "composing and arranging music within specific guidelines." In some instances, children's compositions may be notated as part of an assessment task. When this is required, the task addresses National Content Standard number 5, "reading and notating music" (MENC, 1994, p. 27).

Creative activities in general music involve the children in a creative process that results in a created *product*. For assessment purposes, tasks that involve children creatively should be designed to examine the product of the task or the musical skills that are engaged to create the musical product but not creative ability itself. It is recommended that judgments never be made about *levels* of creativity within a given work or the possession of more or less *creative ability* in children as evidenced in classroom-administered assessment tasks. There are several reasons for this. First, the content standards do not address the creative process; instead, they address the production of music through creative activity. Second, the creative process is a very personal, internalized event for each child and is elusive to anyone seeking its measurement. The assessment tools available to the general music specialist—observation of behaviors, listening, and examination of products—do not provide adequate information to allow a judgment to be made on creative ability. Third, there is not yet a standardized measure of the creative process or creative ability, although research continues (Webster, 1992; Webster & Hickey, 1999). Musical creativity and creative ability is difficult to define and to measure objectively, as will be shown in the following "Glimpse at the Research."

The Nature of Musical Creativity: A Glimpse at the Research

There are a number of theoretical conceptions of general creativity, and reviewing these is beyond the scope of this chapter (the interested reader will find many books on this subject); however, the wealth of conceptions of general creativity has not yet been fully transferred to the domain of music. Theoretical conceptions and their procedural definitions remain a major need in the domain of music, as Webster (1992) emphasized when he stated that "*the* most important need that faces researchers interested in this topic is the development of better theory" (p. 278).

Defining Musical Creativity

A surge of interest in creativity in music education occurred in the 1960s. Four major projects in music education guided the profession toward the identification of problems and their suggested solutions, and these projects provided a vehicle through which creativity in music was defined.

In 1959 the Contemporary Music Project (CMP) was the first of several efforts to incorporate novel and creative music programs in the public schools. The CMP placed young composers, under thirty-five years of age, in public school systems to serve as composers-in-residence. Of the four publications that arose from this project, two were devoted to reporting the results of pilot projects in musical creativity. In the foreword to the fourth report, William Mitchell provided a definition of creativity as it was applied in these two projects:

> *Creativity and innovation have a literal meaning in the
> Ithaca and Interlochen projects; creativity refers to the
> act of composing [emphasis added], innovation to the
> discovery and use of relatively unfamiliar materials.*
> (Benson, 1967, p. vii)

One of the five topics undertaken at the Tanglewood
Symposium (July 23-August 2, 1967) was "The Nature and Nurture
of Creativity." The committee, chaired by Karl D. Ernst, explained
creativity as follows:

> *Creativity comes into existence in many different ways. It
> is a human characteristic existing in all, varying only in
> degree. It may result from a unique way of looking at a
> problem—musical or otherwise. It may be simple or it
> may be complex. The same creative behavior may be
> observed in children as well as in composers. The differ-
> ence is in degree of complexity.* (Ernst, 1968, p. 129)

This statement acknowledged the perspective that creativity in
music may involve innovative problem-solving procedures as well
as compositional processes and products. In terms of personality
characteristics, the creative student was described as: (1) a
nonconformist who may act out grievances and not make an
attempt at endearment to the peer group or teacher; (2) not
necessarily the most intelligent student in the class; (3) one who
engages in divergent rather than convergent thinking; and (4) one
who is independent, seeking to find a personal style. This committee also expressed the importance of the child's environment in
the development of creativity.

The Manhattanville Music Curriculum Program (MMCP) took
place from 1965 through 1970 and was sponsored by the U.S.
Office of Education. The purpose of this project was to develop a
sequential music curriculum from the elementary grades through
high school. The *MMCP Synthesis* (Thomas; n.d.) was the project's
curriculum guide for grades three through twelve; the *MMCP*

Interaction (Biasini, Thomas, & Pogonowski, n.d.) was produced for the primary grades. These two curriculum guides defined musical creativity as follows:

> *Creativity in music. This term refers to activities in which the pupil uses aural imagination, aural insights, and aural judgment to fashion sounds into music. The term does not apply to skill-drills in notational formulae or activities where the imagination is focused on other than aural expression.* (Biasini, Thomas, & Pogonowski, n.d., p. 107; Thomas, n.d., p. 38)

In a study of writings about creativity as an objective of music education, Hounchell (1985/1986) concluded that there *was* no clear definition of creativity in music. However, he revealed that the term "creativity" was most commonly used in relation to composing and that creativity was often used as a means of building support for ideas regarding music education.

Music education philosopher David Elliott (1995) makes a clear distinction between his conceptions of creativity and originality. For Elliott, creating is "a particular kind of making or doing that results in tangible products or achievements that people deem valuable, useful, or exceptional in some regard" (p. 216). Originality, however, is achieved when a work of art is "simultaneously similar to, yet different from, its relevant ancestors" (p. 217). Originality is not the sole determiner of creativity; the product or achievement's significance to its domain is of equal importance. His perspective is related to Csikszentmihalyi's "systems" view of creativity (Csikszentmihalyi, 1988, 1996), wherein a creative act or product exists within a specific domain and is shaped and judged by the forces of a cultural and societal "field" that determines the exact nature of what is to be considered "creative." Elliott's view remains praxial (practice-based) in its overall conception; the creative musical achievement is a result of music making or, to use Elliott's term, *musicing.*

Regarding spontaneous musical generation in children, Elliott believes that this musical behavior is

> ...*more a matter of spontaneous originality [emphasis added] and this, in turn, is largely a matter of innocence, or lack of knowledge. Spontaneous originality usually has no relationship to recognized domains of practice except, perhaps, in a naive, exploratory way.* (p. 221)

Elliott further suggests that while the creating individual may not know what the end result of his or her creative activity will be, the activity itself is goal-directed and intentional. That is, the creative effort is put forth to create something tangible that can be judged as significant to the domain by persons knowledgeable within that domain. From this perspective, children who are *original* with sounds and sound combinations may not always be musically *creative.*

This brief exposition of the evolving definition of musical creativity informs teachers to the extent that it makes clear the continuing effort to adequately address this issue within the profession. The elusive and strikingly individual nature of creativity in music not only makes it difficult to define but also poses challenges for those who wish to develop theoretical descriptions of the creative process. What follows is a brief introduction to some of the work of music education researchers toward building creative theory and models of the creative process in music.

Musical Creativity: Theories and Models

Margery Vaughan (1973) developed a four-stage view of the musical creative process that expresses these stages as levels of energy. The first level *(acquisition)* denotes the gathering and storing of knowledge for later use. The second *(combinational)* level is reached when the child begins to reassemble this acquired knowledge in new ways to generate new musical ideas. At the third *(developmental)* level, the individual employs insight and intuition in the generation of novel relationships between ideas and new sounds. The fourth *(synergistic)* level of this process is reached when the individual accounts for and meets what his or her society requires to accept a new musical work as "creative."

Webster (1987a, 1988, 1991) has been instrumental in the development of a conceptual base for creativity in music and has developed a model of the creative thinking process in music. In Webster's view, the creative process begins with the individual's *product intention*, a composition, performance/improvisation, or analysis. Once this intention is established, the creator calls upon available thinking skills, or *enabling skills*. These include musical aptitudes (such as tonal and rhythmic imagery, sensitivity to the musical whole or musical syntax, musical extensiveness, flexibility, and originality), conceptual understandings, craftsmanship (the ability to apply factual musical knowledge to a complex musical task), and aesthetic sensitivity. A number of nonmusical conditions also influence the creator's thinking process in music; these are the *enabling conditions* of motivation, subconscious imagery (a hypothesized condition referring to mental activity apart from the conscious mind that may help the creative process), the environment (e.g., family and financial support), and personality characteristics (such as the willingness to take risks). These enabling skills and conditions are connected to creative production through *divergent* and *convergent* thinking. During the divergent thinking phase of the process, many solutions are generated and tested, with or without regard to traditional practice. Eventually, one idea is converged upon as the best, and this becomes the final creative product.

While Webster (1987a,b) admits that this model "is not designed in developmental terms" (p. 167), he notes that several developmental characteristics are implied. Product intention is doubtless different for the young child, who relies primarily on intuition and chance for performance/improvisation. The enabling skills that are vital to the model are developing in children, implying that creative products may be differently affected by these conditions at different ages. The same is true of the gradual acquisition of conceptual understanding in music, achieved over a period of time. Another important implication of the model is the equal importance of environments that encourage both divergent and convergent thinking in music; both are essential to the model.

Swanwick and Tillman (1986) and Tillman (1989) have proposed an eight-step sequence of children's creative development in music based on their study of over 700 children's compositions. Conceived as a spiral, this sequence has four levels through which development occurs: (1) *mastery,* (2) *imitation,* (3) *imaginative play,* and (4) *metacognition* (Swanwick, 1988, 1994). Within each level there are two steps, or *modes,* which demonstrate the child's transformation from initial, intuitive explorations to conscious, deliberate actions. Swanwick (1994) describes the first mode at each level as the *intuitive* phase and the second mode as the more *analytical, cognitive* manifestation of these intuitions. As children grow through these levels, the intuitive modes are transformed through experience into the analytical/cognitive modes, and the child gains control of the application of this knowledge.

1. At the *mastery* level (newborn through age four), the child's main interest is taking delight in the materials of music making. The intuitive mode at this level is the *sensory mode* (step 1), wherein the child simply explores sounds for his or her sensory input. The *manipulative mode* (step 2) follows around age four or five, characterized by the increasing ability to manipulate sounds.

2. During the ensuing *imitation* level, the child's focus shifts to expressiveness. The intuitive *personal mode* (step 3) is exhibited when the child creates pieces that are spontaneous and personal musical expressions. The *vernacular mode* (step 4) begins around age eight or nine and is characterized by a more analytical approach and the use of more common musical conventions; simple meters emerge and compositions may contain some repetition of phrases and sequential patterns.

3. Around age ten, the *imaginative play* level is reached, where the child's focus shifts to consideration of formal structures. The *speculative mode* (step 5), attained at the beginning of this level, is characterized by the deliberate introduction of pattern deviation, and again there seems to be evidence of a very personal type of music that is created. The *idiomatic mode* (step 6) is characterized by the return of more conventional musical production and an interest in creating music in a particular idiom such as rock or jazz.

4. The final *metacognitive* level of the spiral, reached around age fifteen, is manifested through musical valuing, having to do with the growing recognition of music as a symbolic form of discourse. The *symbolic mode* (step 7) is marked by the use of technical mastery to communicate musical ideas in a coherent, expressive, and well-formed composition. The last step on the spiral is the *systematic mode* (step 8), wherein the child's composition is based on a novel array of musical materials, such as new scales or harmonies, resulting in an expansion of the musical language.

Elliott (1995) offers a model of general creativity in music that is placed within the context of musical practice. In Elliott's view, creativity in music is energized by both *enabling abilities,* which are a result of genetic predisposition toward musical intelligence, and *promoting abilities,* which result from an individual's acquired musicianship that promotes creativity. Promoting abilities include a "promise detector," pertaining to the ability to sense the promise or significance of new musical ideas, and "plans," which refers to the individual's working patterns while involved in musicing. For

Elliott, a creative event is the result of the "effort expended, expertise deployed, promises realized, and enjoyment felt" (p. 230).

The Measurement of General Musical Creativity

One of the central problems relating to the measurement of musical creativity has been the identification of valid and measurable constructs that capture the complexity of this behavior. The four divergent production abilities identified in Guilford's (1967) Structure of Intellect model have provided the basis for corollary musical constructs that have served as the foundation for the construction of tests of musical creativity. Guilford's components are:

1. *Fluency,* defined as the ability to provide multiple answers from the same information within a certain amount of time;

2. *Flexibility,* described as the ability to produce shifts in meaning from the same information;

3. *Originality,* which referred to the production of responses that were novel and remotely associated with the information given; and

4. *Elaboration,* defined as the ability to provide a higher level of detail and complexity of information than that called upon for the response.

Within these components, three specific factors were identified as important for artistic creativity:

1. *Expressional fluency* was identified as the ability to integrate ideas into a single product.

2. *Spontaneous flexibility* was identified as the basis for creative imagination.

3. *Adaptive flexibility* denoted the ability to reject familiar patterns and attain new ones.

Guilford's identification of four components of general creativity led to the development of numerous musical creativity tests (Gorder, 1976, 1980; Vaughan, 1971; Wang & Kageff, 1985). Peter Webster (1977, 1987a,b) has developed the most thoroughly researched tests of creativity in music. His first measure, *Thinking Creatively with Music* (Webster, 1977), was designed for and administered to older students. His later research produced the *Measure of Creative Thinking in Music (MCTM)* (Webster, 1987b), suitable for younger children. The four musical factors assessed in this test were: (1) *musical extensiveness,* the amount of actual clock time spent on a given musical task (measured in seconds); (2) *musical flexibility,* the extent to which a child can freely move from one extreme to the other with one of three musical parameters: low to high, soft to loud, and fast to slow; (3) *musical originality,* the extent to which a child manipulates musical phenomena in a unique fashion; and (4) *musical syntax,* the extent to which a child manipulates musical phenomena in a logical and inherently musical manner, with attention to the shaping of the whole response and not just a single part.

Webster's newest test, *Measure of Creative Thinking in Music — Version II (MCTM-II)* is a three-part, ten-item test with a brief warm-up. The first part, *Exploration,* is three items long and is designed to test the musical flexibility of the child. The second part, *Application,* is four items long and tests multiple factors in exploratory tasks on single instruments. The final section, *Synthesis,* is three items long and employs the child's usage of all instruments (temple blocks, piano and nerf ball, and voice with microphone). The final three tasks are scored for all musical factors. The test takes twenty-five minutes to administer. This test is one of the most researched of its kind, and Dr. Webster has agreed to make it available to interested general music specialists. If you are interested in administering the MCTM-II, contact Dr. Webster via email at pwebster@nwu.edu, or via regular mail by writing to: Peter Webster, School of Music, Northwestern University, Evanston, IL 60208. His internet website is located at the following address: http://pubweb.nwu.edu/~webster. At the time of this printing, the test is being revised again by both Dr. Webster and Dr. Maud Hickey using MIDI-based technology (personal communication, June 4, 1999).

This brief review informs the general music practitioner that while musical creativity is important as a process and as a framework for learning and assessment activities, a widely accepted definition and theory remains elusive at the present time. The development of adequate measures and testing of creative ability in music is also in its early stages.

Therefore, it is recommended that the *judgment* of creativity or creative ability never be a component in an assessment task. Children who are composing, improvising, and arranging should always be encouraged to be as "creative as possible" when completing their tasks, but their creative works should only be assessed for the performance process or creative evidence they provide.

Determining What Is Important to Assess

The first step in developing assessment tasks within the creating artistic mode is to determine the assessable components that comprise these activities. These components are directly related to the focus of the assessment task, whether it is the musical skills involved in the process of the task or the product that is the end result of the task. The assessment of musical skills employed during a composing, improvising, or arranging task, such as steady beat, evenness of tempo, instrumental or vocal technique, follows the same guidelines set forth in chapter 3 for assessing the performing child musician. The assessable components of compositions, improvisations, and arrangements fall into five task target areas: (1) *melodic,* (2) *rhythmic,* (3) *structural,* (4) *theoretical,* and (5) *aesthetic.*

1. When assessing *melodic* features of a composition, improvisation, or arrangement, task targets include *range, melody type, closing tone, presence of repeated melodic motives,* and *presence of developed melodic motives.*

Melodic *range* has to do with the distance from the highest to lowest pitch in the melody and is expressed in terms of the interval which represents that distance.

The *closing tone* is simply the last note of the melody. In certain tasks, this may be assessed as an important indicator of a child's sense of tonality.

Melody type is determined by assigning the description of *conjunct, disjunct,* or *combined* to the melodic motion. A good rule of thumb is that a melody can be considered *conjunct* when approximately 60 percent or more of the intervals employed are a major third or smaller, and *disjunct* when approximately 60 percent or more of the intervals used are a perfect fourth or greater. It follows, then, that a melody possesses *combined melodic motion* when its intervals are from 40 to 60 percent a perfect fourth or greater *and* 40 to 60 percent a major third or smaller. In the melodies where two pitches are performed simultaneously (for example, the improvisation of a child who uses both mallets simultaneously at a barred percussion instrument), it is recommended that the highest pitch be considered in this determination.

A *melodic motive* is generally considered to be two to six pitches that form a distinct pitch pattern.

A *developed melodic motive* is a melodic motive that demonstrates changes in pitch that are different from, but perceptually similar to, a previous melodic motive (Kratus, 1985).

2. Task targets for *rhythmic* features fall into three areas: (a) *beat divisions/note and rest values,* (b) *presence of repeated rhythmic motives,* and (c) *presence of developed rhythmic motives.*

The type of *beat division* present in a composition or

improvisation can be categorized by whether or not this division occurs as part of a rhythmic pattern. A rhythmic pattern can be identified as a set of durations that demonstrate a sense of pulse and cohesiveness, and appear to be intentionally organized. For child musicians, there are three types of beat division that can be identified: (a) the single division of the beat, or eighth notes and rests; (b) the double division of the beat, or sixteenth notes and rests; and (c) the triple division of the beat, or triplets and rests. Beats that are unevenly divided, such as dotted quarter and dotted eighth notes and rests, can be considered divided beats at the highest level of division. For example, if a child's composition contains a dotted quarter/eighth note or rest combination, this can be considered a single division of the beat; the dotted eighth note/sixteenth note or rest combination should be considered a double division of the beat. Other note and rest values that can be targeted for assessment are quarter, half, dotted half, and whole notes and their corresponding rests.

A *rhythmic motive* is generally identified as two to six pitches that form a distinct durational pattern; a *developed rhythmic motive* is a rhythmic motive that demonstrates changes in duration that are different from, but perceptually similar to, a previous rhythmic motive (Kratus, 1985). The presence of repeated and/or developed rhythmic motives can be measured by counting the number of measures in which these occurred or by simply making a bi-level determination of whether or not they are present.

3. When assessing the *structural* features of a child's composition, improvisation, or arrangement, four task targets can be identified: (a) *form,* (b) *presence of phrases,* (c) *presence of antecedent/consequent phrases,* and (d) *sense of closure.*

A *phrase* is a series of sequenced or different melodic motives that create a complete musical idea or thought.

Antecedent/consequent phrases are two phrases of equal length that are complementary to one another. The first step in the assessment of these features involves determining whether or not phrases are present. If phrases are present, then a determination can be made as to whether or not they expressed an antecedent/consequent relationship.

160

A *sense of closure* exists when there is a clear-cut conclusion to the child's composition or improvisation. This can be expressed in numerous ways, such as the presence of the tonic as a closing tone and/or a rhythmic final point.

4. *Theoretical* task targets primarily have to do with the components of *scale, harmony,* and *notation.* In some instances, composition and arranging tasks may require the student to choose and then employ a particular scale or pitch-set, include a particular harmony change, or notate the composition. If these are a focus of the task, then they become assessable components. The teacher predetermines these components for most tasks as part of the task design (see *Guided Composition* later in this chapter).

5. When assessing children's compositions, improvisations, and arrangements, *aesthetic* task targets are those that relate to the appropriateness of the musical and movement choices made in response to the task.

For compositions, this has to do with the subjective qualities of the finished product—such as *listener appeal, emotional effect,* and *overall impact.*

For movement improvisation, these task targets include *sense of space, appropriateness of the movement, balance of motion,* and *body positions* used.

For musical arrangements, the task targets are *expression* and *instrumentation.*

For literature-based arrangements, task targets include *expression, instrumentation, sound association,* and *dramatic movement. Expression* relates to the child's choice of dynamics and articulation in the created work. *Instrumentation* refers to the appropriateness of the child's choice of musical instruments in the arrangement. *Sound association* pertains to the child's sense of appropriateness about sounds that represent events in a literary dramatization. *Dramatic movement* relates to the child's choice of movement to enhance a literary work, specifically the use of gesture, space, balance, and body position. These assessable components are summarized in Figure 4-1.

Assessable Components for Creative Musical Products

Product Type: **Task Target Areas:**	Composition/ Improvisation	Arrangement/ Musical or Literature-based

Melodic	range
	melody type: conjunct,
	    disjunct, combined
	closing tone
	repeated melodic motives
	developed melodic motives
	scale
		range
		melody type: conjunct,
		    disjunct, combined
		closing tone
		repeated melodic motives
		developed melodic motives
		scale

Rhythmic	beat divisions/note values
	    and rests
	rhythm patterns
	repeated rhythmic motives
	developed rhythmic motives
		beat divisions/note values
		    and rests
		rhythm patterns
		repeated rhythmic motives
		developed rhythmic motives

Structural	form (use of contrasting
	    sections)
	phrases
	antecedent/consequent
	phrases
	sense of closure
		form (use of contrasting
		    sections)
		phrases
		antecedent/consequent
		phrases
		sense of closure

Theoretical	scale or pitch set harmony changes notation	scale or pitch set harmony changes notation

Aesthetic	subjective qualities:
	    listener appeal
	    emotional effect
	    overall impact
	use of dynamics
	articulation: staccato, legato
	movement: body positions/
	    sense of space/
	    balance of motion/
	    appropriateness
		expression
		instrumentation
		sound association
		dramatic
		    movement

Figure 4-1.

Models and Techniques

The following suggestions for the assessment of children's compositions, improvisations, and arrangements are presented as models. The use of specific materials and contextual conditions is the prerogative of the teacher. As in chapter 3, each model or technique is discussed using specific terms as task design parameters. Component definition of the task target has to do with specifying the component to be assessed. The focus of most assessment tasks in this response mode is the musical product, but in some instances, the focus is the musical process. The assessment tools most appropriate for product assessment are listening and post-performance examination of a notated score; for process-focused assessments, listening and observation are most appropriate. The assessment context refers to the general type of material or performance condition that is best for observing or generating the assessment target.

Assessing Children's Compositions

When teaching composition or providing composition experiences for general music students, teachers use a variety of approaches and techniques. One overall goal of teaching composition is to provide students a variety of experiences so that they are comfortable with both the process and the products they produce. Children experience a great deal of joy in the process of creating new music and are proud of their newly created works. A number of researchers have examined children's compositions for their characteristics and the processes that children employ while composing. The following section presents some of this research.

The Nature of Children's Compositions: A Glimpse at the Research

In the early 1940s, Dorothea Doig (1941, 1942a, 1942b) studied the compositional strategies used by children ages six through sixteen prior to their receiving any composition training. She found that most of the children composed in duple meter and that older students were better able to maintain a sense of consistent meter throughout their compositions. Older children used fewer tones in their compositions. While the compositions of the six- to nine-year-olds demonstrated a sense of cadence, the older children's compositions showed more consistent and conventional melodic closure, with the majority ending on the tonic pitch.

John Kratus (1985; 1985/1986) examined the rhythm, melody, motive, and phrase characteristics of children's original compositions. He found the compositions of five-year-olds to be "very much like improvisations, in that the children cannot replicate them (reproduce them once they have been performed)" (p. 224). These compositions displayed weak metric organization, little attention to the steady beat, and were unlikely to end on the tonic pitch. Seven-year-olds produced similar compositions but showed greater frequency of ending on the tonic and repeated rhythmic motives. The compositions of the nine-year-olds displayed the greatest variance in musical characteristics. At that age, most (but not all) children produced compositions within the steady beat and within an organized metrical structure, and displayed a greater sense of tonal center and more frequently ended on the tonic pitch. Eleven-year-olds produced the most musically organized compositions, exhibiting consistent tempo, strict meter, and development of rhythmic and melodic motives. Kratus also noted that "about half of these children can replicate their songs" (p. 225), in contrast with the five-year-olds who could not. Thirteen-year-olds produced pieces that varied widely, and only half of the compositions appeared to be tonally organized.

Kratus (1989) later examined the compositions of sixty (60) seven-, nine-, and eleven-year-olds for the amount of time they spent involved in the processes of exploration, development, repetition, and silence during a ten-minute compositional period. The results showed that eleven-year-olds devoted the most time to development and repetition, and seven- and nine-year-olds spent most of their time exploring. These results led Kratus to recommend that the seven-year-olds' first creative experiences be improvisational rather than compositional because subjects this age appear to lack the enabling skills (Webster, 1987a,b) necessary to replicate original music. Kratus further interpreted his results to indicate that the older students were *product-oriented* rather than *process-oriented* in their approach to solving the musical problems posed by composition.

Kratus (1995) has also researched the effect of composing tempo, or speed, on the compositions of forty (40) nine-year-olds. The students were given ten minutes to create a composition on a Casio CZ-1000 full electronic keyboard, and composing "tempo" was determined by counting the number of times a subject played a note on the keyboard while composing during the first, fifth, and tenth minutes of the task. Students with faster composing tempos tended to compose longer, less structured music. Kratus (1994) later examined the relationship of children's music audiation (as measured by Gordon's *IMMA*, a version of the Musical Aptitude Profile, discussed in chapter 2) and their compositional processes and products. Participants with higher audiation scores composed pieces that were more metrically and tonally organized, exhibited greater use of developed rhythmic patterns, and contained narrower ranges.

Wilson and Wales (1995) collected the compositions of seventy-three (73) second and fourth grade students (seven and nine years old) that were created on a computer. The students were shown how to create music using a mouse and *Music Works* software. Results revealed that rhythmic development in the compositions seemed to proceed more slowly than melodic development; the suggested reason for this was that "the computer task of this study did not draw upon the motoric component of rhythmic development" (p. 107). This study is one of the few that has attempted to examine children's compositions that were created strictly through technological means. (For a more qualitative examination of this process, consult Upitis, 1989.)

This research informs teachers in that it provides a research-based view of children's compositional products and processes. In the 1940s, Doig was able to show that older children were better able to maintain consistent meter throughout their compositions than younger ones. It is not surprising that Kratus's research shows that older children spend more time developing musical ideas while younger children spend more time exploring and that the compositions of five-year-olds are much less musically organized than those of eleven-year-olds. Wilson and Wales reveal that rhythmic development appears to be impeded when composing with only a computer mouse, without the bodily-kinesthetic involvement of instrument playing or singing.

Compositions for Assessment

In order for a composition to be produced for assessment, it is important for the teacher to provide a clearly articulated composition task that targets specific assessable components. It is important to emphasize here that this book is addressing the composition experience for *assessment* purposes. These steps, which are summarized in Figure 4-2, are designed to help teachers devise tasks that will target relevant assessment components. It is recommended that numerous, less-restricted composition opportunities be provided for instructional purposes.

First, the teacher must *decide whether the composition will be rhythmic or melodic.* Rhythmic compositions may be produced with unpitched percussion instruments or with body percussion (snapping, clapping, patting the knees, and stamping being the most common elements). Melodic compositions may be produced on an instrument or by voice. Vocal compositions generally take the form of songs, and the song may have words or be sung on a neutral syllable ("la," "lie," "lo," etc.). Vocal compositions may also consist of series of vocal sounds that are not songs.

Steps for Designing Composition Tasks

1. Determine the type of composition to be completed —rhythmic, melodic, instrumental, vocal — and whether or not it will be accompanied.

2. Choose the assessable components for the task.

3. Decide the minimum length of the composition, either in measures or in minutes.

4. Determine the context of the task: single instrument (includes voice), unaccompanied; multiple instruments, unaccompanied; multiple instruments, accompanied.

5. Determine the amount of time (the number of lessons) to be devoted to the task.

6. Decide how or if the composition will be notated.

7. Develop the rubric for the task and prepare it for distribution to the students.

Figure 4-2.

Second, the *task's assessable components must be determined and articulated.* This is the point at which the teacher decides what is most important to examine in the finished composition; this can be as many or as few components as deemed necessary. For example, if a group of third graders has been learning about the single division of the beat (eighth notes) and how to notate this type of beat division, the teacher may choose to include in the composition task a specific requirement that the finished composition present eighth notes.

Third, when dealing with a composition task, *students will need to know how long the composition should be.* While a *minimum* length should be assigned, it is best not to assign a maximum. However, if time is a factor, a length restriction is appropriate for assessment purposes, either in minutes (for example, compositions must not exceed two minutes in length) or in measures. It is appropriate and reasonable to assign a number of measures for students who are familiar with this terminology, because limiting the number of measures (usually to four through eight) automatically limits the time involved in listening to and assessing the finished products. For students unfamiliar with the concept of measures, a time restriction in minutes may be more appropriate.

Fourth, the *context of the task must be determined.* Because composing involves instruments or voices, the primary contextual conditions have to do with the number of instruments/voices involved and their function within the composition. There are many contexts for composition in the general music classroom, but for assessment purposes, three are recommended: (1) *solo instrument* (includes the voice); (2) *multiple instruments, unaccompanied;* (3) *multiple instruments, accompanied* (includes a solo instrument or voice with accompaniment). For most composing tasks, the context will be an unaccompanied single instrument. In some instances, a teacher may assign a task to a group of children who create their composition for more than one instrument to be performed in unison and unaccompanied. A more complex context involves the composition of a melody and an accompaniment, also requiring the use of multiple instruments.

Fifth, *the number of lessons to be devoted to the composition task should be determined.* As stated in chapter 2, integrated projects such as this require several weeks for adequate completion. Composition takes time, and the task will require two or more lessons. It is helpful to remain somewhat flexible if the children need more time to create and experiment.

The Notation Question

Next, a decision should be made as to *whether or not the child's composition will be notated*. This may or may not be a desired goal in the assessment task. If the curriculum states that a certain grade level must obtain certain standard notation skills, a teacher may decide to include standard notation as part of the assessment task. The decision to include standard notation of the composition will affect each aspect of the task and how it is designed (see *Guided Composition* later in this chapter). However, if the teacher chooses not to include notation, the composition will only exist in performance, and therefore it is suggested that an alternative means of preserving the composition be prepared (such as a video- or audio-cassette recorder).

An alternative to standard notation of compositions is *invented* notation. In a composition task, the teacher may decide to have the children write their compositions down in a way that makes sense to them. Several researchers have used this approach to study the development of children's musical cognition (see Bamberger, 1991; Davidson & Scripp, 1988; and Upitis, 1992 for some examples). For example, Davidson and Scripp told their participants to "write the song down on paper so that someone else who doesn't know the song can sing it back." This practice relieves the child of having to deal with the precision of musical notation, especially if this is not a desired goal of the task. The disadvantage is that for every child there may be a different notation scheme for the teacher to later interpret.

A primary advantage of including notation by hand in the task is that the task then addresses National Content Standard number 5, which is concerned with notating music, as well as the Literacy learning area. This adds the assessable component of *correct standard notation*, which includes notehead placement; stem directions; note beaming; the placement of rests, measure bars and clefs; meter and key signature placements; and dynamic markings. When a composition with an accompaniment is notated, the teacher may also assess the child composer's ability to align notes within a grand staff. If notation software is available, it is advisable for the children to use this only after their hand-notated scores have been completed. For assessment purposes, it is recommended that students experience hand writing music notation before being assisted by technology.

Scoring Guides and Data Collection for Compositions

Finally, *the rubric for the task must be developed and prepared for distribution to the students.* The design of an appropriate scoring guide for a composition is directly related to the assessable components targeted in the composition task. If a composition is assessed only through performance, then the targeted components can be assessed most efficiently with a bi-level scoring guide. Because most composition tasks target multiple components, a bi-level, multiple-criterion guide is most effective, with each criterion corresponding to one of the targeted components. However, it is recommended that teachers assessing compositions by listening only to performances limit themselves to three components per performance. Listening for and assessing more than three components is difficult, and reliability suffers.

For example, if a teacher were to assign a task that requires a child to compose a piece that employs quarter notes, eighth notes, and quarter rests, then the bi-level, multiple-criterion scoring guide would look like this:

Key: "+" = yes; "–" = no

1. The composition uses eighth notes.

2. The composition uses quarter notes.

3. The composition uses quarter rests.

Once the child has performed the composition, the assessment results would then be recorded on the data collection form by encoding the symbols that correspond to the presence of these components in the finished composition, yielding a result such as "+/+/–."

In some cases, it may be necessary or advantageous for a teacher to employ a multi-level, multiple-criterion scoring guide when examining several components of a *notated composition*. Multi-level scoring of a composition can be most successfully completed only if the teacher has access to the child's written music along with the performance. For example, let's say that a teacher decides to create a composition task for the recorder that will assess her fourth grade students' knowledge of single beat divisions (eighth notes), quarter notes, and quarter rests, phrases, notation of the G-pentatonic scale, sense of closure, and recorder playing skills for low D and low E. The task was designed like this:

[The teacher says:] *Your task is to compose a piece for the soprano recorder in the G-pentatonic scale. When your composition is finished, you are to write it down in standard notation on the music paper I will give you. I will assess your composition on the following characteristics: it must be at least four measures in length in 4/4 meter; must contain (but is not limited to) eighth notes, quarter notes, and quarter rests; must use all five pitches of the G-pentatonic scale, B, A, G, low E, and low D; contain at least two musical phrases; and present a sense of closure on pitch G. When you perform your piece, I will also assess your ability to play low E and low D on the recorder. Here is the rubric I will be using to assess your work.*

This task is an integrated project, designed to assess composition as well as performance skills. The composition context is a single, unaccompanied instrument, the soprano recorder. The task contains six assessable components: length (four measures), beat divisions (eighth notes, quarter notes, quarter rests), scale (five notes of G-pentatonic), phrase usage, sense of closure, and recorder playing skills. If the notation is also assessed, then a seventh component is added to the rubric.

The multi-level, multiple-criterion rubric shown in Figure 4-3 is recommended for assessment of this finished piece. The criterion-by-criterion design is recommended for composition rubrics because all of the criteria may not require assessment on three or more levels of achievement. Furthermore, the child composer will find it easier to understand this type of rubric when given the rubric at the start of the task. In this example, there are two bi-level criteria, length and playing skills; one three-level criterion, beat divisions; sense of closure, phrase usage, scale, and notation are four-level criteria. Other sample composition assessment rubrics can be found in Hickey (1999). Hickey's sample rubrics are designed for high school composers, and they are fine examples of multi-level, multiple-criterion scoring guides for this purpose. For the performance of the compositions (in this example, checking the fingering skill for low E and low D), the guidelines for performance assessment set forth in chapter 3 should be followed.

Guided Composition

One general approach to developing children's compositions for assessment is *guided composition* (Brophy, 1996). Guided composition is the act of composing music with as many parameters prescribed as the young composer needs in order to guide the composer toward successful notation of his/her composition.

Multi-Level, Multiple-Criterion Rubric for the Sample Composition Task, Criterion-by-Criterion Design

Assessable Component	Level: 4	3	2	1
Length	*	*	4 or more measures	less than 4 measures
Beat divisions (*eighth notes, quarter notes/ rests*)	*	used, in a pattern	used, not in a pattern	not used
Scale	all 5 tones employed	4 tones employed, including low E and low D	4 or less tones employed, but only one required tone, low E or low D, in the melody	3 or less tones employed, no low D or low E in the melody
Phrase usage	phrases are antecedent/ consequent	phrases are used, but are not related to one another	phrases are incomplete	no evidence of phrase structures
Sense of closure	closes on G, with a rhythmic final point	closes on G, no rhythmic final point	does not close on G, has a rhythmic final point	does not close on G, no rhythmic final point
Notation (*if assessed*)	piece is perfectly notated	notation contains a few minor errors	notation is flawed and contains more errors than correctly notated symbols	no evidence of any correct notation
Recorder playing skills				
low E	*	*	correctly played	incorrectly played
low D	*	*	correctly played	incorrectly played

Figure 4-3.

In guided composition, a *parameter* is defined as a *rhythmic, structural,* or *theoretical* component that is prescribed in the task as a control that helps ensure a successful notation experience. Within the guided composition approach there are three primary models: the *pathway model,* the *given rhythm model,* and the *composed rhythm model.* These guided composition models provide an authentic assessment in that the learning and assessment contexts are the same. Guided composition involves children in the act of being a composer, faced with developmentally appropriate challenges that allow them to think like a composer; as they learn about composition and notation, their musical productions also serve as assessments.

When designing a guided composition task, the teacher may decide to control any of the assessable components presented:

1. For student composers, the *rhythmic* components are most often controlled as follows: (a) the actual rhythm can be given, (b) the beat divisions/rests to be included may be specified, and (c) the meter signature may be predetermined.

2. *Structural* components that are most often controlled include (a) the length of the composition (and the number of repetitions), (b) the phrase structures (when the rhythm is prescribed), and (c) the form of the piece.

3. *Theoretical* components that can be predetermined are (a) the scale or pitches employed (which in turn controls the melodic component of range), (b) the clef used for notation of the melody, (c) the accompaniment pattern used, or (d) a harmony change.

4. The *melody* of the composition is never prescribed, with the exception of the range, which can be controlled by the use of a particular scale or pitch-set. The melody should remain the sole creation of the young composer. However, if the teacher deems it acceptable or necessary, the final tone of the composition may be specified in order to ensure that each composer ends his or her piece on the tonic pitch. For novice composers, internal phrase endings may also have specified ending pitches if so desired.

While these controls help to guide the notation experience, they still permit children to be as creative as possible within these parameters in the composition of their melodies.

The first step in the guided composition process is to *plan and determine exactly what parameters need to be set to ensure a successful composing and notation experience.* If the students are beginners, then it is advised that every aspect of the composition be prescribed except the melody. Here is what you should do to design a guided composition task:

> **1.** *Contextual considerations: instrumentation and accompaniment.* First, decide which instrument(s) the composer will use. Good choices include any classroom melody instrument with which the children have attained enough skill to play comfortably, such as barred percussion instruments (e.g., Orff-type instruments), recorder, or keyboard. Older students may have expertise on instruments from private lessons (often string or band instruments) that are not classroom instruments, and these can be brought into the classroom to complete the task if the teacher permits. However, the music specialist must be aware of and ready to assist students whose instruments are notated with different pitches than those that sound (clarinet, French horn, etc.), and in clefs other than treble and bass. It is also important for the teacher to decide ahead of time whether or not the composition will be accompanied.

> **2.** *Rhythmic considerations: rhythm and meter.* Next, the teacher must determine a rhythm and meter signature commensurate with the students' level of skill and understanding. More advanced students can be given a choice of meter signatures (such as 2/4, 3/4, 4/4, 6/8), and beginning around fourth grade, students should be able to create original rhythms from prescribed note values. For example, the teacher may give older children instructions to create a

rhythm that uses half, quarter, and eighth notes and rests (see the sample composition task for another example). Younger students and novice composers, however, will benefit from having a prescribed rhythm and meter signature that the teacher feels is at the students' level of expertise. For example, second graders may compose to a rhythm in 4/4 meter that is all quarter notes and rests, such as:

Whereas third graders might compose using a more age-appropriate rhythm:

3. *Theoretical considerations: scale, harmony, and notation.* It is important that the theoretical aspects of the composition task, most often having to do with choice of scale and whether or not a harmony change is to be part of the task, be predetermined. For younger student composers, teachers should generally prescribe the scale or group of notes that are to be used in the composition. However, some younger students who have training outside of the school music program will possess a higher level of understanding about music theory and therefore be knowledgeable enough to choose their own scale. Teachers of older students may choose to assign a scale or allow the student to do this, in a manner commensurate with the students' training and experience. The choice of scale or pitch-set is based on several factors, such as instrumental skill, notation considerations, and student familiarity with the scale. For example, a teacher may design a recorder composition task for a class that can only play B (b_5), A (a_5), and G (g_4), and limit the composition to using those pitches. The pentatonic scale is good for beginners who are using Orff-type barred percussion instruments; for example, the teacher may choose to have second graders complete their first composition task in F-pentatonic because the entire scale (f_4-d_5) is notated within the five lines and four spaces of the treble clef without the need for ledger lines (the tonic F is written on the first space of the staff; the d_5 is written on the fourth line). However, the next year in third grade the students may be ready to notate ledger lines, and the teacher may choose to design the composition task using the C-pentatonic scale (c_4-a_4), in which the tonic pitch c_4 is written on a ledger line below the staff. In fourth grade, the task may involve the G-pentatonic scale because the students know those pitches on the recorder (see the earlier sample composition task for an example). By fifth grade, children who begin this process in the second grade are ready to compose using two staves, perhaps with a prescribed accompaniment, in a pentatonic scale. If the sixth grade curriculum includes the study of scales and tonic-dominant harmony, then the composition task could include composing a melody (perhaps with a given accompaniment as an additional control) that presents a tonic-dominant harmony change in a major scale, using two or more staves.

The teacher must then decide what clef the children will use for their notation. For most child composers, this will be the treble clef. When the children are presented a task in which an accompaniment must also be notated, then (and, again, this depends on the curriculum) it may be appropriate to introduce bass clef notation. For older, more experienced composers, multiple staves (more than two) may be appropriate for multiple melodies and accompaniment. The addition of one or more unpitched percussion instruments requires the addition of a single line for each instrument between the melody and accompaniment staves.

4. *Structural considerations: form, length, repeats, and phrases.* It is important to determine the number of measures or the length of time for the composition and whether or not there will be any repeats. This controls the length of the piece and keeps the task manageable for the children; it also controls the amount of time spent on assessment. Adding a repeat to a prescribed rhythm accomplishes two goals for the teacher: it gives the student the opportunity to notate the repeat sign within an original piece and it doubles the length of the finished piece without doubling the amount of work required for the student to complete the task and for the teacher to assess it. With respect to the presence of phrases within a piece, this can be predetermined if the rhythm is given, or the assignment may contain a requirement for music to be composed in phrases. If the task target is the demonstration of musical contrast, then form can be ascribed as a parameter; ABA is the simplest for assessment purposes, with B presenting different, contrasting material from A.

5. *Aesthetic qualities.* For most composition tasks, aesthetic qualities are mentioned and encouraged, but the assignment of these qualities as a task target is not recommended. For most student composers, the composition experience is self-directed toward the production of a piece that is aesthetically acceptable to the student and his or her audience. Judgment of aesthetic qualities is possible with more experienced composers (again I refer the reader to Hickey, 1999) but not recommended for younger composers.

6. *The rubric.* Finally, once the task has been designed, it is essential to develop the rubric for scoring the task and then give the rubric to the composers at the start of the task. This essential aspect of any assessment procedure should never be overlooked. The wording of the rubric should be clear and in terms the students will easily understand. For some tasks, a teacher may decide to help the class devise its own rubric for the finished compositions; this can be quite effective and will be discussed in the next chapter.

Figure 4-4 presents one possible sequence for guided composition from grades two through six. Tasks for kindergarten and grade one students are generally sequencing tasks (discussed later); composition for grades seven through twelve becomes increasingly more self-directed and less guided. This is presented as a model for development rather than a prescription.

Once the task has been designed, the next step is to *implement the task*. First, it is recommended that a guided composition be completed with the entire class first, as a class project. This process provides the students an opportunity to all experience the

Suggested Sequence for Guided Composition Tasks

Key
If deemed important by the teacher or the curriculum and included in the task:

Yes	=	this component should be prescribed in the task
No	=	this component should be created by the student as part of the task
Can be	=	the teacher may choose to prescribe this or leave this up to the composer
N/A	=	this component is not age-appropriate

Component	Grade 2	Grade 3	Grade 4	Grade 5	Grade 6
Contextual					
instrumentation	yes	yes	yes	can be	can be
accompaniment	N/A	N/A	N/A	can be	can be
Rhythmic					
prescribed rhythm	can be	can be	no	no	no
beat divisions/ note values	yes	yes	yes	yes	yes
meter	yes	yes	yes	can be	can be
Structural					
form	can be	can be	can be	can be	can be
length	yes	yes	yes	yes	yes
repeats	can be	can be	can be	can be	can be
phrases	yes	yes	yes	can be	can be
Theoretical					
scale or pitch-set	yes	yes	yes	yes	yes
harmonic changes	N/A	N/A	N/A	yes	yes

Figure 4-4.

same task at once and to achieve the goals of the composition experience as a group before attempting a task individually. For children, this class composing experience is highly beneficial and helps to build the confidence and skill necessary to complete an assessment task. Following are the steps for leading a guided composition experience, either as a class project or as an individual assessment:

1. *Verbally describe the task to the children and present the rubric.* It is important that this aspect of the task be carefully completed. The teacher should answer all questions and use terminology that is musically correct and with which the children are familiar. One of the goals of this experience is to achieve success in composition and notation, and this success will be facilitated if adequate time is taken at the start of the task to explain it thoroughly, to go over what is expected, and to show how it will be measured. During the introduction of the task, the teacher should also present the instrument(s) to be used in the task.

2. *Teach the predetermined rhythm or present the required note values.* If a predetermined rhythm has been built into the task, then it is time to teach the children this rhythm in whatever manner the teacher prefers. If the teacher is requiring that the composition contain particular note values, then these should be introduced at this time.

3. *Present the scale or pitch-set to be used in the composition.* Next, the teacher should introduce and review the scale or pitch-set. To help establish the tonal context of the piece for the children, it is recommended that the children perform the scale or pitch-set on the instruments they are using for the task. For example, if the task is to compose a piece for recorders in G-pentatonic, then the pitches of G-pentatonic need to be reviewed and played prior to beginning the task. In instances where the scale is pentatonic and the rhythm is prescribed, then the class can improvise together to the assigned rhythm. Students preparing to perform in a major scale should perform the scale together or perhaps review pieces already studied in that major scale.

4. *Add additional controls if they are part of the task.* Once the rhythm and the scale are presented, it is then time to add other controls such as phrase ending pitches, closing tones, rhythmic final points, etc. Once the controls are added, the teacher must be sure to review all aspects of the task again to ensure that the students understand these additions.

5. *Composing and creating the "rough draft."* At this time the teacher should present the students with a blank sheet of paper; the teacher may choose to provide pencils or have the children bring them to class.

a) The children must clearly write their names as well as the date on this sheet, as this will become a portfolio entry.

b) If the rhythm has been prescribed and is written on the board, the children should write this rhythm on their blank sheets as neatly as possible. If available, individual chalkboards (available from most school supply stores) provide an excellent medium for rhythm writing practice before placing it on the blank paper. If the task requires that the composers use an original rhythm created from specified note values, the rhythm can be composed first using the blank sheet or chalk-board as a sketchpad.

c) Once this is done, the students should be given time to compose their melodies—to experiment and impro-vise with the given or composed rhythm on their instrument—until they have created a melody with which they are satisfied. The teacher must be prepared to expect a great deal of sound in the classroom during this process, and children may want to move to different areas of the classroom in order to better hear themselves. During this process, students who have composed their own rhythm may want to revise the rhythm to suit their melodic ideas, or vice versa; this is a natural part of the composition process.

d) Once the pitches of the composition have been determined, the students should then place the letter name of the pitch underneath its corresponding rhythmic note value on the blank sheet or chalkboard. This copy becomes the "rough draft" of the composition.

e) At this time the children may also choose to name the composition.

6. *Notating the "final copy."* Once the piece is completed in draft form, the teacher should then hand out staff paper for the notation of the "final" copy of the work.

a) The students should practice the notation before placing it on staff paper. To practice the notation, individual chalkboards or dry-erase boards with staff lines (also available from most school supply stores) are recommended. Otherwise, additional staff paper for practice may be necessary.

b) The teacher may also choose to write a "helping staff" on the board to assist children in finding the staff locations of the pitches in their compositions. The helping staff presents the notes of the scale or pitch-set written on the staff in their proper locations and with their letter names underneath.

c) The students should then complete the final copy of their piece by notating the draft copy on the staff using the predetermined clef(s). The teacher should be prepared to help students who have difficulty making the connection between the letter name of a note and its placement on the staff.

d) The teacher should also make sure the copy is clearly marked with the child's name and the date, for portfolio purposes.

e) Once the draft and final copies are completed, they are ready for display in the hall as well as for the portfolio (see chapter 6).

7. *Perform the piece with accuracy and musicianship.* Each composer should then be allowed to perform his or her piece for the class. This may or may not be an assessed performance; that decision is up to the teacher. To extend the performance activity, students can be sent to other class-rooms and to the principal's office in small groups to perform their pieces. Children who do this will need to take an instrument on which to perform (a small glockenspiel or recorder is best) and their notated copies with them to show their work.

Kindergarten, First Grade: Sequencing and Organizing Tasks Using the Pathway Model

With young children, a guided composition task generally does not lead toward the notation of the melody or rhythm created. It is recommended that students in these grade levels be given time for composition *experience* only; notation should wait until second grade or higher. However, pre-notation in the form of icons can be effectively used, and the composition experience can be guided to help students organize compositions effectively. It is important that the teacher lead the children through one or more group compositions before expecting students to undertake the task individually.

The Pathway Model

In this composition model, children are provided a way to assign instruments or melodic patterns to an icon, and are directed to temporally and visually organize their musical choices using a predetermined pathway. The pathway can take many different forms, limited only by the teacher's imagination and the needs of the curriculum. The following suggestions are not meant to be a complete list of possible pathway model examples, but they should provide the reader with several starting points for original ideas.

The "Tree" Task:

Materials:
- Green construction paper "pine trees" glued to white paper backgrounds (or simply copy a tree design onto white paper)
- 3-4 colored markers or "stick-on" colored dots (those backed with pressure-sensitive glue), one color per instrument used

In this task, children (either individually, in pairs, or in small groups) are presented with a set of three or four rhythm instruments and, if desired, a melodic percussion instrument (Miller, 1999). Using the instruments, the children create a short piece that uses each instrument correctly only once. (You may choose to let them use the instruments more than once, but this can get confusing.) To "write down" their pieces, the children assign a color to the instrument; they then decorate the tree with the stick-on colored dots or draw dots using the colored markers as if they were colored balls used to decorate a Christmas tree. The composer then "connects" the dots in the correct order by drawing a "garland" (line) on the tree that stretches between the dots. At the bottom of the picture, the child's "key" is written as a series of small dots of the appropriate color in a row that represents the order of performance. If desired, the composer can also draw a "miniature" picture (or write the first letter of the name) of the instrument to be played when that dot is indicated. Performance of the piece requires the child to point to the dots on his/her tree while other players perform.

For those who find themselves in situations where the Christmas tree idea is inappropriate, apple trees are a good substitute; instead of different-colored Christmas ball decorations, different-colored apples (red, yellow, green) can be used to represent the different instruments or sounds of the child's composition. The child can then connect the apples in the correct order for performance by drawing a line that indicates the order in which the instruments or sounds are to be performed.

The "Ladder" Task:

Materials:

- White sheets of paper with a ladder drawn on each
- Different types of white shoe cutouts (to be colored by the children)

Another composition task for young children is the "ladder." One of the strengths of this task is that it more directly implies a definite beginning and ending to the composition. In this model, each child receives a sheet of paper with a ladder, preferably six to eight rungs tall, printed on it. The children use three or four instruments for their composition, preferably pre-selected by the teacher. To "notate" the order of their instruments or melodic patterns, the children use different types of shoe cutouts (preferably cut out ahead of time), which they have colored themselves. As the children compose, they place the shoes on the ladder climbing up, indicating "duration" by the number of rungs skipped between the different shoes (i.e., the more rungs skipped, the longer the duration). Once the shoes have been arranged on the ladder in the order that the composer wishes, the teacher can tack them down with a dab of glue.

The "Shapes and Colors" Task:

Materials:

- Blank sheets of paper
- Paper cutouts in different shapes and colors

A more straightforward task makes use of shapes and colors to represent different instruments or melodic patterns. In this model, the child assigns an instrument a familiar shape (square, triangle, circle, etc.) and color. The shapes are then drawn or glued to a clean piece of paper in the order the child wishes to have the instruments performed.

Storage:

Many times a composition task may take longer than the time allotted for a single music class. Because young composers may have multiple parts of their work (such as unattached dots, shoes, or shapes) left over at the end of class, it is recommended that the teacher have a gallon-sized Ziploc (or similar) sealable bag ready for each child, with the child's name on it. Everything that the child has left over can be safely put in the bag, sealed, and saved for the next class. Young children can be trained to manage their personal items in this manner.

Suggested Rubric for the Kindergarten/First Grade Tasks:

At this age, the purpose of the task is to give children experience in organizing and sequencing created music and keeping track of that organization through manipulation of icons. One suggested bi-level, multiple-criterion scoring guide for assessing these types of tasks follows:

The child:
1. Assigns a specific icon or color to a specific instrument/melodic pattern consistently.
2. Completes a "key" that indicates understanding of the instrument order.
3. Successfully completes the task on paper.
4. Successfully directs or performs the piece for the class.

Record Keeping:

+ = criterion met
− = criterion not met

The Given Rhythm Model

Figure 4-5 presents a sample guided composition lesson for beginning students. This task is an example of the *given rhythm model,* which should be used when the teacher feels that the students' notation success will be greater if they do not generate their own rhythm. In this model, the teacher predetermines the rhythm that students will use in their compositions, then teaches the rhythm to the class before the composition experience begins. The scoring guide for this task is in Figure 4-6; it is to be given to the students at the start of the task. This model is quite effective with students in second or third grade.

The Composed Rhythm Model

When children are comfortable with musical notation and generating original rhythms that they can write themselves, they are ready for the composed rhythm model. In this model, the composers are instructed to create their own rhythm using various note values that are prescribed or recommended. This model marks a step toward musical independence for the composers because they are now responsible for generating both an original rhythm and an original melody.

In the previous section of this chapter, a recorder task for fourth grade was presented that is an example of a guided composition task within the composed rhythm model. In this task the composers are instructed to use eighth notes, quarter notes, and quarter rests. They are to remain in the G-pentatonic scale, use all five pitches of that scale, and close on the home tone G. The scoring guide for this task is in Figure 4-3. It is to be given to the students at the start of the task; it is clear and easy to follow.

Figure 2-5 (chapter 2) presents a guided composition task as an integrated project for sixth grade that is constructed within the composed rhythm model. However, the composers are instructed that there are minimum requirements for their use of rhythmic values; they are to include at least ♩, ♪, and ♪ rhythms in their compositions. Other parameters, such as meter signature and scale, are also less prescribed than earlier grades. The scoring guide for the task presents eight criteria for scoring, and it is also to be given to the composers at the start of the task.

Guided composition is an excellent technique for building confidence in your students' creative and notational skills. Although you must start with numerous parameters prescribed for beginning composers, over time students gain more musical knowledge, become more skilled and quite comfortable with the process of composing, and can create completely original works of increasing sophistication (including the addition of accompaniments, harmony changes, and lyrics to create songs). The end result is a positive, hands-on authentic assessment experience that gives students the opportunity to become personally involved with music notation in a satisfying and successful manner.

Sample Guided Composition Lesson with Melodic Percussion: Given Rhythm

Remember, always start a guided composition task with the rubric and a verbal explanation of what will be expected. Here is a sample rhythm that has been successfully used with third graders for a guided composition experience with melodic percussion.

After the students practice the rhythm through speaking (using rhythmic language, such as "ta" for quarter notes and "ti" for eighth notes) and clapping, invite them to practice writing the rhythm down on individual blank chalkboards or blank paper. Once this is completed and everyone is comfortable with the notation, have the children set up the C-pentatonic scale on the melodic percussion instruments (Orff instruments, bells, etc.). Then have the students improvise melodies using this rhythm on their instruments, as a group. (You will get many different melodies, but the sound will be pleasing because of the pentatonic scale.) When this has been done several times, add this to the rhythm on the board.

Figure 4-5.

Conduct a group improvisation to the given rhythm again, coming to the G at the end of phrase one and the C at the end of phrase two. The children should then write the letters C and G underneath the correct rhythmic values on their chalkboards. At this time, instruct them to compose a melody that fits the rhythm and ends on the G in phrase 1 and the C in phrase 2, and to write down the letter names of their melodies underneath the correct rhythmic value on their chalkboard. They should be allowed to do this any way they like; that is, they may write down note names first and try the melody afterwards, or try a few melodies and write down the one they like best, or whatever method suits them best. They should be free to create a melody in the manner that suits them most comfortably.

Once the students are comfortable with this and have a piece with which they are happy, they should be informed that the piece on their chalkboard is a "draft" copy of their composition. Then, hand the children a sheet of blank paper and ask them to make a "permanent" copy of the draft in pencil, one that can be turned in and handed back in the next lesson.

The next step is the transcription of the "draft" copy onto the staff in order to make a final copy. This can be started with individual music slates (chalkboards with blank staves on them) or blank staff paper for practice. At this time, show the children how to make a treble clef and the 4/4 meter signature, and allow ample time to practice making these symbols. Next, draw a helping staff on the board, as follows:

C   D   E   G   A

With the helping staff serving as a reference, allow the students ample time to practice transcribing their drafts into standard notation using their music slates/practice staff paper. Once success in writing the piece on the slate/practice paper is achieved, hand the students a piece of blank staff paper and allow them to make their best permanent copy to be turned in for their music portfolios. (It is recommended that teachers create their own staff paper for guided compositions; this can be done in any word processing software using the smallest font size and the underline button.)

Figure 4-5. (continued)

Multi-Level, Multiple-Criterion Rubric for the Sample Melodic Percussion Composition Task Using the Given Rhythm Model, Criterion-by-Criterion Design

Assessable Component	Level: 4	3	2	1
Scale	all 5 tones employed	4 tones employed	3 tones employed	2 or less tones employed
Notation	piece is perfectly notated	notation contains a few minor errors	notation is flawed and contains more errors than correctly notated symbols	no evidence of any correct notation
Performance Mallet skills	*	alternates consistently	alternates inconsistently	does not alternate
Accuracy of piece	*	completely accurate	mostly accurate	completely inaccurate

Figure 4-6.

Assessing Children's Improvisation

Composing music and improvising music are related in that both involve children in the creative process; however, they are fundamentally different in a very important way. The child composer creates music with the intent of revising and reworking his or her piece until it meets his or her needs or satisfaction. The child improviser, on the other hand, creates music with no intention or expectation to revise: what is initially created is the final product. Improvisation is a spontaneous act and improvised music exists *only for the time during which it is being performed,* unless the performance is preserved via recording. For the general

190

music specialist, this fundamental difference between composition and improvisation means that the assessment of improvisation must be treated primarily as a performance event.

To better understand improvisation and improvisatory behavior in children, the following is a brief overview of some of the theory and research related to improvisation. Following this, recommended procedures for assessing student improvisations will be introduced.

The Nature of Children's Improvisations: A Glimpse at the Research

The research and theory building with respect to improvisation has centered around both *process* and *product*. The products of children's improvisations have been examined (Brophy, 1998/1999; Flohr, 1979/1980, 1984; Reinhardt, 1990) as well as the process of improvising (Moorhead & Pond, 1941/1978; Prével, 1979). In an early study of preschool children, Moorhead and Pond (1941/1978) observed that young children were primarily interested in the tone color of the instrument on which they were improvising. In reference to playing (and improvising with) barred percussion instruments, they observed that young children might not possess the "muscular coordination which would enable them to play with precision and at the same time maintain an uninhibited rhythmic flow to their music" (pp. 44-45).

In two studies involving children ages two through eight, John Flohr (1979/1980, 1984) concluded that there were differences in young children's improvisations that were related to chronological age. He identified three stages of improvisational development: (1) *motor energy*, characterized by plodding and accented durations, (2) *experimentation*, and (3) *formal properties*, characterized by the use of repetition and larger formal structures. Similar results were obtained by Reinhardt (1990), who examined rhythmic elements of the alto-xylophone melodic improvisations of 105 preschoolers ages three, four, and five for (1) use of steady beat, (2) meter, (3) durations used, and (4) use of rhythm patterns. All but one of the subjects maintained a steady beat and meter. Use of different durations and rhythm patterns increased at each age level.

Martin Prével (1979) examined over 2,000 children's improvisations that were created in a free and unstructured environment. He observed that "children's very first improvisations reflect their motor energy" (p. 14), and that "what counts for the child is identification with the overall effect of his own production" (p. 14). Once children gain the ability to restrain their own movements, "they begin to alternate different colours of sound, vary the intensity of volume, and make accents, conclusions, and even introductions" (p. 15). Overall, Prével noted that children's musical productions are the products of motor energy at several stages, unrelated to age. He reasoned that the development of children's musical productions owes more to their kinesthetic development than their auditory perception.

John Kratus views improvisation as "a variety of different behaviors that develop sequentially" (1996, p. 30). He has theorized a seven-level sequential model that is independent of age. The first level is *exploration,* when the improviser appears to be making seemingly random sounds without regard to creating a product for an audience to hear. The next level, *process-oriented improvisation,* occurs when some structural characteristics begin to appear, such as repeated patterns. However, at the process-oriented stage, the improviser is still viewing the act of improvisation as "doing" rather than "making." The third level is *product-oriented improvisation,* during which the improviser begins to view the act of improvisation as the creation of a musical product that must be shaped to conform with acceptable sounds in the improviser's society. The next level, *fluid improvisation,* occurs when the improviser gains enough technical control of the improvising instrument to render playing the instrument automatic, allowing the improviser's emerging musical ideas to be more easily transformed into sound. *Structural improvisation,* the fifth level in this continuum, begins when the improviser is able to apply structural techniques, such as development and variation, to the improvisation. The sixth level is *stylistic improvisation,* wherein the improviser has mastered one or more improvisational styles. The seventh level, rarely reached, is *personal improvisation.* At this level, the improviser transcends current styles and creates a new, original improvisational style.

Children's improvisations have been generally described in one of two ways: *process-oriented* or *product-oriented.* Process-oriented improvisers focus primarily on the act of musical creation, whereas product-oriented improvisers focus upon the musical creation itself with the intention of creating a pleasing result. Kratus (1991b) believes that this orientation is a result of fundamental (and possibly age-related) differences in a child's musical perspective.

Brophy (1998/1999) examined 840 melodic improvisations of 280 children ages six through twelve for age-related differences in their musical characteristics. Participants improvised three eight-measure melodies on an Orff alto xylophone within the specific context of the C-pentatonic scale, as the B, C, and D sections of a seven-part rondo for the Orff instrumentarium. The participant's class performed the A-section of the rondo, improvising in the C-pentatonic scale to a given rhythm on a variety of Orff instruments. The rondo, both the class portion and the solos, was accompanied by a simple, broken bordun (c_3-g_3) on the bass xylophone.

Developmental trends were indicated for the rhythmic and structural characteristics of the improvisations but not the melodic characteristics. Mallet facility and age were also shown to be significant predictors of the characteristics of the improvisations. The combined characteristics of the improvisations were shown to change significantly with age regardless of mallet facility, with a fundamental change occurring between ages eight and nine. At age nine, the improvisations moved toward increased motivic repetition and development, greater attention to the pulse, increased generation of rhythmic patterns, and greater structural organization. This change was followed by a period of stasis from ages nine through eleven. Development appeared to resume at age twelve.

This review informs teachers with respect to the challenges involved in researching (and assessing) children's improvisations. Because improvisation is spontaneous, preserving children's improvised music for later study has been a major challenge. Researchers have also employed a variety of contexts in which to gather their data, from free improvisation based on word imagery to highly structured musical forms such as rondo. There is also evidence that children's improvised melodies become significantly more highly structured and musically organized at age nine. These findings all have implications for the assessment of children's improvisations.

Improvisation for Assessment

For the general music specialist, the assessment of improvisation is complicated by a number of factors. First, the time for assessing this skill is at a premium, especially when a teacher serves six to eight (or more) classes a day, for thirty to sixty minutes per week. Second, when each class has twenty to twenty-five (or more) students, individual versus group assessment of improvisation becomes an issue. Third, determining if the improvisation will be preserved for later assessment through technology or assessed during the improvised performance plays an important part in the choice of assessable components and the approach the teacher takes to scoring the improvisation. Finally, the musical context of an improvisation for assessment is of great importance because the context, to a large extent, shapes the improvised musical product.

The teacher, therefore, must address these factors prior to designing an improvisation assessment task. Given the time allotted for teaching, the number of students served, and the demands of the curriculum, the teacher must decide how often improvisation should be assessed and the extent to which it is examined. Because improvisation is a performance behavior, there are two possible foci for assessment: *process* and *product*.

The steps for designing improvisation tasks are the same as those for designing composition tasks, with a few important exceptions:

- Notation is *never* a component of an improvisation task.

- Musical context assumes a greater importance in task design since the context of the improvisation shapes the response to the task.

- The process or product focus of the task is also of primary importance in both task design and the judgment of the responses.

Again, it must be emphasized here that the following suggestions are for the development of assessment tasks; these are not recommendations for teaching improvisation. (For recommendations on teaching improvisation music in general music, I refer the reader to Brophy, in press, *Music Educators Journal*.) Teachers can develop instruction in improvisation by following these guidelines if they choose, but lessons in improvisation do not need to be so strictly controlled.

1. *Determine the focus of the assessment as either process or product.* For the purposes of designing assessment tasks, improvisation process tasks are those that focus on the performance elements of the improvisation while it is in progress. When a teacher is examining improvisation process, the process can serve as a vehicle for the assessment of performance task targets (as discussed in chapter 3). The process can also serve as an indicator of whether or not the student can improvise within the established context. For children under the age of nine years, a simple bi-level determination of ability to improvise—whether a child can or cannot spontaneously generate music within a given context—may be all that is necessary or desired. This depends on the expectations of the teacher and the curriculum.

Product-focused assessment tasks target a specific component of the improvised melody, rhythm, or movement. Assessing the melodic, rhythmic, and structural characteristics of improvised rhythms and melodies parallels the assessment of those characteristics in compositions. However, the assessment of components such as range, melody type, the presence of melodic and rhythmic motives, motivic development, and type of phrase requires the post-performance examination of a recorded or notated improvisation. Videotaping facilitates the assessment of improvised movement, but if the task is well structured and designed, movement can be adequately assessed during performance.

2. *Determine the assessable components.* Because improvisation is a performance event, it is recommended that no more than three criteria be assessed at one time and that each criterion be assessed at only two levels of achievement (bi-level). More complex assessment is possible only when reviewing a technologically preserved improvisation performance.

For example, a teacher may choose to examine originality of rhythm and closing tone during a child's improvisation on a melodic instrument, if these were components to be assessed in the task. Two criteria are easily judged during real-time performance; additional criteria make such judgment difficult and unreliable.

3. *Clearly define the medium and musical context of the improvisation task.* The teacher must first decide if the improvisation medium will be instrumental, vocal, or movement, and if instrumental or vocal, whether or not the task will generate a rhythmic or melodic improvisation. The context of the task can then be one of the following: (a) a *response to word cues,* (b) a *response to musical cues,* or (c) a *free improvisation* within a given musical form.

When a task targets musical *responses to word cues,* the child is expected to create a rhythm or melody as a reaction to reading or hearing a specific word. This approach was used by John Flohr (1979/1980), who engaged his participants in a game of "pretend," and the children were asked to play as if they were "glad," "mad," "scared," or "sad." In what Flohr called "programmatic improvisation" (p. 10), children were asked to improvise sounds like "rain," a "lion," "lightning," a "train," and a "cat." When administering this type of assessment task, the teacher must be prepared for a number of different responses and should not expect to hear one "right" or "wrong" response. It is recommended that a bi-level, single-criterion scoring guide be used to assess this type of improvisation; that is, the child should be assessed only as being able to improvise or not being able to improvise in this fashion. The appropriateness of the improvisation may be assessed using a multi-level, single-criterion guide if the teacher so chooses, but this is not recommended. If appropriateness is a problem that the teacher feels must be addressed, then it is best for the teacher to simply question children at an age-appropriate level about their choice of response. Care must also be taken that the word images used are ones that the children can recognize and for which they possess a mental image. For example, while all five-year-olds may have a conception of "lightning" and could probably improvise a sound that represents lightning to them, they may not all hold a conception of "lion" or "train." The teacher needs to know the students well enough (and have provided enough instructional experience) to create a meaningful list of words.

For assessment purposes, improvising in *response to musical cues* has to do with generating consequent musical phrases to antecedent phrases given by the teacher. Often called "question and answer," this can be achieved both rhythmically and melodically, and instrumentally or vocally. For the assessment of vocal-rhythmic improvisation, the recommended context is nonsense speech, during which the teacher simply speaks a short, rhythmic nonsense phrase to the child or class, then the child or class responds back with another nonsense phrase as an "answer."

During a typical task involving responses to musical cues, the teacher performs an antecedent phrase vocally or instrumentally, and the child (or class) responds vocally or instrumentally with a spontaneously generated consequent phrase. For example, young children respond well to singing a response to the teacher's sol-mi greeting, or to other sung instructions. Older children, on the other hand, respond well to instrumental or body percussion cues. For example, if the teacher claps a two-measure rhythm in 4/4 as a musical "question," the child's response should be two measures long and come to a final point. The teacher's antecedent phrase should not have its own final point; it should end on the final beat of the second measure, requiring the response to pick up the unfinished musical thought and bring it to its conclusion. The child's improvised response can then be assessed for the components predetermined for the task.

The assessment of *free improvisation* within a given musical form is best accomplished through a class rondo or other simple, sectional form. The rondo form, which alternates a recurring section ("A") with differing sections ("B,C,D," etc.) between each "A." The form of the rondo is ABACADAEA, etc., until the task is completed. For the assessment of solo improvisation in the general music classroom setting, the "A" section can be a melody or rhythm performed by the entire class, and the differing sections a solo improvisation on a rhythm or melody instrument for a specified number of measures. For balance of form, all sections should be the same number of measures as the "A" section of the rondo. Setting up this type of context requires the teaching of the "A" section to the class. The "A" section may be instrumental, rhythmic, or vocal[1]. A sample instrumental rondo improvisation assessment task is presented in Figure 4-7; a suggested scoring guide for this task is presented in Figure 4-8.

Other possible solo improvisation assessment contexts include the *twelve-bar blues* and the *variation game*. The twelve-bar blues is particularly well suited for vocal improvisation with older children who have studied and know this jazz form. To do this, first present the child with a set of lyrics with which to impro-vise, then play a twelve-bar blues accompaniment as the child performs. If the students are familiar with this style and it is important to the task, lyrics do not need to be given, and the child can improvise vocally on invented syllables (called "scat" singing.) Assessment of this performance is again best limited to bi-level scoring, unless the teacher or the curriculum requires more complex data.

The assessment of a child's ability to improvise musical varia-tions is best accomplished with a familiar piece, and songs can be used if the children are old enough to understand that the varia-tion to be improvised is melodic and not a new set of words. The context may be accompanied or unaccompanied. A good model for developing variation assessment tasks is the *variation game*. The steps are as follows. First, explain to the class that they are being assessed for their ability to create variations, then have them perform a familiar melody together. For example, if students have learned the folk song "Hot Cross Buns" well on the soprano

Sample Instrumental Rondo Improvisation Assessment Task for Melodic Percussion

First, explain to the class that they will be improvising and that their improvisations will be assessed, and present the rubric. You will observe proper mallet technique, a final point on the tonic, and a rhythm that is different from the "A" section. Then, ask the children to stand and echo-speak the words "Very nice, very nice, nice today," as follows:

After repeating this procedure, have the children speak words simultaneously as they clap the rhythm. Repeat this procedure. Then clap the rhythm only, with the class echoing once more, and repeat this procedure. Next, instruct the class to clap the rhythm four times in a row, and repeat this procedure. Then pat the rhythm in the lap four times, and stamp the rhythm four times in place.

Ask the students to sit down at their instruments and to look at the bars (note: this playing task assumes that each child has a barred percussion instrument and that the bars have been preset by the teacher to C-pentatonic). Have them read aloud the names of the bars in unison, c_4-d_4-e_4-g_4-a_4-c_5-d_5-e_5-g_5-a_5 (the C-pentatonic scale). Then instruct the class to pick up their mallets and to demonstrate the proper way to hold them. The students should then click the "very nice" rhythm four times using the mallet handles. After this, ask each member of the class to make up his or her "best" melody on the instrument to the "very nice" rhythm, using any of the bars on the instrument and alternating the mallets. Two synonym phrases for "alternating mallets" can be used for students who are unsure of the meaning of "alternating." These are (1) "changing the mallets for each note you play" and (2) "switching the mallets back and forth for each note you play." Students can then review or be taught the word "improvise," using the definition "making up your own music as you go along." After this, instruct them to play the rhythm four times once again, improvising their best melody.

Have written on the board the following rondo form: ABACADA. Explain the order of the rondo sections; also explain that the class will perform the "A" section all together and that the remaining sections will be improvised solos. Have the students then perform the complete rondo, with a volunteer performing the B, C, and D sections. Two students with good beat competency can be assigned to play a broken bordun, c_3-g_3 on quarter notes, as an accompaniment on bass instruments (if they are available). Otherwise, a simple steady beat on an unpitched percussion instrument is fine.

Figure 4-7.

At the start of the rondo, have three students ready to be assessed. Instruct the students being assessed to only play their assigned B, C, or D sections, and to remain quiet during the A section. Remind them to perform their best and most beautiful, creative melodies, to make up a rhythm different than the A section, and that the bass xylophone will accompany their solos. If you are recording the performances, inform the children of this. Otherwise, assess these as they are performed.

Figure 4-7. (continued)

Bi-Level, Multiple-Criterion Rubric for Sample Instrumental Rondo Improvisation Task

Assessable Component	Level	
	2 (or +)	1 (or –)
Mallet technique *(performance component)*	correct	incorrect
Rhythm different than the "A" section	yes	no
Rhythmic final point	yes	no
Ends on tonic	yes	no

Figure 4-8.

recorder on the notes B (b_5), A (a_5), and G (g_4), have them review and perform this as a class. They can then be instructed that they are about to play a game with "Hot Cross Buns," where each of them will individually play the song "in a new way, so that *you* know it is still 'Hot Cross Buns' but someone else might not recognize it, or only recognize part of it." This can be accompanied by the teacher or a student on a classroom instrument, or left unaccompanied. In most tasks, bi-level scoring is also best for this assessment; for the general music teacher, it is likely to be enough to know that a child can or cannot create a variation. The variation

game also offers opportunities to assess performance components, particularly with respect to instrumental or vocal skills and
the ability to improvise within the steady beat.

It is important to take this opportunity to address the assessment of children's improvised movements. It is common for
general music curricula to contain references to children's creative
movement in response to music, and most children are naturally
drawn into movement when hearing or performing music.
Movement is often an integral part of teaching general music, and
it can serve many purposes, from helping children to remember
words to a song and adding visual impact to music programs, to
reinforcing musical concepts and knowledge.

However, the music specialist is not always trained to be a
movement teacher, and of those who are trained in movement
techniques (such as teachers of Orff Schulwerk and Dalcroze
Eurhythmics), only a few are trained dancers. The question for the
teacher then becomes: "When do I assess movement? Is it even
necessary for me to assess improvised movement?" For most
teachers, the curriculum should provide the answers to these
questions. If there is a movement component to the music
curriculum, then the music specialist should plan to assess what is
expected. If movement is used only as a tool for learning and
reinforcing musical knowledge, then it would not be necessary to
assess movement unless the teacher chose to do so.

Children's improvised movements are best assessed as bi-
level, single-criterion performance events. That is, the child is
assessed as being either able to improvise movement or not able
to do so. Questions of appropriateness of movement should be
addressed by asking the child for reasons behind a particular
improvised movement; it is not recommended that assessment of
levels of appropriateness be attempted. However, if appropriateness
is an issue, then a bi-level approach to scoring is best, where the

child's improvised movement is determined to be either *appropriate* or *not appropriate*.

When developing movement improvisation assessment tasks, the *word cue* and *musical cue* contexts are most appropriate. Responding to word cues through movement follows the same procedures as those for responding through an instrumental medium; the teacher simply says a word, phrase, or reads a short section of a poem or story and the movement is created spontaneously. When students are improvising movement to musical cues, they are not creating a consequent phrase to a given antecedent as in vocal and instrumental improvisation. Instead, the teacher presents a preselected musical phrase or short piece (this can be a recorded or live performance) and the children are instructed to improvise movement to this example. The type of task is also best scored as a bi-level, single- or multiple-criterion assessment, and the criteria must be clear and understood by the children at the outset of the task.

Because the assessment of improvisation is primarily a performance event, the task parameters are summarized in a similar fashion to those presented in chapter 3. The chart is shown in Figure 4-9.

Assessing Children's Arrangements

Arranging music has to do with either the creation of a new presentation of a familiar piece or song or the creation of a musical enhancement of a literary work, such as a story or poem. Music-based arrangements involve the development of new accompaniments or interpretations of a known work. Literature-based arrangements primarily consist of sound effects and rhythmic or melodic phrases that represent events or characters in a story or poem.

Task Design Parameters: Improvisation Contexts

Context / Parameter	Component Definition	Assessment Focus	Assessment Tool	Medium	Scoring Guide	Record Keeping Strategy
Word Cues	carefully choose words to be used as stimuli	product	listening/teacher observation	voice, instrument, movement	single-criterion/ multiple-criterion (bi-level)	grade book, class list, seating chart; + or -
Musical Cues	design and create appropriate antecedent rhythmic/melodic phrases	product	listening	body or unpitched percussion, melodic instrument, vocal questions and answers	single-criterion/ multiple-criterion (bi-level)	+ or -
Free Improvisation–Performance	predetermine performance skill elements to be examined	process	teacher observation/ listening	instrumental rondo or other piece with embedded improvised solos	single-criterion (bi-level)	+ or -
Free Improvisation–Product	carefully define melodic, structural, rhythmic, theoretical, or aesthetic features to be assessed	product	teacher observation/ listening	instrumental rondo; twelve-bar blues for vocal improvisation	multiple-criterion (bi-level or multi-level)	+ or -; or number corresponding to assessed achievement level
Variations	determine exactly what product is reasonable to be expected	product	listening	a familiar, simple piece or song; melodic or unpitched instrument	single-criterion (bi-level)	+ or -

Figure 4-9.

204

Arranging is actually a hybridized extension of two already familiar creative musical acts: *composing new music* and *improvising variations*. The child arranger must be very familiar with the material to be arranged, as well as have a working knowledge of various instruments and their sounds. This discussion will examine the assessment of *arranging skill* as well as the *finished arrangement* as a musical product (much like a composition), within both the musical and literary arranging formats.

Assessment of arranging skill is process-focused, whereas the assessment of a finished arrangement is product-focused. Arranging skill, in similar fashion to other musical skills, is best assessed as a bi-level, single-criterion performance event; that is, children are assessed as either being able to arrange or not able to arrange. It is not recommended that students be assessed for more than two levels of arranging skill. The teacher's primary assessment information will come from a performance of the finished arrangement. A finished arrangement may seem very much like a composition in that it is, to an extent, a newly created work. However, it cannot be assessed only as a composition. The assessable components for an arrangement have more to do with the student's aesthetic and musical decisions than the rhythmic, melodic, structural, and theoretical characteristics of the new musical presentation.

To review, the aesthetic task targets for arrangements include (1) *expression*, which has to do with the child's choice of dynamics and/or articulation; (2) *instrumentation*, which has to do with the appropriateness of the child's choice of musical instruments in the finished arrangement; (3) *sound association*, which pertains to the child's sense of appropriateness with respect to the sounds selected for the arrangement; and (4) *dramatic movement*, which has to do with the child's choice of movement to enhance a literary work, specifically the use of gesture, space, balance, and body position. For music-based arrangements, the recommended assessable components are expression and instrumentation; for literature-based tasks, all four components are recommended. However, because arrangements are assessed during performance, the number of components targeted in the task should be limited to that which the teacher can comfortably assess.

It is important here to stress that the term *appropriateness* refers to the student's sense of the musical suitability of his or her choices; in some cases, it may be necessary to ask a child to explain his or her choice in order for the teacher to assess its suitability. The teacher must be very careful when doing this so as not to give the child the idea that the teacher feels that a musical choice is "wrong." Therefore, it is recommended that these criteria be assessed at three levels of achievement, as follows. A "+" can be recorded if the criterion is determined to be appropriate without question. A check mark (✓) can represent the teacher's decision to deem the child's choice appropriate after his or her explanation of the choice. A "–"should be reserved only for those students whose choices are deliberately poor, who purposefully do not select a sound, or who do not seem to understand the exercise. These decisions are made at the time the arrangement is performed.

In addition to the determination of the assessable components to be included, the development of assessment tasks in musical arrangement requires the teacher to make the following considerations: (1) *the selection of appropriate material for the arranging exercise*, (2) *the scope of instrumentation to be used*, (3) *whether the task will be completed in groups or individually*, and (4) *whether or not the arrangement task will include a notation component.*

1. When designing an arranging task for assessment, the most important decision that the teacher must make has to do with the *selection of the material to be arranged.* If the arrangement task is music-based, then the melody or rhythm

to be arranged must be very familiar. The children should be able to perform the melody or rhythm easily and, if possible, perform it on more than one instrument. For example, if a fourth grade class knows how to play "All Through the Night" on the soprano recorder using the pitches g_4-a_5-b_5, then it is helpful to them as arrangers to also know how to play the melody on other classroom pitched instruments, such as Orff instruments, melody bells, or keyboards, if these instruments are available. A high level of familiarity with the rhythm or melody will facilitate the arranging task; it can be a favorite from an earlier grade level or from earlier in the school year.

The *selection of an appropriate literary work* for an arranging task is equally important. The selected literature should be relatively short. A good rule of thumb is to limit stories to approximately four paragraphs and poems to no more than four stanzas (approximately sixteen total lines). The age of the child is also a guide to the length of the work selected; shorter selections are more appropriate for younger children. For example, short nursery rhymes are good choices for the early grades, and fables are more challenging for older students. Fairy tales and contemporary children's books are often too long for assessment tasks but can be excerpted for this purpose (although this would never be done when presenting a lesson on literature-based arranging to a class). The literature chosen should possess clear musical cues and at least one primary character that can be illustrated musically.

2. The *scope of the instrumentation to be used* in a task has to do with the teacher predetermining the *selection of sounds available to the child.* Many general music specialists have a number of different instruments available, and predetermining the set of instruments streamlines the time needed to complete the task. Children will take a great deal of time in selecting their own instruments for arrangements if allowed to do so, and managing twenty-five or so children who are looking for particular instrumental sounds can become counterproductive to the completion of the task. For music-based tasks, the teacher should carefully preselect a small group of instruments, at least three, that the children will use for the arrangement. For example, using the recorder example of "All Through the Night," the task may require that the new arrangement use only the recorder, the soprano glockenspiel, and the triangle; the teacher would simply have ready those instruments and present them to the child with the task instructions. For literature-based tasks, the teacher should prepare in advance a box, basket, or bag of instruments that can be presented to the child at the start of the task. The instruments should represent a cross-section of the sounds and timbres available in the class—wood, metal, skin (drums), pitched, unpitched, etc. If dramatic movement is a component of the task, the teacher may also choose to include some selected costume items with the instruments, such as hats, scarves, etc.

3. The teacher must also determine *whether the task will be completed in groups or individually.* Arranging tasks are best done in small groups in most general music classes. Individual arranging tasks are possible if the teacher has the ample number of instruments available and the time to listen to each individual arrangement. However, most arrangements require more than one student for the performance, and performance is the primary medium through which arrangements can be assessed. Therefore, groups of three to five students are preferable for these tasks.

4. Finally, the teacher must decide *whether or not the arrangement task will include a notation component.* Notation of an arrangement is not recommended. This can get complex and defeat the purpose of the arranging task. However, if notation of a music-based task is desired, the final score can be assessed as if it were a composition. If notation is desired for a literature-based task, then it is recommended to have the children use an invented notation approach, where they create their own notation to represent their work. The parameters for designing arranging tasks are summarized in Figure 4-10.

Task Design Parameters: Arrangements

Parameter	Arrangement Type: Music-based	Literature-based
Material Selection	a relatively short, familiar melody or rhythm	children's story (no more than 4 paragraphs, or excerpt from a longer story) or poem (no more than 16 lines in length)
Scope of Instrumentation	three or more preselected melody or rhythm instruments, presented at the start of the task	a small set of melody and rhythm instruments that represent a cross-section of sounds available in the classroom
Recommended Components	expression and instrumentation	expression, instrumentation, sound association, dramatic movement (to facilitate dramatic movement, selected costume props may be presented with the instrument set)
Scoring Guide	multi-level, multiple-criterion (three levels recommended)	multi-level, multiple-criterion (three levels)
Record Keeping Strategy	in the grade book, seating chart, or class list: + or –	in the grade book, seating chart, or class list: + or –

Figure 4-10.

Summary

- Children involved in creative musical activities produce one of three musical products: (1) a *composition,* (2) an *improvisation,* or (3) an *arrangement.*

- Creativity in music has been defined and researched by a number of scholars, and a commonly accepted view is still being developed. For this and other reasons, the assessment of children's creative ability should not be attempted. However, the products of the creative process can yield a great deal of valuable assessment data, and the creative process is

209

an engaging avenue through which children can demonstrate their accumulated musical knowledge.

- Children's creative musical products provide melodic, rhythmic, structural, theoretical, and aesthetic assessable components that serve as potential assessment task targets.

- Because children's created music is presented most often in performance, it provides an additional opportunity to observe performance behaviors.

- Composing music involves the application of a child's musical knowledge toward the creation of a new musical work. Assessment tasks in composing also provide an authentic opportunity for children to produce musical notation in the form of a finished score.

- Compositions are assessed using multi-level, multiple-criterion rubrics.

- The general approach to designing composition tasks is *guided composition*. In guided composition, teachers plan composition tasks with as many parameters prescribed as the young composer needs to help ensure the successful notation of his or her composition.

- Improvising music is the spontaneous generation of music without the intent of revision.

- Improvisation assessment tasks never involve notation; improvised music only exists for the time in which it is performed, unless preserved for later study through technological means.

- Improvisation tasks for children are designed in one of four contexts: (1) *responses to word cues,* (2) *responses to musical cues*, (3) *free improvisation within a specific form*, and (4) *variations of a familiar melody.*

- Because improvisation is assessed primarily during perform-ance, bi-level, single- or multiple-criterion scoring guides are recommended.

- No more than four components should be assessed at one time during a child's improvisation performance.

- Children's arrangements are either *music-based* or *literature-based.* Arrangements can be assessed for their *expression, instrumentation, sound association,* and *dramatic movement.*

- Designing assessment tasks in arranging requires careful choice of the musical material or literature, and control of the scope of the instrumentation through the pre-selection of instruments to be employed.

- Arranging tasks are best conducted in groups of three to five students, which facilitates the performance of the arrange-ment once the task is completed.

- Assessment of arrangements is done with a multi-level (three levels are recommended), multiple-criterion rubric.

Questions for Clarification

1) Children involved in creative activities generally produce a/an _____, _____, or _____.

2) Assessment of creative ability or skill should be limited to a _____ - _____ judgment of whether the child does or does not participate in the creative process.

3) Assessable components for creative musical products fall into the _____, _____, _____, _____, and _____ task target areas.

4) The recommended model for developing composition assessment tasks is _____ _____.

5) When designing guided composition tasks, _____ components should never be prescribed.

6) Of the three creative musical products that children produce for assessment, composition is the only one for which _____ is a reasonable task target area.

7) The composition tasks are generally scored with _____ - _____, _____ - _____ rubrics.

8) The four recommended contexts for improvisation assessment tasks are _____, _____, _____, _____, _____, _____, and _____.

9) Because improvisation is almost always assessed as a performance event, a _____ - _____, _____ - _____ scoring guide is recommended.

10) Children's arrangements are either _____ - _____ or _____ - _____.

11) The aesthetic task target areas for assessment of arrangements are _____, _____, _____ _____, and _____ _____.

12) When designing arranging tasks, teachers need to consider carefully the selection of appropriate _____ for the arrangement as well as the scope of the _____ to be used.

13) Arrangement tasks are almost always assessed during performance, but the _____ - _____, _____ - _____ type of scoring guide is recommended.

Questions for Discussion

1) This book recommends that children's creative ability or skill not be assessed when tasks are administered involving the creative process. Do you agree with this? Would you ever want or need to assess a child's creative ability? If so, how would you do it? Under what circumstances might it be necessary or desirable?

2) Discuss the differences between involving children creatively in music lessons as opposed to assessment tasks. Is it important for a creative assessment task to have certain controls or prescribed parameters? Why do you think this is important, or why do you not? Can you think of a creative assessment task appropriate for general music students where there would be no controlled parameters at all?

3) This chapter presented some of the many extant definitions and conceptions of musical creativity. How do you define musical creativity? Is creativity important to your philosophy of music education?

4) This chapter presented some of the research in children's compositions and improvisations. Discuss the value of this research to the instruction and assessment of musical creative activities. Does research help music teachers with their daily work? Are there connections between what music education researchers seek to explore and the classroom music teacher's concerns?

5)   This chapter recognizes three primary musical creative products: composition, improvisation, and arrangements. Of these, which are you most comfortable (or feel you would be most comfortable) teaching? Assessing?

6)   In your view, is movement something that is important to music education? Is it important to assess movement? Why or why not?

7)   With respect to the assessment of a particular literature-based arrangement, a teacher strongly believes that the sound of the rattlesnake in the story should be played by the shaking of the maracas. Instead, the child uses a tambourine. The teacher marks the child with a "–" because the chosen instrument is not "correct." Do you agree with this teacher's thinking? Do you disagree? Why? Support your response.

Assessment Practice

Composition

 1)   Assessment Figures A-1 and A-2 present the draft and final copies of Megan's hand-notated third grade composition in C-pentatonic. Megan does not study music privately. The requirements were to: (1) use all of the pitches of C-pentatonic, (2) notate the melody correctly on the staff in the treble clef, (3) end the piece on C (c_4), and (4) perform

the composition correctly. Create a rubric for this composition, then assess the piece according to your rubric. Is the
draft copy of any assessment value? Is spelling important in
the title (the title is "What am I supposed to do when I want
you in my world")? How would you assess the notation?

Amy **2)** Assessment Figure A-3 presents three third grade guided
compositions. Kyle and Joshua composed to the same given
rhythm, and Logan composed to a different given rhythm.
The boys do not study music privately and completed the
notation themselves on the classroom computer using
notation software. The requirements of the composition
task were to: (1) create a melody in the F-pentatonic scale
using all five pitches (the c_5 at the end of phrase 1 and the f_4
at the end of phrase 2 were given), (2) notate it correctly, and
(3) perform it correctly. How would you assess these
compositions? Of what assessment value are these
Rami musical scores?

3) Assessment Figure A-4 is Dan-Ying's hand-notated fourth
grade composition for recorder. Dan-Ying is an accomplished pianist and has received extensive private music
training. The requirements for this composition were to: (1)
create an original rhythm in 4/4 meter that is at least four
measures long, (2) compose a melody to this rhythm in G-
pentatonic using all five tones, (3) close the piece on a final
point, and (4) perform the piece correctly. Create a rubric and
score this composition. Does the fact that this child studies
Tindall music outside of school affect your assessment?

4) Assessment Figure A-5 is a fifth grade guided composition
by Douglass, Jacob, and Robert; only Douglass studies
music privately. The boys notated this themselves using the
classroom notation software. In this composition, they were

215

required to: (1) create an original rhythm using eighth, quarter, half, and/or whole notes and their rests in a meter of their choice, (2) create a melody to this rhythm for recorders in G-pentatonic using all five tones of the scale, (3) bring the composition to a final point on the tonic pitch, (4) align the melody with a given bordun on a bass xylophone (g_3-d_4), (5) make the composition four to eight measures in length, and (6) perform the composition correctly. Create a rubric for assessing this score, then assess the score assuming that the performance was adequate. What does this composition tell you about the acquired musical knowledge of these students?

5) Assessment Figure A-6 presents Whitney's hand-notated sixth grade guided composition for recorder, piano, and xylophone. The requirements for this composition were to: (1) create a four-measure or longer piece utilizing a I-V harmony change in the key of C major (the bass accompaniment was given and implied the harmony change, (2) employ at least one melody instrument in the piece, (3) include a rhythm and melody that was original, (4) notate the piece to demonstrate alignment of the accompaniment and the melody, and (5) perform the piece correctly. Develop a rubric for this composition, then assess the composition. What does this student know about the tonic-dominant harmony change? How do you know?

Improvisation

6) Assessment Figure A-7 presents the notation for three eight-measure alto xylophone improvisations created by eight-year-old students. The children were instructed to: (1) create a melody that used all of the bars of the instrument, (2) alternate the mallets, (3) attend to the beat, and (4) make their best and "most beautiful" music. What is the assessment value of these notated improvisations? Devise a rubric to assess these. What are the assessable components you have chosen? Why?

---

[1] One particularly appropriate song for an "A" section is "Solo's Here for Everyone," from the Orff/ *Keetman Music for Children, Volume 1,* Margaret Murray edition. Published by Schott.

Megan's Draft Copy

Assessment Figure A-1.

Megan's Final Copy

Assessment Figure A-2.

Computer-Notated Compositions
by Kyle, Joshua, and Logan

Assessment Figure A-3.

Dan-Ying's Recorder Piece

Assessment Figure A-4.

Computer Notation of "Candy"

Assessment Figure A-5.

Whitney's Piece for Three Instruments

Assessment Figure A-6.

Computer-Notated Improvisations

Assessment Figure A-7.

Chapter 5

Assessing the Critically Thinking/ Responding Child Musician

This chapter will focus on the purpose, design, and administration of tasks that involve children in the responding assessment mode. When involved in this mode of assessment, children are placed in the role of audience member who *listens, evaluates, and forms opinions and criticisms about musical events.* Students respond verbally through oral description or writing.

Embedded within the responding assessment mode is the process of critical thinking in music. Critical thinking in music, however, is not limited to the responding assessment mode; critical thinking can and does occur within the performing and creating assessment modes. Because critical thinking plays such an important role in the development of both oral and written assessment responses, it will be addressed at some length in this chapter.

Related National Standards

The responding assessment mode is best suited for student responses to tasks related to National Standards 6 through 9. Content Standard number 6 has to do with listening to, analyzing, and describing music. Content Standard number 7 deals with evaluating music and music performances, and Content Standard number 8 states that children should develop an understanding of the relationships between music, the other arts, and disciplines outside the arts. Content Standard number 9 has to do with understanding music in relation to history and culture (MENC, 1994, p. 29).

This chapter will begin with an examination of critical thinking in music. Following "A Glimpse at the Research," critical thinking and its application in the general music classroom will be presented. The chapter will close with a detailed look at appropriate assessable components and assessment models for the responding assessment mode.

Critical Thinking in Music: A Glimpse at the Research

Critical thinking in music is founded within the general body of theory and knowledge pertaining to critical thinking across all subject domains. This complex area of educational theory, philosophy, and practice has developed into an individual but substantial subject only within the past forty years and, in many respects, is still in its formative stages. Furthermore, any discussion of critical thinking in music becomes first a task of "making sense of the concept as viewed through the lenses of a variety of researchers" (Richardson & Whitaker, 1992, p. 546).

With the publication of *Dimensions of Thinking* in 1988, Marzano et al. described the fifth (and final) dimension as the relationship of content-area knowledge to thinking. In an initial effort to apply the framework set forth in *Dimensions of Thinking* to the content area of music, *Dimensions of Musical Thinking* (Boardman, 1989) was published. In this book, the dimensions articulated in the 1988 publication were explored and placed within a musical context.

DeTurk (1989) describes good critical thinkers in music as those who can

> *...rely upon conceptual musical evidence as the basis for their evaluations...they critically evaluate a particular*

> *work by understanding the music and the merits of its parts and its totality...in this way evaluation is derived from musical evidence rather than from peer pressure, whim, or fashion.* (p. 22)

In this view, critical thinking in music requires three components. First, critical thinkers must understand the elements of music. Second, critical thinkers in music must possess a storehouse of musical experiences from which to draw toward the comparison of other works of music. Last, critical thinkers must possess a metacognitive strategy or disposition; they must wish to, as well as know how to, make critical musical decisions. DeTurk contends that music instruction that teaches for critical thinking needs to address each of these characteristics.

Two major efforts at defining and describing thinking in music were undertaken by May (1989) and Beane (1989). May describes musical "experts" as engaging in several activities:

> *...they compose music; perform as musicians or vocalists; conduct others in the performance and interpretation of music; know how to appreciate music created by others; make informed judgments about musical works; arrange and orchestrate music for others to interpret and perform; or, through criticism, engage others in the examination of particular music forms or trends and the value of these forms or trends in social and historical contexts.* (pp. 84-85)

May (1989) recommends that students should be

> *...engaged in activities that promote their abilities to analyze the structural content of music by responding to elements, principles, or other sensory qualities in these forms; perceive and interpret symbolic or expressive subtleties (mood or feeling) in musical forms; and become aware of their own and others' perceptions, responses, feelings, and interpretations of musical forms.* (p. 80)

227

May also states that the social and historical contexts of music are necessary knowledge bases for critical thinking in music, as well as the ability to participate in effective musical criticism. Musical criticism is defined as "evaluating the effectiveness, worth, or success in generating specific responses to musical forms" (p. 82). In her view, critical thinking in music should not be taught in isolation, as a separate musical activity; it is best employed as a continuing exercise throughout the music curriculum.

Beane (1989) describes a set of critical thinking skills for the arts as follows: (a) metacognition, (b) epistemic cognition (the examination of another person's thinking processes), (c) classification, (d) comparison and contrast, (e) pattern recognition, (f) causal relationships, (g) making connections, (h) identifying the main idea, (i) sequencing, (j) developing criteria for judgment, and (k) synthesis. Most of these critical thinking skills are corollaries of the core thinking skills proposed by Marzano et al. (1988), with the inclusion of *epistemic cognition* and *pattern recognition.* Epistemic cognition can be viewed as a musical application of Paul's (1984) notion of dialogical, or multiperspectival, thinking. Pattern recognition in music is key to the understanding of musical structures and forms. Figure 5-1 presents the critical thinking views of DeTurk (1989), May (1989), and Beane (1989) as lists of general features.

There has been limited research in the area of critical thinking in music and music education, and only a few of these will be mentioned here. DeTurk (1989) explored the relationship between a student's number of years of performing music and his or her musical critical thinking skills. Two hundred seventy-nine high school juniors were asked to write essays in which they were to

228

Conceptions of Critical Thinking Skills in Music

Beane (1989)
Critical thinking skills:
Metacognition
Epistemic cognition
Classification
Comparison and contrast
Pattern recognition
Causal relationships
Making connections
Identifying the main idea
Sequencing
Developing criteria for judgment
Synthesis

DeTurk (1989)
The critical thinker must:
Understand the elements of music
Possess a storehouse of music experiences
Employ a metacognitive strategy or disposition

May (1989)
Facets of critical thinking:
Analysis of structural elements
Interpret symbolic/expressive subtleties
Knowledge of social/historical context
Effective musical criticism

Figure 5-1.

discuss, evaluate, and compare two musical selections. The essays were rated according to the SOLO (Structure of Observed Learning Outcomes) taxonomy. The taxonomy consisted of five levels, as follows:

1. *Prestructural*—essays do not accurately respond to the task;

2. *Unistructural*—essays rely upon a single, lower-level musical concept or fact (simple rhythm, tempo, dynamics, or performance medium;

3. *Multi-structural*—essays employ several not well-defined concepts or facts of the same type as the unistructural essays;

4. *Relational*—essays display both a grasp of higher level concepts (such as form, orchestration, style) and present unified arguments that successfully incorporate evidence from several concepts into convincing answers that deal with the assignment as narrowly defined; and

5. *Extended abstract*—essays meet the relational criteria but exceed the assignment in a musically correct way. (DeTurk, 1989, pp. 25-26)

Results indicated a significant association between years of performing group experience and critical thinking as measured by the essays, but post hoc (that is, after the study was completed) comparisons revealed that at least six years of experience were required before a significant difference was shown.

Several studies have attempted to build a theoretical and/or philosophical base for critical thinking in music. Elliott (1995) presents a view of critical thinking in music that is based on the "procedural essence of musicianship" (p. 55). Elliott identifies four classifications of knowledge involved in procedural musicianship: (1) formal musical knowledge, such as concepts, theories, etc.; (2) informal musical knowledge, described as the ability to reflect critically in action, make judgments, and achieve an understanding of the musical context in which the music is embedded; (3) impressionistic musical knowledge, which is likened to intuition; and (4) supervisory musical knowledge, defined as "knowing how to manage, guide, and advance one's musicianship in and over time" (p. 66). In this view, music making is at the heart of what music is, and "music making is a matter of musical knowledge-in-action" (p. 66). Among Elliott's recommendations for music educators to facilitate the teaching and learning necessary to develop musicianship in students are:

1. *Progressive problem solving,* the presentation of musical challenges that confront students with genuine musical problems to be solved in context;

2. *Problem finding,* having to do with locating "what counts and what needs to be done musically in relation to a given musical challenge" (p. 73);

3. *Problem reduction,* the careful guidance of students in the reduction of performance difficulties while still focusing upon problem solving; and

4. *Evaluation,* wherein a student's level of musical understanding demonstrates itself in the quality of his or her music making.

Elliott's view of critical thinking in music as occurring "in action," or procedurally, accounts for the temporal nature of musical experience and the internal decision-making processes involved in performance. He claims that his view does not completely disavow the importance of verbal musical understanding and knowledge but that "a musical performance ought to be valued for what it is: the embodiment of a student's musical understanding of a given musical work and its related practice" (p. 76).

Woodford (1994/1995) presents a view of critical thinking that is derived from Dewey's concept of reflective thinking. He proposes that because music is political, and hence results in musical belief systems that are rejected or accepted by individuals within or outside of a group, critical thinking is "essentially about defining one's musical 'self' in relation to some musical group or groups" (Woodford, in press). Woodford (1994/1995) identifies five phases of musical reflective thinking that occur in no particular order:

1. The first phase is musical suggestion and suggested musical actions, invoked by the need to resolve doubt and uncertainty, and used by the musical "self" to guide actual musical thought and action.

2. The second phase is intellectualization of the musical problem, occurring when an individual, upon sensing a possible musical problem, begins to intuitively yet purposefully utilize musical suggestions and suggested musical actions toward some musical end.

3. Phase three, the formation of a guiding musical hypothesis, is when "full reflective thinking is reached" (p. 441). At this point, the emotional quality of the musical challenge or problem is converted to a more definite form of propositional or procedural knowledge about the problem as a whole. It is at this stage that reflective thinking takes on a metacognitive quality in that the individual is aware of the thought processes being invoked.

4. Musical reasoning is the fourth phase, having to do with making connections between musical events, actions, ideas, and conceptions through inference and association such that a sequence of musical thought is established.

5. The last phase of reflective thinking occurs when the musical hypothesis is tested through overt action or in the imagination.

Embedded in this process are four inseparable general thinking skills, identified as (1) musical observation, (2) judgment, (3) analysis and synthesis, and (4) musical imagination.

Brophy (1995) has synthesized these conceptions of the critical thinking process in music into a three-phase model as follows (see Figure 5-2).

1. First, there is an attempt to *identify the musical problem or situation* that is the origin of the critical thinking experience. During this phase, core thinking skills are employed in order to describe and observe this problem.

2. If the problem or situation has meaning for the individual, he or she then enters the second phase. The second phase is one of *general reflection* that is directed toward the generation

232

of a solution to the problem or situation. During this phase, the critical thinker engages the application of both core thinking skills and metacognitive skills within a disposition conducive to generating solutions, testing them, and keeping or discarding them.

3. The generation of an adequate solution allows the individual to enter phase three, which is a *musical production or performance* that is both meaningful to the individual and to the musical collective and based on sound musical judgment supported by evidence.

Three Phases of the Critical Thinking Process in Music: A Synthesized View

Phase One
Identifying a musical problem or situation through describing and/or observing

Phase Two
Reflection, wherein solutions
are generated and tested

Phase Three
Musical production or performance
that is meaningful and based on
sound musical judgment

Figure 5-2.

What *Is* Critical Thinking in Music?

This brief review reveals that while some progress has been made toward solidifying the conception of critical thinking and its components, there is still much to be accomplished in defining and clarifying critical thinking as it occurs in music. For this book, critical thinking in music shall refer to the ability to *consciously apply* cognitive processing to musical experiences, whether thinking *about* music (reflectively), thinking *in* music (procedurally), or thinking about one's own personal musical growth (metacognitively).

Critical thinkers in music have three primary avenues of expression: (1) *reflection*—the examination of previous musical experience in relation to present experience (includes critical review, preference, evaluation); (2) *metacognition*—thinking about one's own thinking, learning, and/or development; and (3) *procedural application*—thinking in performance, updating and altering musical performance to suit the immediate musical conditions or context.

Figure 5-3 presents a trilateral model of these three avenues of critical thinking expression. Metacognition is placed at the top of the triangle because it is a global thinking process that can occur within all musical learning areas. The left side of the model denotes musical "thinking in action," and procedural application of critical thinking in music is placed at the lower left point of the triangle. The right side of the model denotes musical "contemplation," and reflection is placed at the lower right corner of the triangle. The critical thinker—in this case, the child musician—is at the center of the triangle, and the arrows present the various directions that critical thinking can be directed within a task. The next section explains these directions more fully.

Critical Thinking in Music: A Trilateral Model

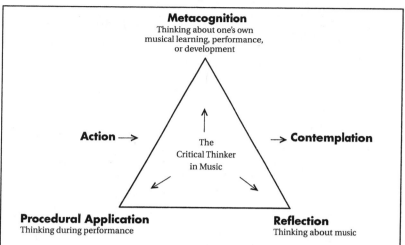

Figure 5-3.

It All Begins with a Prompt:
Steps for Planning Critical Thinking Tasks

To design assessment tasks that involve critical thinking skills, teachers must follow certain steps. The following paragraphs explain these steps.

> **Step 1:** *Plan the time for thinking into your lesson and determine the format of the responses.* If you are planning a reflective or metacognitive activity, plan at least ten minutes for thinking and writing. For children in kindergarten, first, and the first half of second grade, the time for thinking may need to be adjusted because the children's responses will be verbalized in a class discussion rather than written. Younger children (late second grade and third grade) need more time for writing because they are less experienced with the process and mechanics of writing. Older students may need longer than ten minutes because their written responses are more involved and include more detailed information than those of the younger students.

To prepare for these types of writing assignments, students should get into the habit of bringing a pencil and journal to each music class, even though writing is not a part of each and every music lesson. This practice should be started at the beginning of the school year, and teachers should include these materials on their music supply lists that are given to parents at registration prior to the opening of the school year.

Students will also want to know about the expected length of their written responses. The teacher may or may not want to prescribe a number of sentences for a response; this depends on the class and the manner in which the students' classroom or subject area teachers normally present writing assignments. Some written responses may require a paragraph, while others may require only one or two sentences. Music teachers are advised to familiarize themselves with the students' other teachers' presentation formats for writing assignments and use this as a starting point for developing a writing assignment approach for music class. However, students should always be instructed to write responses (1) in complete sentences, (2) using proper capitalization and punctuation, (3) with appropriate subject-verb agreement, and (4) using neat and clear handwriting (penmanship). A good rule of thumb is to ask the children to write their responses in such a manner that they could be placed on display in the school hallway, either outside the music room or, in the case of the traveling teacher, a specially designated area where such displays are permitted (often outside the children's homeroom or regular classroom).

Step 2: *Determine the direction in which to guide the students' thinking.* Ask yourself: Which thinking direction is best for the lesson—reflection, metacognition, or procedural application—or a combination of these? The critical thinking direction for any task is related to the learning area in which it falls. Figure 5-4 presents some suggested directions for guiding students' critical thinking for each musical learning area.

Some Guidelines for Directing Musical Thinking

Lesson Focus/ Content Area:	Reflection	Metacognition	Procedural
Musical Skills			
singing	x	x	x
playing instruments	x	x	x
improvising	x	x	x
composing	x	x	
arranging	x	x	
Literacy			
reading music	x	x	
notating music	x	x	
History and Literature			
musical form	x	x	x
musical styles	x	x	x
historical periods	x	x	
specific composers/ works	x	x	
Analysis and Preference			
musical structures	x	x	x
timbre	x	x	x
criteria building	x	x	
evaluating performances/ products	x	x	
presenting logical arguments	x	x	
Related Arts and Humanities			
describing relationships between music and culture	x	x	
making connections between music and the other arts, and disciplines outside the arts	x	x	

Figure 5-4.

Reflective and metacognitive thinking skills can be included in the design of tasks embedded within each of the musical learning areas. *Reflection* is applicable to all learning areas because it occurs after a musical activity has been completed; the child can respond to questions such as the following: How did I do today? Did I enjoy the musical experience? What did I learn? What meaning did this musical experience have for me? *Metacognitive skills* can be applied to tasks within each learning area because metacognition involves the students in reviewing their own learning processes, and students can respond to questions such as: What did I do to learn this? What process did I go through to obtain this knowledge or skill?

Procedural critical thinking occurs during musical performance and therefore is limited to performance-related musical learning areas, which include singing, playing instruments, and improvising. However, critical thinking during performance can also require students to incorporate knowledge of musical form and styles, as well as musical structures (motives, phrases, periods) and musical timbre. Critical thinking during performance occurs when a child draws upon all available musical knowledge and skills to alter and adjust a performance to suit the style or interpretation of the music, as well as to adjust to directions given by a conductor or to contextual clues presented by the accompanist or other performers.

Step 3. *Identify the specific musical behavior(s) and learning area(s) in the lesson, and then determine the critical thinking process(es) involved in completing the behavior(s).* At this step, the teacher first identifies the specific musical behavior(s) that the children demonstrated in order to complete the lesson. These specific behaviors are related to those listed within each category of the musical learning areas (refer to Figure 2-2) and are the basis for the specific behavioral objectives in the lesson. The next step is to examine the lesson context and its influence on the behavior(s) observed and to identify the specific critical thinking skills that are involved in the execution of this behavior within the context of the lesson. Figure 5-5 presents a list of the critical thinking skills proposed by Beane (1989) as they have been adapted for general music.

Beane's (1989) Critical Thinking Skills (Processes) in the Arts, Adapted for Music

1. **Epistemic cognition**
   assuming the role or viewpoint of another person; examining another's thought processes

2. **Classification**
   grouping according to common attributes

3. **Comparison and contrast**
   finding inherent similarities and differences between separate musical events

4. **Pattern recognition**
   observing sets in a designated order or arrangement

5. **Causal relationships**
   finding cause and effect, examining the particular forces that influence specific events

6. **Making connections**
   finding commonalities among seemingly disparate musical events (making associations)

7. **Identifying the main idea**
   finding the central point or idea of a creative work

8. **Sequencing**
   arranging attributes into a connected series or successive order according to a given criterion

9. **Developing criteria for judgment**
   defining goals, determining the steps to reach the goals, and establishing criteria for assessing the quality of that achievement

10. **Synthesis**
    organizing previously separate ideas into a new and different (sometimes better) whole

11. **Metacognition**
    thinking about one's own thinking and learning

Figure 5-5.

Step 4. *Target the lesson content area that will become the focus of the response.* Each lesson that is taught has specific content that is integral to the lesson. This content includes (but is not limited to) the songs, instrumental pieces, listening selections, dances or movement, compositions, and improvisations which are the basis for the activity that the lesson presents to the children. At this step, it is important to select specific content or material that will be the focus of the critical thinking processes that will be called upon to respond to the task.

Step 5. *State the prompt clearly and simply, in the form of a question or a "challenge statement."* Once steps 1 through 4 have been completed, the prompt must be formed as either a question or challenge statement. A challenge statement is simply a declarative statement of the task.

Some Examples of Critical Thinking Prompts

The following are examples of critical thinking prompts that were developed using the five-step approach discussed in the previous section.

Kindergarten

Time allotment
about 5 to 7 minutes for discussion

Lesson content
In this lesson, the children have played with the steady beat in three different ways and have learned the term *steady beat.* First, they formed a circle and passed a yarn ball around the circle to the steady beat as they played a name game. Then, they patted the beat in their laps as they sang "Georgy Porgy Puddin 'n' Pie" and "Peas Porridge Hot." Third, they went on a "walk to school" with the teacher leading them in this activity using the sound of a hand

drum as the steady beat for walking (they "matched their feet to the sound of the drum").

Lesson content target for the prompt
the steady beat

Critical thinking process
making connections (between seemingly disparate musical events)

Critical thinking direction
reflection; thinking about previous musical experiences

The prompt
Today we played the name game with the yarn ball, sang some of our favorite songs, and went on a walk with the hand drum. When we moved during these activities, what musical term describes what we were showing? (The term *steady beat* should emerge in the discussion.) Was there a steady beat in everything we did today? From here, the teacher should guide the discussion toward the realization that the steady beat can be expressed in different ways.

First Grade

Time allotment
5 to 7 minutes for discussion

Lesson content
In this lesson, the class has experienced the form of Kodàly's "Viennese Musical Clock." In this activity, the students (after preparation by listening to the theme) are divided into 4 groups, each forming a circle by holding hands. Group 1 is assigned to move clockwise in the circle when the "A" section is playing, and Groups 2, 3, and 4 are assigned to move in their circles only when the B, C, and D sections are playing (respectively). Eventually, the ABACADA form of the piece is discovered by the children and written on the board.

Lesson content target for the prompt
the recurrence of the "A" section

Critical thinking process
identifying the main idea; sequencing

Critical thinking direction
reflection; thinking about a past musical event

The prompt
Today we listened to the "Viennese Musical Clock" and discovered the way the sections of the piece were put in order by the composer, Zoltan Kodàly. I would like each of you to share with me which section you think was the composer's favorite and why. (Class discussion follows.)

Second Grade

Time allotment
15 minutes for writing

Lesson content
In this lesson, the class has experienced writing down dictated rhythms using standard notation for the first time. Prior to this, they have written iconic notation only. They are introduced to the term *standard notation*.

Lesson content target for the prompt
notation process

Critical thinking process
comparison and contrast

Critical thinking direction
metacognition; thinking about one's own learning

The prompt
Today you used standard notation to write down rhythms using quarter and eighth notes, and quarter rests. Describe how this is different for you and what you had to do to write

standard notation. Do you find this kind of notation easier? Why or why not?

Third Grade

Time allotment
10 to 15 minutes

Lesson content
The singing game "The Closet Key"; the class played this game and each child was assessed for vocal pitch accuracy.

Lesson content target for the prompt
matching pitch on mi, re, and do while playing the game

Critical thinking process
pattern recognition (recognizing and recreating the patterns do-mi and mi-mi-re-re-do)

Critical thinking direction
metacognition; thinking about one's own learning

The prompt
Today we played a singing game, and I told you that I would be listening for how well you matched the pitches do, re, and mi. How do you know when you are matching pitch?

Fourth Grade

Time allotment
10 minutes

Lesson content
In this lesson, the class sang the American folk melody "Way Down Yonder in the Brickyard" (a call-and-response song) and "Mongolian Night Song" (a song from China). (Both of these songs are found in the fourth grade book of the McMillan/McGraw-Hill *Share the Music* series.) The

lesson focused on finding the phrases in each song; these were traced in the air and located on the written page through the examination of phrase markings in the scores. The class discovered that the phrases in the American song were all equal in length, while the Chinese song contained phrases of unequal length.

Lesson content target for the prompt
phrase lengths

Critical thinking process
comparison and contrast

Critical thinking direction
reflection; thinking about a previous musical experience

The prompt
Today we performed two songs, one from America and one from China. We discussed the phrasing in both songs and made some discoveries about the lengths of the phrases in each song. Why do you think these songs have different phrasing?

Fifth Grade

Time allotment
10 minutes

Lesson content
In this lesson, the class sang the Ghanian song "Everybody Loves Saturday Night" (McMillan/McGraw-Hill, *Share the Music* series, Book 5) in English and in Ga (the language of Ghana). They then played a recorder countermelody to the refrain and learned the new note F-natural (Baroque fingering) as part of this countermelody.

Lesson content target for the prompt
the new F-natural fingering

Critical thinking process
comparison and contrast; causal relationships

Critical thinking direction
metacognition; thinking about one's own learning

The prompt
Today we learned a new song from Ghana and played a harmony part to the song with the recorder. We played the note F-natural for the first time. What did you have to do in order to perform the F-natural as best as you could?

Sixth Grade

Time allotment
10 to 15 minutes

Lesson content
In this lesson, the class was introduced to the "Piece in d minor" for the recorder. To play this, they learned the new recorder note Bb.

Lesson content target for the prompt
"Piece in d minor"

Critical thinking process
sequencing; comparison and contrast; making connections

Critical thinking direction
procedural application (changing the piece as it is performed); reflection

The prompt
Today we have learned the "Piece in d minor" on the recorder and the new recorder note Bb. Now play the piece with B-natural and switch all of the high D's to low D's, and vice versa. How does this change the piece? Is it easier or harder to play this way? Why do you think so?

Critical Thinking and Assessment

Assessment of Critical Thinking Skills

Now that a great deal of time has been spent on understanding *critical thinking* and the design of critical thinking prompts, it is imperative that the terms *critical thinking* and *assessment* not be used interchangeably. While a response-mode assessment task may employ specific musical critical thinking skills, the student's *level of engagement* in particular critical thinking skills should *not* be assessed.

Oral or written responses that employ musical critical thinking skills can be assessed for their content, as well as whether or not there is evidence of particular critical thinking skills in the final product, but they should not be assessed with respect to the degree to which those specific critical thinking skills may have been employed. Critical thinking skills are the tools used to facilitate musical responding, and at the present time, there is not an adequate measure of *levels* of musical critical thinking skills. The internal mental processes that comprise musical critical thinking skills are literally impossible to measure with reference to their level of engagement at any one time. Additionally, standardization of such process assessment would be theoretically and philosophically weakened by the fact that children's musical processing is an individualized and constructed event, and is subjected to developmental forces that at the present time are still under exploration.

However, one can certainly make assumptions as to what product evidence reflects the engagement of critical thinking skill. These assumptions form the skill-related criteria that can be used when assessing oral and written responses. Qualitative differences in children's oral or written responses can be observed when appropriately designed criteria are used for these judgments. However, since the critical thinking processes involved in any

246

particular response are used in the service of retrieving information and interpreting problems, assessment of the *level* of skill engagement remains elusive.

In other words, strong responses to critical thinking exercises can be judged to differ from weak responses in the quality of the information they present and the degree to which they meet the other skill-related product qualities that are outlined in the assessment criteria. However, a teacher must be very careful to avoid suggesting that the student who wrote a strong response was more "highly developed" in a particular critical thinking skill than one who produced a weak response. It is best to use a bi-level judgment of "present" or "not present." For example, if a teacher is examining critical writings for evidence of synthesis, the judgment of the presence of synthesis would be made using a scoring guide that specifically lists criteria for evidence (this is discussed in detail later). The teacher should not attempt to judge whether or not one response evidences *more* or *less* synthesis than another; the judgment needs to remain criterion-referenced. Until there is a better theoretical and philosophical foundation that tells us what critical thinking actually is, it is recommended that teachers stay away from such judgments in the general music classroom.

On the other hand, the way in which musical critical thinking is assessed at the district and state levels is important to the music specialist and should be investigated and understood by the teacher so that he or she can prepare students for such assessments. If a school district or state designs and administers assessments that involve critical thinking in music, the appropriate administrators are responsible for providing teachers with the curricula that include and identify the specific skills that are to be assessed.

Therefore, it is recommended that general music teachers use a scoring process that allows for a maximum of three levels when judging each criterion designed to gauge the employment of critical thinking skills within a particular response. It is both valid and valuable to assess whether or not the response presents evidence of a particular process or skill using a bi-level scoring guide (indicated by a "+" or "−" in the grade book). It may also be valuable in some instances to include a third level, one that is between "does not show evidence of the targeted skill" and "shows adequate evidence of the targeted skill." Such a level might be "shows inconsistent evidence of the targeted skill," indicated by a checkmark (√) in the grade book. The general music specialist should not try to assess critical thinking skills beyond these levels.

Critical Thinking Directions and Task Purpose

Responding mode assessments generally are conducted for one of three purposes: (1) *direct content assessment,* (2) to provide *evidence of the employment of critical thinking skills,* or (3) for *self-assessment of achievement and personal growth.*

Direct content assessment is done primarily through reflective critical thinking; that is, the student is asked to think back on a particular event or lesson and write about or discuss the experience. Embedded in such a response is specific musical content that the teacher targets for assessment; the responses are then examined for the presence of this content. Again, teachers may choose to give objectivist-based tests or quizzes for content assessment, and this is perfectly appropriate at certain times. However, this book is focusing on assessment formats that involve higher levels of thinking from students.

Evidence of the employment of the specific critical thinking skills that serve to facilitate both the retrieval of targeted musical content and the formation of musical judgment can be achieved through reflective and procedural critical thinking tasks. Teachers can establish evidence criteria (as shown in Figure 5-7) that will help them to recognize whether or not students have employed critical thinking skills. For reflective exercises, this evidence is presented in oral or written form. For procedural exercises, the evidence is in the form of performance components (see chapter 3) or components related to epistemic cognition.

Self-assessment and personal musical growth is gauged through metacognitive tasks. Metacognition is the thinking direction through which musicians come to "know themselves," and the purpose of metacognitive tasks is to help students become stronger, more independent musicians through self-understanding. The teacher is not going to be concerned with the musical content of such tasks but rather the child's ability to be truthful and aware of his or her progress and achievement.

Therefore, responding mode assessment tasks produce three primary types of responses in the general music classroom: (1) *metacognitive writing or discussion,* (2) *reflective writing or discussion,* and (3) a *musical performance in response to a specific critical thinking prompt.* For this book, written and oral responses are both categorized as *verbal responses.* Because the purpose and use of procedural tasks, as well as their assessment as musical performances, has been previously discussed, it will not be reviewed here. (However, in the section that follows on establishing evidence of critical thinking skills in assessment responses, nonverbal performance demonstrations are discussed when appropriate.) Figure 5-6 graphically displays this critical thinking direction/task purpose relationship.

Metacognitive and reflective verbal responses can be assessed with appropriate criteria, and this will be the focus of the next section. First, general issues involving developing criteria for assessing reflective responses will be discussed, followed by issues pertaining to verbal metacognitive responses.

Alignment of Thinking Directions and Responding Mode Assessment Tasks

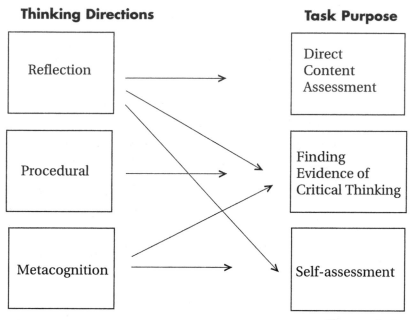

Figure 5-6.

Establishing Product Evidence of the Musical Thinking Process in Critical Thinking Responses

Written and oral responses to responding mode assessment tasks provide a rich and varied source of assessment data. This data is embedded in oral statements and reports, as well as in written sentences, paragraphs, and reports. These types of reports—both written and oral—are categorized as *verbal* responses because they have to do with responses that are word-based. Performance demonstrations of a response to a responding mode assessment task are categorized as *nonverbal* or *performance* responses. In order to effectively and accurately assess such responses, the data must be gathered systematically and applied to certain criteria that the teacher has selected or developed to ascertain the student's level of response to the task.

One of the challenges facing general music teachers who evaluate children's responding mode assessments is deciding what product data best shows evidence of the targeted musical content and/or critical thinking skills. Establishing the form this evidence takes (and its related assessment criteria) requires that the teacher make important connections between the content and skills embedded in the tasks and their possible verbal or nonverbal representations. This connection is usually based on assumptions at first; that is, the teacher has to predict the responses that may be forthcoming and develop criteria based on those predictions. The criteria for assessment must be developed prior to the assignment of the task and shared with students so that the students know what is expected of them. The following steps are guidelines that can be followed to help facilitate criteria development in these situations.

Step 1: Identify the Specific Content Targeted in the Task and Expected in the Response

With the exception of self-reflection and self-assessment (metacognitive tasks), every responding mode assessment task focuses upon specific musical content or skill that has been previously taught or learned. Therefore, if the teacher is looking for specific facts, references, or materials, these should be specifically mentioned in the assessment criteria.

The choice of words used for describing expected content in assessment criteria is important. For example, if a teacher is asking students to reflect upon their study of Mozart's music, one of the criteria for distinguishing levels of achievement might be the

251

number of specific works mentioned in the response. If this is the case, then the teacher needs to determine next what number or type of works mentioned will represent a particular achievement level. For example, if the teacher is using a four-level rubric, then he or she may decide that the lowest level of response (level 1) would include no mention of any specific works, a level 2 response would mention one or two specific works, a level 3 response would mention three or four specific works, and a level 4 response five or more works. This type of criterion is very specific and helpful for students. It is much less helpful to use subjective terms such as "poor," "adequate," "small number," "large number," etc., to describe the numbers of works mentioned. Students will interpret these terms in many different ways, and older students (and some parents) can get argumentative over subjective distinctions. This specificity is also helpful when asking students to support their opinions and preferences with content knowledge.

Step 2: Know the Expected Verbal and Performance Outcomes of Critical Thinking Skills

When devising criteria statements, the teacher must consider as best as possible the typical verbal outcomes of specific musical critical thinking skills. This requires experience with identifying the skills at the lesson planning stage, as well as knowing what verbal responses are typically associated with the employment of specific critical thinking skills. Musical critical thinking skills, by their nature, are typically *goal-enabled*; that is, they are employed in the pursuit of a particular goal or outcome. The skill itself, then, also serves to suggest an array of responses that could be expected. However, because verbal and performance responses are open-ended and can vary widely, a definitive set of *typical* or *prototype* responses and assessment criteria is not feasible.

However, some generalizations regarding responses are possible and useful as the bases for criteria development, as shown in Figure 5-7 and explained in this section.

Epistemic Cognition:

Epistemic cognition can be evidenced in a performance or written assessment, when children are actively engaged in role-playing as part of a task. If this process is being employed during or within a response, the teacher can look for the following in the student's role-playing: (1) references to the work of the person whose role is being assumed, (2) knowledge of the personal and professional relationships of the assumed individual (where important), (3) first-person statements that reflect the viewpoints, opinions, and/or beliefs of the assumed role, (4) dramatic characterization of the role that authentically reflects the individual, or (5) the use of objectivity when examining the thought processes of others. Generalized criteria might include:

The response

1. Refers to the work or works of the person whose role is being assumed;

2. Expresses knowledge of the important professional and/or personal relationships of the individual;

3. Contains first person statements that reflect viewpoints, opinions, and/or beliefs of the assumed individual;

4. Presents dramatic characterization of the role that authentically reflects the individual; and

5. Is objective when examining, discussing, or presenting the thought processes of the assumed individual.

Example: Pairs of students are given a task in which they are to assume the roles of music critic and a famous composer. The critic is to interview the composer regarding at least two different works that the composer created.

To account for evidence of epistemic cognition in the response, the generalized assessment criteria might include (but not be limited to) statements such as:

1. The critic provided questions pertaining to specific works of the composer.

2. The composer provided accurate responses to the critic's questions.

3. The student behaved in a manner typical of that composer.

These generalized criteria could then be made more specific by the teacher to include references to targeted content, such as specific works or numbers of works referenced in the task.

These types of criterion statements can be assessed with either a bi-level or multi-level scoring guide, depending on the teacher's skill and time taken to assess these types of tasks. For most tasks, evidence of epistemic cognition is best assessed as either *observed* or *not observed*, using a bi-level scoring guide.

Classification:

Evidence of *classification* can be found in performance (through demonstration) or in oral statements or written lists (verbal responses) of categorized objects or musical phenomena. For example, young children may be asked to "find one of each kind of unpitched wooden instruments in our class and collect them together at your place." In this performance response, the young child is categorizing instruments by their materials and demonstrating the process of classification. Older children can also demonstrate classification of objects through similar tasks, but teachers interested in this process will find it less time-consuming to have these students write their responses as lists or paragraphs. Older children can categorize musical motives, phrases, themes, melodies, rhythms, styles, and forms according to common attributes. These attributes include (but are not limited to) melodic direction, melody type (e.g., primarily stepwise, skipping, or a combination of these), structural relationships, note and rhythmic values, pitch, key signature, harmony, types of form, and historical period. Some general criteria for assessment might include:

The response

1. Specifically mentions the musical objects or phenomena that are being classified;

2. States the common attribute or attributes that serve as the basis of the sorting/categorization/classification activity; and

3. Provides a clear list, statement, or demonstration of the classified musical objects or phenomena.

Example: Students listen to a series of six short melodies and classify them according to their melodic direction, either upward, downward, or staying the same.

Assessment criteria for this task might include (but not be limited to):

The response

1. Uses the term melody to describe what is being classified;

2. Describes the directional attribute—upward, downward, staying the same—that is used to categorize the melodies; and

3. Presents statements or lists of the correct classifications.

Evidence of the classification process is best completed with a bi-level scoring guide, since most classification tasks are either *correctly* or *incorrectly* completed.

Comparison and Contrast:

Comparison and contrast is evidenced in verbal responses. When looking for evidence of this process in oral or written work, the teacher should look for (1) specific mention of the two events or works being compared and contrasted, (2) specific attributes of the two events or works that are used as focal points for comparison and contrast, and (3) statements that reveal points of similarity and difference between the two events or works. Generalized criteria might include (but are not limited to):

The response

1. Includes the names of the events or works being compared and contrasted;

2. States a (specified) number of specific points in the events/works that are the foci of the comparison and contrast; and

3. Includes statements that clearly describe the points of comparison and contrast.

The teacher can then design these to be specific to the task by including reference to the content that forms the basis of the exercise. For example, a fifth grade task might state: "Using at least one example of each from the pieces we have studied, compare and contrast the rondo and sonata allegro forms." The criteria for assessment might include (but are not limited to):

The response

1. Includes the names and composers of a work in rondo form and a work in sonata allegro form;

2. Pinpoints at least three specific features in the named works with respect to their function in the form of the piece; and

3. Clearly describes these features in terms of their similarities and differences.

Sample response to the above task: I would like to compare and contrast the use of form in the *Rondo alla Turca* by Mozart and the first movement of Beethoven's *Fifth Symphony*. The opening of the *Fifth Symphony* has a short

256

introductory passage, and the rondo does not. The A-section of each work returns, but in the rondo it returns five times and in the symphony it returns only once as a recapitulation. When the A-section returns in the rondo, it is exactly the same each time; the recapitulation is longer in the symphony, so it is not exactly the same.

Such paragraph responses can then be judged with the type of scoring guide that best suits the time available to the teacher and the depth with which the teacher wishes to review the responses. A music teacher with hundreds of students will do well to employ a bi-level scoring approach, and place a "+" or "−" in the grade book/data collection form for each criterion assessed. The sample response above would be encoded as "+/+/+" because it met all three criteria listed in the rubric.

Pattern Recognition:

Pattern recognition is evidenced through performance and verbal responses. In performance, students simply indicate through movement, singing, or instrument playing that they recognize a pattern of notes (such as a motive or melody) or durations (rhythm). For example, third graders may be asked to play a particular pattern of pitches on melodic percussion (such as mi, re, do) each time they hear it in a melody; to do this, they must employ pattern recognition. Verbal responses should include reference to (1) an arrangement of musical objects or events that is repeated or (2) a particular order in which these objects or events occur. Generalized criteria for assessment of pattern recognition might include (but is not limited to):

The response

1. Refers to a specific arrangement of notes, durations, instruments, or other musical objects or events; and

2. Refers to the particular order in which specified notes, durations, instruments (or arrangements of these), or other musical objects or events occur.

This process is best assessed using a bi-level scoring guide, because the outcome of a pattern recognition task is usually *recognized the pattern* or *did not recognize the pattern.*

> **Example:** A teacher has taught a class a particular ostinato pattern that travels from the triangle (playing a quarter note), to the tambourine (playing a quarter note), to the suspended cymbal (playing a half note). The class has learned this ostinato as part of the accompaniment to a song. The class has divided into trios and all have had a chance to perform the ostinato and become familiar with it. To check for pattern recognition, the teacher then has three students come forward to play the instruments. She asks the remaining children to close their eyes and to raise their hands when they hear the ostinato pattern. The three instrument players are instructed to play their instruments when the teacher points to them; the teacher then points to the instrument players "out of order" and "in order" several times, resulting in an incorrect and correct ostinato pattern being played several times. The teacher can then mark in the grade book or data collection sheet (using a "+" or "–") which students did or did not recognize the timbre pattern.

Causal Relationships:

Evidence of *causal relationships* is found primarily in verbal responses. When the teacher is seeking evidence of this process in oral and written work, he or she should look for (1) mention of the two musical agents that are the source of the cause and effect relationship, (2) the actions involved in instigating the cause and effect relationship, and (3) statements that clearly describe the cause and effect. Generalized criteria might include (but are not limited to):

The response

1. Specifically mentions the causal agent and the object or event that is affected;

2. States the action of the causal agent that results in the effect on the specified object or event; and

3. Clearly describes the cause and the effect with proper terminology.

These responses can be judged using a bi-level or multi-level scoring guide. The teacher can design these criteria to specifically refer to targeted content. An example is the fifth grade critical thinking exercise mentioned earlier in this chapter, wherein the children were asked to describe the playing of the "F" on the Baroque soprano recorder (in the exercise, the children played the pattern A-G-F-G-A). In this task, the assessment criteria might include:

The response

1. Mentions the fingering as the causative agent, the soprano recorder as the object affected, and the note "F" as the effect of the new fingering;

2. States that the placement of the fingers on the recorder determines the note produced; and

3. Using proper terminology, describes that the length of the vibrating air column within the recorder results in the pitch of the note, and the pitch F is lower than the pitch G because the addition of the three fingers of the right hand lengthen the air column.

This task can be efficiently scored using a bi-level guide for each criterion, recorded as a series of "+" or "–" markings in the data collection instrument.

Making Connections:

Evidence of *making connections* is found in verbal responses. This process allows students to find commonalities in separate events or phenomena within a particular discipline or between disciplines, including (1) musical works, performances, or concepts; (2) music and the other arts; and (3) music and disciplines outside the arts. When examining oral or written responses for evidence of this process, teachers should look for:

1. Mention of the specific events or phenomena;

2. Mention of shared or related characteristics between or among the events or phenomena, which can be *aesthetic* characteristics, referring to the use of artistic elements or concepts in the service of producing an object or event within a particular domain (for most general music teachers, this domain will be music only); *structural* characteristics, which have to do with the properties of form and/or structural organization of specified events or phenomena; or characteristics related to *function* or *purpose,* which have to do with why the event or phenomenon exists and how it serves the domain in which it occurs; and

3. Statements that are clear descriptions of these connections.

General assessment criteria might include (but not be limited to):

The response

1. Specifically mentions the events or phenomena and the relevant discipline(s);

2. States the shared characteristics of the events or phenomena in terms that are appropriate for the discipline(s) in which they occur; and

3. Clearly describes the connections that result in the designation of the specified characteristics as "shared."

These general criteria can then be designed to (1) include specific content that has been taught and is the basis for the task and (2) include the relevant disciplines (if this is part of the task) that the connections are made between.

These criteria can be scored using either a bi-level or multi-level scoring guide, and the number of criteria for each specific task may help the teacher decide how many levels of achievement he or she will assess.

> **Example:** A fourth grade class has been studying perspective in visual arts and listening to Gregorian chant in music. Through their study of Gregorian chant, they have reinforced the concept of unison singing. The teacher places a fifteenth century painting that employs a two-dimensional ("flat") perspective before the class and plays a Gregorian chant for the class as they look at the painting. The students are asked to discuss what the painting and the chant may have in common in terms of perspective.

> **Sample response:** "The painter used a perspective that does not give depth to the picture; the faces, animals, and everything else in the painting is flat. The music is in unison, and even though there are many voices, they are all singing the same melody. This unison sound does not give depth to the sound like it would if it had harmony or an accompaniment, making it seem like the musical version of 'flat.' Even though the painter and the composer used different art forms, they both have applied a 'flat' perspective to their work."

The assessment criteria for this example task and response might include:

The response

1. Mentions the specific works of art; and

2. Discusses and makes appropriate connections between the ways in which the composer and the artist used perspective to achieve their final products.

These criteria can be assessed quickly with a bi-level scoring guide, with the sample response above being encoded as "+/+" in the grade book or data collection instrument.

Identifying the Main Idea:

Evidence of *identifying the main idea* is found primarily in verbal responses. This process allows students to find and recognize the central point of a musical work or event. The central point can also be aesthetic, structural, or related to the function or purpose of the work or event. When seeking verbal evidence of this process, teachers should look for (1) mention of the specific work or event being considered, (2) a clear statement of the central idea, and (3) supporting statements that reinforce the student's statement of the central idea. Generalized criteria for assessment might include:

The response

1. Refers to the specific work being considered;

2. Clearly states or recognizes the main idea or point of the musical work or event; and

3. Presents concise statements that support the validity of the main idea.

These criteria can then be designed to include the specific content that is the focus of the task. The first two criteria can be easily assessed with a bi-level scoring guide, as either *observed* or *not observed*, and recorded as "+" or "–" in the grade book. The third criterion may be judged with a multi-level scoring guide if the teacher wishes to do so. The multiple levels could be designed to account for numbers of supporting statements used and/or the quality of the statements. An example of this process was presented earlier in the first grade example of critical thinking prompts. In this example, the first graders were given the opportunity to move to the sections of Kodàly's "Viennese Musical Clock." The piece is in rondo form, ABACADA. The children were prompted to discuss which part was Kodàly's "favorite" and why. Because this assessment task is a discussion, the responses will be oral, not written; this is the recommended format for young children. The criteria for assessing the children's responses might include:

The response

1. Mentions the composer's name or the name of the piece;

2. Indicates the main theme as the main idea (the A-section theme); young children will likely sing the theme to indicate this; and

3. Presents valid statements supporting this as the main idea.

Appropriate responses to the third criterion include (but are not limited to):

1. References to the fact that the "A" section (which contains the main theme) was featured four times in the work;

2. The instruments used in the main theme resemble the sound of European musical clocks; and

3. Association of the "happy" sound of the main theme, with the fun associated with watching the clock's hourly display of moving characters.

The third criterion can be scored with a multi-level guide if time permits, but it is easiest to use a bi-level guide. The resulting data for each response would then be a series of three markings, one for each criterion. The first two criteria can be assessed most readily with a bi-level scoring guide, with "+" representing *observed* and "–" representing *not observed.*

Sequencing:

Evidence of the process of *sequencing* can be found in both performance and verbal responses. Evidence of sequencing takes many forms and is one of the most common critical thinking processes employed in the music classroom. Because music occurs in time, many musical phenomena naturally occur in sequences. The process of sequencing allows children to place or arrange musical attributes in a series or order according to a given or prescribed condition. When seeking evidence of sequencing, teachers should look for (1) mention of the attribute(s) being sequenced and the condition(s) under which the attributes are being sequenced, (2) manipulation of the attributes in concordance with the given condition(s), and (3) an appropriate statement or product demonstration of the completed sequence. Generalized criteria for assessment might include:

The response

1. Mentions the attributes and the sequencing criterion;

2. Demonstrates or explains how the attributes are changed in order to meet the sequencing criterion; and

3. Demonstrates or states the final form of the completed sequence.

In the first grade critical thinking example presented earlier, the sequencing process is also demonstrated when the children place the sections of the form of the "Viennese Musical Clock" in the correct order. Another example of a sequencing task is one in which children are asked to order pitches according to a given criterion, such as from high to low, low to high, etc., or to aurally recognize the direction in which pitches are ordered.

Assessment of each criterion devised for such tasks is best completed using a bi-level scoring guide; these criteria are either *met* or *not met* in sequencing tasks.

Developing Criteria for Judgment:

Evidence of *developing criteria* for *judgment* is going to be presented in verbal form. Of all the processes discussed in this book, this process relies the most upon prior experience. Students require a number of guided experiences in criteria development in order to gain a cognitive storehouse (DeTurk, 1989) of these from which to draw when they develop their own judgment criteria. The first step in this process is to define a specific musical event or work that will be the focus of the criteria to be developed. Next, the student is engaged in designing the specific criteria, based on the desired attributes of the final event or product. Then, the scoring procedure should be determined so that the quality of the final event or product can be established. The student's response to such a task should bear evidence that these steps were taken. The generalized assessment criteria might include:

The response

1. Clearly states the musical event or work that is the focus of the criteria developed;

2. Carefully presents the important attributes of the finished event or product in the form of complete statements that form the criteria for judgment; and

3. Provides a clear and well-supported scoring procedure so that the level or quality of the achievement of each of the developed criteria can be appropriately measured.

These criteria can then be designed to accommodate the specifics of the task. The criteria should cover the important goals of the event or work.

Example: Fifth graders have just completed a composition project in which they had to compose, notate, and perform a melody at least two phrases in length, and they have been assigned the task of creating at least three criteria for judgment that they feel represent the important goals of the project.

Sample response:

1. *The composition is notated correctly.*

Scoring: 3 = the notation is perfect
2 = the majority of the notation is correct
1 = the majority of the notation is incorrect

2. *The composition contains at least two musical phrases.*

Scoring: 4 = the phrases in the melody share an
antecedent/consequent relationship
3 = the melody contains more than two phrases
2 = the melody contains two phrases
1 = the melody is not structured in phrases

3. *The performance of the composition was accurate.*

Scoring: 3 = the performance was perfect
2 = the performance was mostly accurate
1 = the performance was not accurate

The assessment criteria that the teacher would use for this sample task and response might include:

The response

1. Mentions the specific project—composition;

2. Presents at least three criteria that represent important attributes of the completed composition that match the goals of the project; and

3. Provides appropriate scoring guides that allow the quality or level of the criteria achievement to be adequately judged.

These criteria can be assessed using either bi-level or multi-level guides, depending on the teacher's assessment goals for this project.

Synthesis:

Evidence of the process of *synthesis* is found in performance or verbal responses. The synthesis of musical ideas occurs when separate ideas are combined into a new, different, and sometimes better idea. This is also embodied in the "gestalt" effect as it occurs in music, where the *whole* is greater than the sum of its parts. Students engaged in synthesis generally are examining and combining the strengths of several melodic, rhythmic, or structural ideas, or are bringing together established forms or musical practices in new ways. If a teacher wishes to seek verbal evidence of the process of synthesis, he or she should look for the following in a response:

1. The statement of two or more separate musical ideas that are the stimulus of the synthesis;

2. Statements that describe the characteristics of the original ideas that are being merged;

3. A clear description or demonstration of the new, synthesized idea or practice; and

4. Statements that support the synthesized idea or practice as being new and better.

Generalized assessment criteria might include:

The response

1. Presents the musical ideas, thoughts, practices, or materials that serve as the focus of the synthesis process;

2. Lists, categorizes, or states clearly the characteristics of the original musical ideas, thoughts, practices, or materials that are selected for or are part of the synthesis task;

3. Provides a clear statement or demonstration of the newly synthesized *whole* (product or idea); and

4. Presents statements that support the synthesized product or idea as valid, unique, and/or different (sometimes better) than the originals.

These criteria can be judged using a bi-level or multi-level scoring guide. Tasks involving synthesis skills in general music usually

267

General Assessment Criteria for Responses Involving Musical Critical Thinking Skills

Musical Critical Thinking Skill	Response Type(s)	General Assessment Criteria The RESPONSE:	Suggested Scoring Guide(s)
Epistemic Cognition	Performance, Verbal	1. Refers to the work or works of the person whose role is being assumed.	Bi-level
		2. Expresses knowledge of the important professional and/or personal relationships of the individual.	
		3. Contains first-person statements that reflect viewpoints, opinions, and/or beliefs of the assumed individual.	
		4. Presents dramatic characterization of the role that authentically reflects the individual.	
		5. Is objective when examining, discussing, or presenting the thought processes of the assumed individual.	
Classification	Performance, Verbal	1. Specifically mentions the musical objects or phenomena being classified.	Bi-level or Multi-level
		2. States the common attribute or attributes that serve as the sorting mechanism.	
		3. Provides a clear list, statement, or demonstration of the classified musical objects or phenomena.	
Comparison and Contrast	Verbal	1. Includes the names of works, events, or persons being compared and contrasted.	Bi-level or Multi-level
		2. States a (specified) number of specific points in the events/works/lives being compared and contrasted.	
		3. Provides clear statements that describe the points of comparison and contrast.	

Figure 5-6.

Musical Critical Thinking Skill	Response Type(s)	General Assessment Criteria The RESPONSE:	Suggested Scoring Guide(s)
Pattern Recognition	Performance, Verbal	1. Identifies a specific arrangement of notes, durations, instruments, or other musical objects or events. 2. Refers to the specific order in which these occur. 3. Recognizes this specific arrangement in several different temporal locations in music or in other contexts.	Bi-level
Causal Relationships	Verbal	1. Specifically mentions the causal agent and the musical object or event that is affected. 2. States the action of the causal agent that results in the effect on the specified musical object or event. 3. Clearly describes the cause and effect with proper terminology.	Bi-level or Multi-level
Making Connections	Verbal	1. Specifically mentions the events or phenomena, and the relevant discipline(s). 2. States the shared characteristics (aesthetic, structural, or functional) of the events or phenomena in terms that are appropriate for the discipline(s) in which they occur. 3. Clearly describes the connections that result in the designation of the specified characteristics as "shared."	Bi-level or Multi-level
Identifying the Main Idea	Verbal	1. Refers to the specific work being considered. 2. Clearly states or recognizes the main idea or point of the musical work or event. 3. Presents concise statements that support the validity of the main idea.	Bi-level or Multi-level

Figure 5-6. (continued)

Musical Critical Thinking Skill	Response Type(s)	General Assessment Criteria The RESPONSE:	Suggested Scoring Guide(s)
Sequencing	Performance, Verbal	1. Mentions the attributes and the sequencing criterion. 2. Demonstrates or explains how the attributes are changed in order to meet the sequencing criterion. 3. Demonstrates or states the final form of the completed sequence.	Bi-level
Developing Criteria for Judgment	Verbal	1. Clearly states the musical event/work that is the focus of the criteria. 2. Presents the important attributes of the finished event or product in the form of complete statements that form the criteria for judgment. 3. Provides a clear scoring procedure so that the level or quality of achievement of each of the developed criteria can be appropriately measured.	Bi-level or Multi-level
Synthesis	Performance, Verbal	1. Presents the musical ideas, thoughts, practices, or materials that serve as the focus of the synthesis process. 2. Lists, categorizes, or states the characteristics of the original musical ideas, thoughts, practices, or materials that are selected for or are part of the synthesis task. 3. Provides a clear statement or presentation of the newly synthesized "whole." 4. Presents statements that support the newly synthesized "whole" as valid, unique, and/or different from (and sometimes better than) the originals.	Bi-level or Multi-level

Figure 5-6. (continued)

involve direct experience with combining elements of different, known musical materials. For example, a teacher who is having third graders build musical instruments (usually unpitched percussion) may ask the children to create a "new instrument that combines features of two or more instruments that we already have in the room." Another developmentally appropriate task involving synthesis for older general music students might include the combining of specific melodies or rhythms into new melodies or rhythms that share features of the old melodies/rhythms. The synthesis of ideas and thoughts can be started around grade two or three, but most students will not be fully developmentally ready for this type of thinking until they are older.

Assessing Other Forms of Writing

In addition to (and sometimes in conjunction with) the assessment of tasks that involve critical thinking skills or concepts, music teachers often assign written reports, research projects, integrated projects (refer to chapter 2), or journals. The purpose of these is to further learning or, as it is in the case of journal writing, the development of metacognition and self-reflection. The assessment of these written works will be addressed here.

Written reports and research projects in general music are content-focused and most often have to do with specific composers, instruments and instrument families, or a topic related to the musical elements—melody, harmony, timbre, rhythm, and form. Assessment criteria for these types of assignments are largely determined by the specific components that are to be included in the written report. These components include (but are not limited to): (1) coverage of the topic (the scope of the report), (2) research and study involved, (3) appropriate use of musical terminology, (4) organization and presentation, (5) timeliness, and (6) writing skills (there is more later on this topic).

Scoring guides for these criteria can be bi-level or multi-level, depending on the extent to which the teacher wishes to distinguish among the reports. For most music teachers, three levels are sufficient for these criteria: *adequately meets the criterion* (3 or +), *does not meet the criterion* (1 or –), or *somewhat meets the criterion* (2 or √). Sample generalized criteria and scoring guides might include:

1. *The report contains detailed information pertaining to the topic.*

   Scoring: 3 = adequate detailed information on the topic
             2 = presents less than adequate information
             1 = presents little or no detailed information

2. *The report remains focused on the topic.*

   Scoring: 3 = stays on the topic; does not lose focus
             2 = stays on the topic throughout some of the report; loses focus occasionally
             1 = topic wanders; does not stay focused

3. *The report uses musical terms appropriately.*

   Scoring: 3 = musical vocabulary is correctly spelled and properly used
             2 = use of musical vocabulary is inconsistent
             1 = musical terms are misspelled and incorrectly used

4. *The report shows evidence of research and further study outside the music classroom.*

   Scoring: 3 = appropriate research is evidenced in the level of information included in the report, as well as in the bibliography and references
             2 = research has been done, but the report and supporting references indicate it is inadequate for the topic
             1 = little or no research has been completed

5. *The report is organized neatly and presented in an acceptable form, in a timely manner.*

Scoring: 3 = the report is presented (turned in) prior to or on the due date, is neat, clean, and well organized

2 = the report is either untimely or not presented in a neat, clean, and well-organized format

1 = the report is neither timely nor neat, clean, or well organized

6. Optional—*The components of language are used correctly and skillfully.* (See a later section of this chapter for these suggestions.)

These general criteria can then be adapted to the specifics of the report or research project being assessed. The scoring guides can also be adapted to accommodate the desired levels of skill.

The design of assessment criteria for integrated projects is also directly related to the content, scope, and amount of writing required for the project. For example, review the integrated projects that were presented in chapter 2 (see Figures 2-6 and 2-7). The Radio Play project requires specific writing skills and organization throughout the entire project, whereas the Game-Building project requires writing in the form of weekly logs and game rules. The establishment of criteria related to writing in these two projects is necessarily affected by the amount of writing and the importance of the writing to the finished project. The generalized criteria for the writing component of these projects follow the basic form of the report criteria listed above, but adapted to the specifics of the project. The rubrics for the Game-Building Project (Figure 2-7) and the Radio Play Project (Figure 2-6) are located in Figures 5-8 and 5-9.

The Game-Building rubric converts the five requirements for the project into the five criteria for assessment. Each criterion is assessed using a multi-level scoring guide; criteria 1, 2, 4, and 5 are assessed at four levels of achievement; the third criterion is assessed at three levels. The Radio Play rubric presents the expectations for the plays as they were given in the project, and presents two or three criteria for the assessment of each expectation. Each criterion in this rubric is assessed using the same four-level scoring guide (this scoring guide follows the general format presented in Figure 2-8).

Metacognitive writing includes self-assessment, self-reflection, and writing about individual musical preferences, tastes, and opinions. These writing experiences serve the purpose of allowing students time to examine their own learning and thought processes, and to place their accumulated experience with and knowledge about music in a personal context.

Metacognition is considered both a *critical thinking skill* (Beane, 1989) and an important *thinking direction* in which teachers should guide students (see Figure 5-4). Responses to metacognitive tasks are most often written in students' personal music journals. Questions, or prompts, for metacognitive tasks can be generalized as follows (in this list, "I" refers to the student):

1. How did I come to know this?

2. How do I know that I know this?

3. Did I meet the expectations I was supposed to meet?

4. Did I meet my own personal expectations?

5. Did I help, cooperate, or contribute to the best of my ability?

6. Is this something that I would do again?

7. How do I feel about this?

Rubric for Game-Building Project

1. The game has a clear set of rules that are easy to follow.
   The rules:
   4 = are clear, in the correct order, and neatly presented, using correct grammar
   3 = are clear and in the correct order, but there are a few grammar errors
   2 = are not clear and/or not in the correct order, the presentation is not neat, and the grammar is poor
   1 = are incomplete, sloppy, and grammatically incorrect

2. The game has a hand-made game board and set of pieces (cards, spinner, moving artifacts, etc.).
   The game board:
   4 = is superbly designed and drawn, all pieces are well produced and show great attention to neatness and detail
   3 = is adequate for the game, and the pieces and artifacts are useful and practical for playing the game, the design and drawing are acceptable
   2 = is not well designed, seems ineffective for the purpose of the game, and does not show attention to neatness and detail
   1 = is not useful or practical for the game, the design is poor, and the presentation is sloppy

3. The game has an original title.
   The title:
   3 = is original and relevant to the game
   2 = is not original
   1 = is not provided

4. The group consistently turns in a log of the steps taken to create the game at the end of each class.
   The log:
   4 = is exceptionally neat, clear, easy to read, and comprehensive
   3 = is neat and easy to read, but only presents an outline
   2 = is messy and unclear, and leaves out important steps
   1 = is incomplete, messy, and not a representation of a sincere group effort

5. The final presentation and demonstration of the game to the class is easy to understand and involves the entire group.
   The presentation and demonstration:
   4 = is clear, well-spoken, easy to follow, and involves the entire group
   3 = is clear and well-spoken, but does not involve the entire group
   2 = is difficult to understand and follow
   1 = is incomplete or not clear, and makes no sense

Figure 5-8.

Rubric for Radio Play Project

To the judges:

Using the following scale, please rate the following statements for the radio play performance you are about to hear:

> *Scoring Guide:*
> 4 = exceeds expectations
> 3 = meets expectations
> 2 = below expectations
> 1 = no evidence of the criterion

Expectations   **Rating**

The play:

1. **Is engaging and interesting for the listener.**
   a. Each character is clearly introduced the first time he or she is presented. _____
   b. Each character is clearly articulated, easy to understand, and consistently voiced throughout. _____
   c. The story holds the listener's interest and is clearly presented. _____

2. **Is well written and easy to "visualize."**
   a. The writing is clear, specific, and clarifies the action. _____
   b. The scene(s) is(are) presented through appropriate word and action cues. _____

3. **Presents factual content about music that is a natural outgrowth of the story.**
   a. The musical facts are interesting and relevant to the story. _____
   b. At the end of the story, the listener is given the opportunity to check his or her understanding of the story's factual musical content. _____

4. **Uses appropriate musical examples and sound effects to enhance the story.**
   a. The musical examples are well placed, enhance the story, and provide musical illustrations of the story topic. _____
   b. The sound effects are appropriate and enhance the story. _____

5. **Rate the overall effect of the play using the following scale:**
   4 = outstanding
   3 = satisfactory
   2 = less than satisfactory
   1 = completely unsatisfactory

   Total: _____
   (add the ten ratings together)

Figure 5-9.

Using the steps explained earlier in the chapter about devising critical thinking prompts, these questions can then be adapted to the specific content of the music lesson. For example, to engage students in a metacognitive exercise after a vocal pitch accuracy assessment, the teacher might devise a prompt such as: "How do you know when you match pitch?" This is a "how do you know" question that is directed toward the lesson content, which was pitch matching.

Metacognitive responses can be designed in two basic formats: *rated* and *open-ended*. The first is a *rated response*. In such a self-assessment, students are given questions and asked to rate themselves. The scoring guides that students use for this can range from Likert scales, rating themselves from 1 through 7 or higher, with 1 meaning the least level of achievement and 7 representing the highest level of achievement, or with simple word choices like "yes/no/sometimes" or "always/never/sometimes." Figure 5-10 represents a sample self-assessment related to the Game-Building Project discussed earlier. The students were asked to rate themselves from 1 through 7 (a Likert scale) on each of the questions. The criteria for rated self-assessments usually reflect the behavioral objectives of the lesson or project, deal with musical preference, or request opinions.

For most metacognitive tasks, however, the best response format is *open-ended*. In open-ended responses, students are given time to write a few sentences or paragraphs in response to the task prompt. This is dependent on the teacher's intention as well as the activity and its duration; the longer the activity, the more in-depth the self-assessment can be. Earlier in this chapter an example of a metacognitive prompt was presented in the third grade critical thinking task, wherein the third graders were asked: "How do you know you are matching pitch when you sing?" A sample response from third grader John: "I hear the note in my head, then I sing it;

Self-Assessment: Musical Game-Building Project

Name _____ Teacher _____

The other people in my group were:

_____

_____

_____

Rate yourself from 1 to 7 on the following points using this scale:

1	2	3	4	5	6	7
(never)			(sometimes)			(consistently)

Circle one:

1. I fully participated in the building of our game.

1 2 3 4 5 6 7

2. I cooperated with others during the building of our game.

1 2 3 4 5 6 7

3. I contributed to the selection of our game topic.

1 2 3 4 5 6 7

4. I contributed to the fact-finding of our game.

1 2 3 4 5 6 7

5. I helped create the artwork for our game.

1 2 3 4 5 6 7

6. I enjoyed completing this project.

1 2 3 4 5 6 7

7. I have learned more about our topic because of our game.

1 2 3 4 5 6 7

Figure 5-10.

when the note in my head and the sound of my voice are the same, then I know I am matching the pitch."

Because of the nature of these types of questions/prompts, response assessment is best left as a bi-level, single-criterion scoring guide. The teacher should limit his or her interest in assessing only whether or not these responses are completed. That is, when these types of responses are assigned, it is best to encode "+" in the grade book if the student *completes a response* and "–" if the *task is ignored.* Keeping track of these responses serves to keep the teacher informed of the development of musical self-awareness of students and to signal potential problems when a pattern of non-completion emerges.

An Alternative Verbal Assessment: The Concept Map

In chapter 1, the distinction was made between alternative and authentic assessments. To review, an alternative assessment technique in music is one that is *situated within an authentic context other than that in which the musical learning took place.* A particularly effective alternative assessment that is useful for music is *concept mapping.* The concept mapping technique was originally developed as a metacognitive tool to facilitate learning in other disciplines (Novak, 1990a, b; 1991). This tool can be adapted to the assessment of musical content and concept learning.

A concept map is a drawing that serves as a format through which a student's understanding of a particular concept can be exhibited. Another name for this technique, which is summarized below, is *webbing.* During the concept mapping process:

1. A student begins with a blank sheet of paper and in the center writes the name of the concept to be mapped.

2. A circle is then drawn around the word for the concept.

3. Words that represent knowledge related to the concept are then "mapped" around this center term.

4. The student circles these words, then connects related words (ideas) to the center with lines. Lines may also be drawn between and among the outlying words if the student feels that they are related.

5. This process continues until the student feels he or she has achieved an adequate representation of what is known about the central concept and the interrelationships of knowledge within the concept.

When administering a concept map assessment, the appropriate procedure is as follows:

1. Students should draw a "practice" map on a scratch sheet of paper or, if available, an individual chalkboard.

2. The children should then be given time to draw and edit their maps until they feel they have produced the "best one."

3. At that time, the students should redraw the map onto the blank sheet that will be turned in to the teacher.

Concept maps provide a valuable means for the music specialist to assess a child's content knowledge through the terms and explanations the student includes in his or her drawing. The concept map also suggests a child's conceptual understanding through the connections the child makes between and among the relevant terms and information included in the map. Because specific terms are required in a concept map, generalized assessment criteria might include:

The concept map

1. Presents the required terms;

2. Demonstrates knowledge of the concept through appropriate connections between and among terms; and

3. Is neat and easy to read.

These three criteria can then be further specified to include significant distinctions that are important to the teacher administering the task. For example, "presents the required terms" might be expanded to include spelling so that it would read, "presents the required terms, with proper spelling" (there will be more on grammatical specifications in the next section of this chapter).

The first two criteria are best assessed with a multi-level scoring guide, and the third criterion can be assessed with either a bi-level or multi-level guide.

Interpreting Concept Maps

In this section, some concept maps drawn by sixth grade students will be assessed according to a specific set of criteria. These concept maps were drawn in the spring of 1999 at the conclusion of a unit on harmony. The terms studied in the unit and their definitions included:

- *Harmony*—a confluence of pitches that creates a specific sound

- *Scale*—a stepwise progression of tones used in melodies and harmonies

- *Major*—the modality of a scale, triad, or interval, indicated by an uppercase Roman numeral

- *Minor*—the modality of a scale, triad, or interval, indicated by a lowercase Roman numeral

- *Modality*—the sound quality of a scale, chord, or interval that is determined by its arrangement of whole steps and half steps

- *Interval*—two pitches sounding simultaneously

- *Chord*—three or more pitches sounding simultaneously

- *Triad*—a three-note chord

- *Tonic*—the triad built on the first tone of the scale, indicated with a Roman numeral I (major) or i (minor)

- *Dominant*—the triad built on the fifth tone (up from the tonic) of the scale, indicated with a Roman numeral V (major) or v (minor)

The students were informed that the required terms for the concept map were *harmony, scale, interval, chord, triad, tonic,* and *dominant* (and their Roman numeral representations, I or i and V or v), *major* and *minor.* The assessment criteria and their scoring guides were as follows:

1. *The concept map presents the required terms and their definitions.*

   Scoring: 4 = in addition to the required terms and definitions, there are terms present that are beyond the requirements, and these are defined correctly
   3 = the terms are present and defined
   2 = the terms are present but not all defined correctly
   1 = the terms are not all present

2. *The concept map indicates an understanding of the relationships among the harmonic vocabulary through appropriate connections.*

   Scoring: 4 = connections are correct and indicate exceptional understanding
   3 = connections are mostly correct and indicate adequate understanding
   2 = connections are mostly correct but insufficient to indicate inadequate understanding
   1 = connections are mostly incorrect and indicate little understanding

3. *The concept map is neat, easy to read, and well organized.*
    Scoring: "+" = the map is clean, readable, and adequately organized
                 "–" = the map is messy, difficult to read, and shows little organization

Three concept maps are illustrated in Figures 5-11 through 5-13, and each map represents different levels of learning and understanding.

The map in Figure 5-11 presents the required terms but fails to define (or spell) them all correctly. The connections among the terms show some understanding of their relationship to the term *harmony* but not their interrelationships with the other terms; for example, the "triad" and "chord" circles should be connected. This map, however, is neat and well organized. The assessment of this map yielded a rating of "2/2/+," which was encoded on the teacher's data collection instrument.

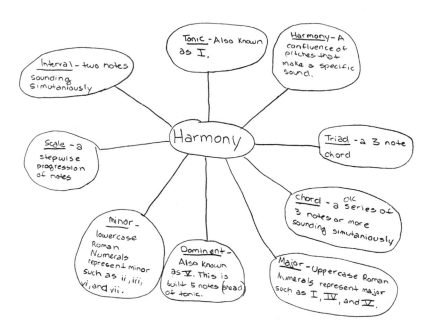

Figure 5-11.

The map in Figure 5-12 presents the required terms and definitions, shows adequate understanding of the relationships through their connections, and is neat and well organized. The teacher made a minor correction: notice in the circle defining "major and minor modality," the student is encouraged to change the words "used in" to "describes." This, however, does not constitute changing the achievement level of the first criterion from 3 to 2. This map was assessed as follows: "3/3/+."

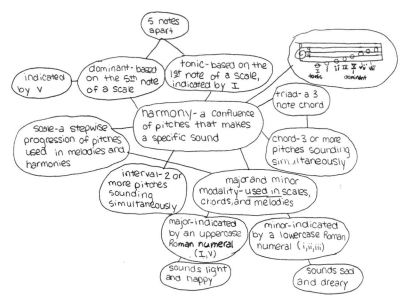

Figure 5-12.

The map in Figure 5-13 presents an extraordinary level of understanding of harmony. There are terms and definitions that exceed what was required, the connections between the terms suggest an exceptional understanding of the unit, and the map is neat and well organized. This student studies music outside of school, and this additional knowledge likely comes from this additional training. This map was assessed as follows: "4/4/+."

Concept maps, however, should never be used as sole measures of concept learning. A thorough examination of a child's

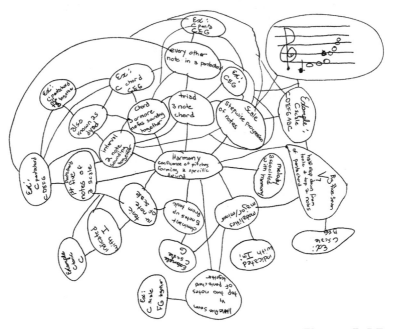

Figure 5-13.

understanding of a concept must include performance observations as well as tools such as the concept map. For example, it would be meaningless for students to know the basic concepts of harmony without being able to perform the harmonic changes themselves as part of the songs and pieces from which the concepts were extracted. Observations and similar authentic assessments help strengthen the reliability of the concept maps—that is, they help to substantiate that the map is not just a drawing of recalled words, but that it is indeed a representation of the child's understanding of the concept. Assessment of both performance *and* conceptual understanding are necessary to gauge the progress of musical learning. A combination of various assessments can provide teachers with a reasonably reliable view of what their students are learning (review "Assessing Musical Concepts" in chapter 3).

Other Considerations

Assessing Grammar and Writing Skills

The extent to which the written responses are assessed for their grammatical and spelling accuracy is up to the music specialist. Several factors may influence the decision to include criteria that pertain to language components (which include grammar, spelling, punctuation, capitalization, penmanship, sentence structure, tenses, subject/verb agreements, etc.).

1. The music teacher needs to explore his or her philosophical views on writing in the music class; this must be viewed as being a valued and important part of music education before it can be successful.

2. If this is deemed important enough to pursue, the music teacher then becomes responsible for becoming familiar with and helping to meet school and district directives with respect to writing across the grade levels.

3. The music teacher also needs to ensure that the writing completed in the music room is of the same quality as that completed in the classroom; some students may write with less attention to the components of language in the music room because they feel that it is "not as important" or "not going to be assessed" as stringently as it would be in the classroom. The approach used by the students' other teachers to writing assignments is important; the music specialist should confer with these teachers to establish common writing requirements. This enables students to link their writing in music to their writing in the classroom and helps students unify the writing experience in both learning environments (I refer the reader to Whitcomb, 1999, for an excellent discussion of language components in music).

A good practice for establishing assessment parameters for language components is to select a representative group of responses written in the music room, present the classroom or language arts teacher with these, and request comments on the use of language in the responses as it compares to language use in the classroom. Most classroom teachers will cooperate well in this procedure. Because writing is a valued and often-assessed skill in the overall curriculum, these teachers will appreciate the music specialist's efforts in furthering language skills. In the rare case where a teacher does not want to cooperate, simply use the information you gather from other classroom teachers to assist in the determination of distinctions between poor, adequate, and good writing across the grade levels. The general criteria for good writing are of importance to the music teacher. The music teacher should never accept sloppy, poorly written materials from students "just because they are writing in music class."

Assessing Other Non-Musical Aspects of Music Tasks

When teachers engage their students in complex tasks such as integrated projects, they are often faced with the assessment of aspects of the project that are nonmusical and not language-based. For example, the Game-Building Project rubric (Figure 5-8) includes criteria that assess the game board design, the artifacts made for the game, as well as their usefulness to the game. The Radio Play Project rubric (Figure 5-9) presents criteria that assess the characterization, voicing, and dramatic skills of the students. Other projects may require the assessment of dance.

In situations where these aspects of the finished product are important enough to be assessed, the music specialist should consult with the "in-school experts" on the topic or skill to be assessed. The music teacher should confer with the visual arts teacher on the assessment of design, the physical education or dance teacher on the assessment of dance, and the English/drama teacher(s) about the assessment of acting, voicing, and character-ization. In some instances, these specialists may actually assist in the assessment of the projects, providing expert judgment in their areas of specialty.

If the school does not have any of these specialists on staff, then it is possible that there are one or two classroom teachers that may be able to provide a level of expertise beyond what the music teacher can do alone. If this is not the case, then there are three possibilities remaining:

1. The music specialist can research and find resources that will help him or her to gain some expertise in the assessment of visual art, drama, or dance.

2. The teacher can assess these aspects of the project with a bi-level scoring guide as either *acceptable* or *not acceptable*.

3. Least desirable, the teacher does not assess these aspects at all. This is least desirable because some students may not put forth their "best effort" in areas that they know are not going to be assessed.

Summary

- Responding mode assessments place students in the role of listener or consumer of music, in which they are asked to *listen, judge, and evaluate musical performances and works*. Embedded in this activity is the process of musical *critical thinking*.

- Critical thinking in music is a very important facilitator of verbal musical responses, whether they are oral or written.

- Teachers can direct critical thinking in music in one of three directions: (1) *procedurally*, (2) *reflectively*, and (3) *metacogni-tively*. *Procedural* thinking occurs during musical performance, when the performer is updating and altering his or her performance to suit the immediate musical conditions or context. *Reflection* has to do with the examination of past musical experience in relation to present musical experience. *Metacognition* occurs when one thinks about one's own thinking, learning, and/or development.

- Critical thinking skills facilitate musical thinking. The specific skills discussed in this chapter are *epistemic cognition, comparison and contrast, pattern recognition, causal relationships, making connections, identifying the main idea, sequencing, developing criteria for judgment,* and *synthesis.*

- When assessing verbal responses to responding mode assessment tasks, teachers may look for specific content or evidence of the critical thinking skills that were employed to formulate the response. The criteria devised for these responses can be assessed with either bi-level or multi-level scoring guides.

- The assessment of other forms of writing such as reports, research projects, and integrated projects is based on task-specific criteria, which include *coverage of the topic, evidence of research and outside study, vocabulary, organization and presentation, timeliness,* and *writing skills.* These criteria can be assessed with either bi-level or multi-level scoring guides.

- Metacognitive writing—self-reflection, self-assessment, musical preferences, opinions, and tastes—is best assessed using a bi-level, single-criterion scoring guide.

- Concept mapping is an alternative form of verbal assessment. These maps are assessed with respect to whether or not they *present the required terms, express appropriate connections among the terms,* and their *organization/neatness.* Bi-level or multi-level scoring guides can be used.

- The music teacher must decide the extent to which grammar and writing skills are assessed.

- When assessing other nonmusical aspects of a project, such as visual art, music teachers may consult with the in-school experts on the topic or skill, or simply assess the criteria using a bi-level scoring guide with respect to each criterion being *met* or *not met.*

Questions for Clarification

1) The work of researchers, philosophers, and theorists all indicate that there is not yet a common consensus on the nature of _____ _____.

2) Critical thinkers in music have three primary avenues of expression, and these are _____ _____, _____, and _____.

3) The first and most important step in preparing to administer a critical thinking task is to _____ _____ _____.

4) Critical thinking prompts are stated in the form of a question or _____ _____.

5) While evidence of critical thinking can be found in children's verbal responses, teachers should never attempt to determine a student's _____ _____ _____ in a particular skill.

6) When establishing criteria for determining product evidence of critical thinking in verbal responses, the teacher must first identify the _____ _____ _____ targeted in the task that is expected in the response.

7) When assessing reports, research projects, or integrated projects, the extent to which writing and grammar skills are assessed is determined by the _____ _____.

8) Concept mapping is a form of verbal _____ _____.

9) The assessment of metacognitive responses is best done using a _____ - _____, _____ - _____ scoring guide.

10) When devising criteria for the assessment of nonmusical aspects of complex tasks that are not language based, the best course for the music specialist to take is to consult with the _____ - _____ _____ on those topics or skills.

Questions for Discussion

1) Discuss the conceptions of critical thinking in music that have been presented in this chapter. In your view, what is critical thinking in music? Can you define it in a way that suits your personal understanding better than the definition offered in this book?

2) Examine a lesson that you teach, or will teach, and determine the critical thinking skills that are required to

complete the musical activity in the lesson. Share this with the group, and discuss your points of agreement and any differences of opinion that may arise. Why do you agree and/or disagree? Can you come to consensus?

3) Using the same lesson, or another lesson, follow the steps given for developing a critical thinking prompt and then devise one for the lesson. Discuss your prompt with the group, including how it was formulated.

4) Discuss the assessment of concept maps and other forms of writing. Do you believe that reports, research projects, integrated projects, and concept maps provide important assessment data for music teachers? How do you feel about assessing the nonmusical aspects of projects? Would you feel comfortable consulting with other teachers regarding assessment in areas in which you are not an expert?

5) When time is at a premium for most music teachers, how do you feel about the time spent in class engaging students in metacognitive tasks? Is the time justifiable? What are the benefits of this type of activity? The drawbacks?

Assessment Practice

Assessment Practice 1

A fourth grade class has experienced and learned about sixteenth notes, the double division of the beat. They have performed, notated from dictation, and practiced reading sixteenth notes as "four sounds per beat," and eighth notes as "two sounds per beat." Their activities have included rhythmic dictation, speaking and using body percussion with the poem "One-Potato, Two-Potato,

Three-Potato, Four," and playing a piece for melodic percussion from the first volume of the Murray edition of the Orff/Keetman *Music for Children* that contains sixteenth notes. After the three lessons, they are asked to write a response to the following prompt in their journals:

> *For the past three lessons, we have performed and written sixteenth notes. How do sixteenth notes differ from other rhythmic values? How do you know this?*

First, determine what critical thinking skills will be employed in the responses. Then, using the general criteria shown in Figure 5-6, devise a set of criteria and scoring guides to assess the predicted responses. Then, assess the following two responses to this task.

Response 1:

I know that sixteenth notes are faster than quarter notes and eighth notes. They can be written in two different ways:

If you multiply 1/8 x 1/2 = 1/16, which is a sixteenth note.

Response 2:

An example of a double division is the sixteenth note. All sixteenth notes need to have a second line (that means it's double division). A double division is as easy as it sounds. It means a note divided by two is a double division. (Note: By "second line," this student means a second "beam.")

Do the responses meet your criteria? Where are they strong, and where are they weak? Are any post-task adjustments to your scoring guides needed?

Assessment Practice 2

In Assessment Figures A-1 through A-6, you will find metacognitive essays written by students at the end of fourth grade and at the end of fifth grade. Figures A-1 and A-2/3 present Student 1's essays, and Figure A-4 (typeset from the child's original) and A-5/6 present Student 2's essays. The topic of each fourth grade essay is "My musical progress in the fourth grade," and the fifth grade essay topic is "My progress from the 3rd to the 5th grade in music." Read these essays carefully. Then reflect on the following questions, and discuss your thoughts with other colleagues.

1) Each student wrote these essays one year apart. What are the differences in the two essays that might be related to learning and skill? What are the differences in the essays that might be related to natural development?

2) Do the essays present information that is valuable to the music specialist? What can you tell about each student's learning and musical progress from what the essay reveals?

3) Do you believe that the essays are truthful and honest? Can you tell from the essay? If so, how? If not, why?

Assessment Practice 3

Assessment Figures A-7 through A-11 present five concept maps drawn by sixth graders in conjunction with a unit on harmony. The required terms for this map were: harmony, tonic (I), dominant (V), scale, chord, and triad (as defined earlier in this chapter in the "Interpreting Concept Maps" section). Assess these concept maps using either the rubric in this book or your own. What can you tell about each student's understanding of harmony from these maps?

Student 1 at the End of Fourth Grade

4th grade

My Year in Music 4th grade

This year in music we learned how to play the recorder. I had fun playing all of the different songs that we learned. I also liked singing the songs, too. We saw movies about famous composers. All in all the year was fun.

Assessment Figure A-1.

Student 1 at the End of Fifth Grade

My Progress in Writing About Music, Composing and Notating Music, and General Knowledge About Music from 3rd to 5th Grade

After looking through my portfolio, I can see an improvement. I can not only see an improvement, I can feel one. I take piano lessons and that has helped me in music class. Also things I have learnt in music class help me in piano. I can also sing much better. I have learnt alot in music class from different composers to how to play a recorder.

Yes, I am a more knowledgeable musican than I was in third grade. I can do many things that I couldn't do then. I can sing on pitch. I can compose and notate music. And I can play music.

Yes, I am a better and more knowledgeable musican. I know more about music and musicans. In fourth grade I couldn't play the recorder very well and wasn't a very good composer. Now I can play the recorder well and read and compose.

Assessment Figure A-2.

Student 1 at the End of Fifth Grade

Yes, I am a better and more knowledgeable musican than I was at the begining of fifth grade. I am a better performen and composer. I know more about composers and the history of music. I think I am a better notater. I think I can judge music better than before, also. I think I have come a long way in music since third grade.

Assessment Figure A-3.

Student 2 at the End of Fourth Grade

My Year in Music – 4th Grade

In fourth grade music I learned many things. I learned the note names and correct fingering on the recorder, the sounds and beats of different notes such as eighth, quarter, and half notes, and even the correct breathing for the recorder. The songs "All Through the Night" and "Hot Cross Buns" were fun to play on the recorder. I even observed the different ways of life from a long time ago. I had a great time in music this year!

Assessment Figure A-4.

Student 2 at the End of Fifth Grade

My Progress

After looking back at my work from third through fifth grade, I have noticed much improvement in writing about music. I have learned to write about everything that happened in music that day and everything I learned. My writing began to be more descriptive after I knew what was expected of me. I have progressed in adding details to my writing, drawing symbols that I have recently learned, and adding any kind of information about composers from the blackboard. I have grown to appreciate the evaluations when class has ended.

I have also seen improvement in composing and notating music. I have noticed that recently I have been using more and different notes in my music. I even had some sixteenth notes in my fifth grade piece. My music has become more complicated to play because I am advancing in my knowledge of notes, rhythm, and beat. I have a better understanding of the importance of the assignments.

In fourth grade, we performed a small number on the recorder. It wasn't a lot, but it made us feel like we had really learned a lot. We had, but in fifth grade we learned a lot more. For our fifth grade performance in choir, we sang four holiday songs with much enthusiasm. Over the years I believe I have become less nervous before performing

Assessment Figure A-5.

Student 2 at the End of Fifth Grade

because I have become more confident in the music, the teacher, and myself.

Lastly, I think that I have progressed in my knowledge of music (such as composers, terms, music symbols, etc.). Often times in music we have listened to the works of great composers from the past, and I have tried to define the different types of music. When we composed and notated music, I learned some basic musical symbols. I have progressed greatly in the game building project. In building our game we had to learn, understand, and write down many terms, musical symbols, and even the work of some composers. I admit, I did not want to participate in this project when I first heard about it, but not only did it turn out to be fun and exciting, but I learned a lot from this project. I must conclude that I have learned very much in music these past years, and I only hope that I can learn more next year!

Assessment Figure A-6.

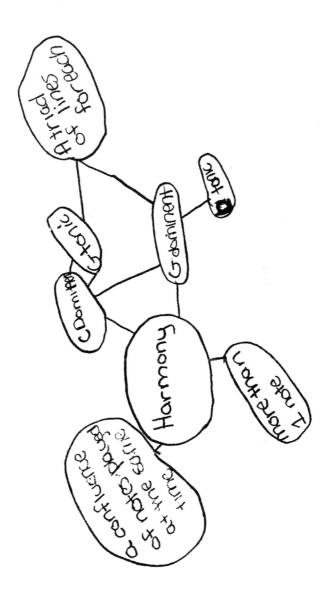

Assessment Figure A-7.

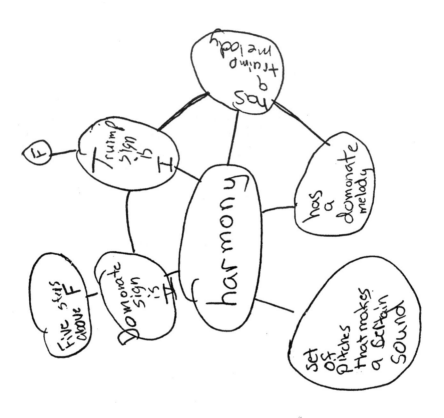

Assessment Figure A-8.

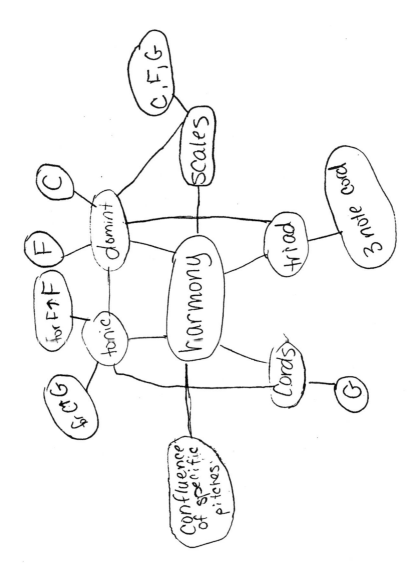

Assessment Figure A-9.

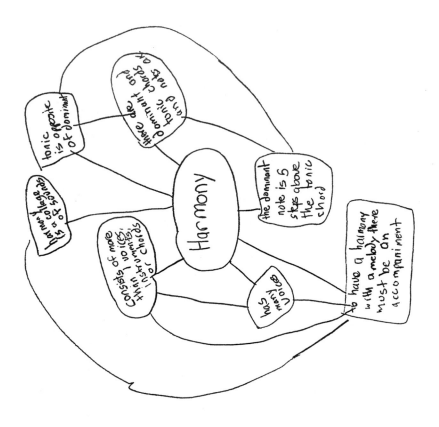

Assessment Figure A-10.

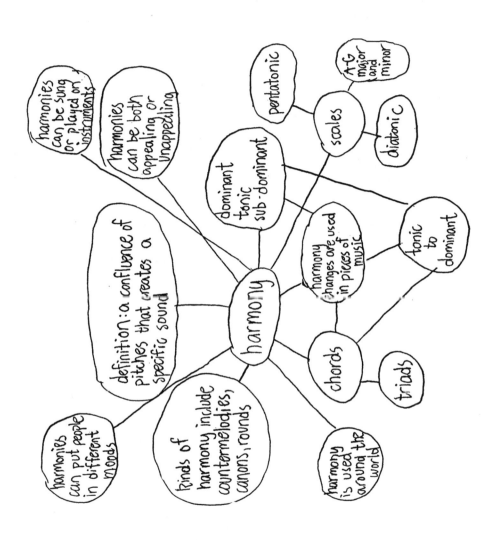

Assessment Figure A-11.

Chapter 6

Portfolios and Profiles: Tying It All Together

The first five chapters of this book have focused upon ways in which classroom music teachers can devise meaningful assessment tasks that are both valid and reliable. The administration of these tasks results in large amounts of data as well as musical materials for each student. In this chapter, the *portfolio* will be introduced as one way in which to manage this data in a manner that is meaningful to the student. Then, this chapter will discuss the *profile system,* a program for organizing data and reporting it to parents through progress reports.

What Is a Portfolio?

A portfolio is a collection of a student's work that he or she feels best represents his or her progress in a particular subject area; it contains examples of the student's work to show the range of skills and abilities possessed by the individual in each area. A portfolio is developed over a period of years in order to show development and growth. It becomes a "case history" of a student's progress. Portfolio entries are not limited to a student's "best work," for if they were, progress from one year to the next would not become evident. A portfolio provides evidence of a student's growth in all of the musical learning areas—*musical skills, literacy, history and literature, analysis and preference,* and *related arts and humanities.* A music portfolio may contain evidence of a student's musical involvement in a variety of contexts: school, home, and community.

Getting Started with Portfolio Building

In the first chapter of this book, the reader was challenged to reflect on personal philosophy of assessment in general music. To get started with portfolio building, one must first examine one's philosophy on the value of this process in general music. The following questions and thoughts can serve as a guide for examining one's beliefs about portfolios and the portfolio-building process:

1. *Do I believe that portfolio building in general music is a good idea?* Children learn in many different ways, and portfolios are one way in which they can examine their work over a period of years to determine their progress and development. Music teachers are in a unique position for guiding students through portfolio development because most teachers serve the same students over a period of as many as six or seven years (from kindergarten through fifth or sixth grade). When students collect and organize their musical work over a period of years, their work assumes a new importance to them.

2. *How do I feel about the portfolio process and its value to a child's musical development?* Students who begin saving musical work from the primary grades learn to be more careful and thorough because they know that it will be kept for them (and parents) to view later. In the upper elementary grades, when the portfolio is actually assembled from these works collected over the years, the process powerfully reveals to students where they *were* musically in earlier grades and where they are *now* in their development and growth. Portfolios provide the evidence that students need to view their own development in music.

3. *Can I give my classes the time to do this without severely impacting their instructional time?* The portfolio-building process is a form of instruction that teaches students several lifelong learning skills. First, students learn the value of keeping track of work over a period of years. Second, they learn that their diligence and care over the years is rewarded with an outcome of which they can be proud: a "book" about their growth and development as musicians. Finally, the portfolio teaches children the importance of organization and neatness, and provides the opportunity to exercise independent selection and choice.

4. *Do I believe that portfolio building is "worth it"?* When students review the work they have collected, they are truly interested and engaged as they build their portfolios. There is a great deal of self-esteem and personal pride placed in the finished portfolio. The portfolio is also a valuable asset for the music specialist, because it provides a comprehensive view of a child's growth and development while under the teacher's instruction. The portfolio provides music teachers evidence of what they have taught over a period of years and can serve as a valuable tool for adjusting and improving instruction.

The portfolio process and the portfolios themselves have valuable and important benefits for the music student and the teacher, as well as the music program itself. Parental interest in the music program is further encouraged when parents are invited to view the music portfolios that their children have constructed. Parents are often limited to viewing the results of music instruction through school performances; the portfolio provides another venue through which they can observe evidence of their child's total musical instruction.

Start "Small"

Because many general music teachers serve hundreds of students and as many as fifty or more classes weekly, it is necessary to first *outline a plan for the gradual introduction of portfolio assessment.* The accumulation of portfolio entries takes place over a period of one or more years, and the long-term nature of this type of project requires careful and steady implementation for success.

How a teacher begins the portfolio process is affected by several factors:

1. The demands of the school and/or the district must be taken into account—will the school or district allow portfolios to be developed gradually?

2. The teacher's schedule and number of schools the teacher serves, number of classes, number of students, and whether or not the teacher "travels" from room to room or has a designated music room affects the manner in which portfolios are started.

In situations where portfolios can be developed gradually, it is recommended that the music teacher *begin with all of the classes at a primary grade level.* A good level at which to begin is second grade, because the children are becoming comfortable with writing and reading. While the teacher can choose to begin with only one class, this is not recommended if it can be avoided. At the end of each academic year, students move to higher grade levels and are assigned new teachers. After one year of starting just one class, the music teacher is then faced with new classes that contain only a few students who have started portfolios.

If the teacher starts with the second grade, each year the portfolios will "move up" with the children until they leave the elementary school (at the end of the fourth, fifth, or sixth grade). As the first year's second grade moves up to third grade, the next year's second grade will start their data collection. This process continues for a period of four years until the entire second, third, fourth, and fifth grade classes (and sixth grade if the elementary school houses these students) are building music portfolios.

Data Collection

Data collection for portfolio development is best started with simple file folders that hold the musical work children complete each year. Students can be asked to bring file folders for music at the beginning of each school year. A request for file folders and other portfolio supplies can be included either on the classroom teachers' supply lists given out at registration at the beginning of the school year or on a special list given out by the music specialist. A sample supply list used by a general music teacher is shown in Figure 6-1.

To get started with file folders, the first thing to do is to *have the students identify the folders with their names.* It is best for the name to be written on the tab at the top of the folder. The best time to accomplish this is during the first lesson of the year, when the groundwork is being laid for classroom practice.

The teacher must also *decide whether one folder will be used each year or over a number of years.*

- If the teacher chooses to have students bring in new folders each year to house that year's work and to keep it separate from the other years' work, the multiple folders can be filed by placing them one within the other, or they can be bound together by a rubber band.

- If the choice is made to house several years' work in one file, then the children need to clearly identify each year's work by grade level. If the combined work is not clearly marked by date and year, the student will be confused about how to organize these entries when the formal portfolio is made in fifth grade. The fifth grader who has collected material since second or third grade will not likely remember the date or grade level at which the work was completed unless it is indicated.

Sample Music Supply List for Portfolio Building

Music Supplies – 1999-2000

August 1999

Dear Parents,

I am pleased to be your child's music teacher for the 1999-2000 school year. Once again I am fortunate to be able to see your child's class for music one hour per week. Your child will need the following supplies for music class:

Grade 3
- one manila file folder
- spiral-bound notebook*
- a sharpened pencil

Grade 5
- one manila file folder
- spiral-bound notebook*
- a sharpened pencil
- a soprano recorder on a necklace

For portfolios:
- 1-inch ring binder notebook
- a set of index dividers
- at least 12 clear page protectors

Grade 4
- one manila file folder
- spiral-bound notebook*
- a sharpened pencil
- In January we will begin recorder, so watch for notices later this year (the recorders will cost around $5.00).

Grade 6**
- one manila file folder
- spiral-bound notebook*
- a sharpened pencil
- a soprano recorder on a necklace
- a set of index dividers
- at least 12 clear page protectors

* This should be a composition-style notebook, suitable for journal writing and note-taking. Please clearly mark (in permanent magic marker if possible) the front of your child's music notebook with the following: name, grade, and classroom teacher.

** If your sixth grader is new to our school and has not created a music portfolio, please follow the fifth grade supply instructions.

If you have any questions, please feel free to call me at school. Thank you for your continued support of our music program!

Sincerely,

Figure 6-1.

The files are best managed by *storing them in a file cabinet in the music room.* Most principals will gladly provide the music specialist a filing cabinet when they know the teacher is guiding students through portfolio building. General music teachers can manage 600 or more student files in two small, two-drawer filing cabinets. Because music specialists see their students thirty to sixty minutes weekly, the files do not fill up rapidly. By the time the files begin to get large, it is time to convert the file folders into formal portfolios.

It is good practice to *train students to do their own filing.* Student access to files is very important, and even very young children can find their files without any trouble as long as they know where they are in the classroom. It is recommended that students be allowed to access their files/portfolios at any time during the school year.

What Can Be Filed: Some Suggestions

Every assessment task that is completed yields data or a product that can be placed in the student's music file. These items include:

- Compositions;
- Notation assessments;
- Copies of progress reports;
- Evidence of performance assessments;
- Responses to critical thinking exercises;
- Metacognitive writings from music journals;
- Evidence of performances, both in and outside of school, such as programs and photos of participation in musical events;

- Evidence of concert attendance, such as programs and written critiques/evaluations of the performances attended;

- Audiotapes of performances—songs, compositions, programs; and

- Anything you or your program deems an important measure of musical progress (for example, many series' books now have pages in their Resource Manuals that can be copied and completed by students as portfolio entries).

For most general music specialists, audio- and videotape management is an issue. Tapes are a requirement for a good *performance* portfolio, but they are not an absolute necessity for a good *general music* portfolio. Unless the school district requires tapes, the decision to include audio- and videotapes is up to the teacher, or this can be left up to the student.

The best method for *storing a tape in a file folder* is to place it in a sealable, sandwich-type plastic bag, then tape or staple the bag to the side of the file folder near the bottom. Make sure that the bag can be sealed and resealed; stapling the inside of the bag closest to the inside of the folder is best. Students should use one tape over a period of years. For each entry on the tape, the student should clearly state the day, date, and year the recording is being made, the grade level, and the title of what is on the recording.

From Files to Portfolios

Once a substantial amount of data is collected in a student's file, it is time to *organize the data into a portfolio.* This can be done as early as the fourth grade, but it is recommended that this take place at the end of the fifth grade. For older students, a portfolio can be constructed as soon as the teacher feels there is enough material gathered to support a portfolio.

The basic materials for portfolio construction are:

- A one-inch three-ring binder;
- Clear page protectors;
- Index dividers (at least three, usually five or six); and
- Markers or other coloring materials.

These materials are all on the sample supply list shown earlier in Figure 6-1. The ring binder serves as the notebook that houses the final portfolio materials. The page protectors provide a means of keeping the pages neat and clean, which is especially valuable if the portfolio is to be kept for many years. Index dividers serve to partition the various sections of the portfolio, and the coloring materials are used to design certain cover pages that personalize the portfolio for each student.

Teachers can provide as many of these materials as they choose. Some items that the school or teacher may be able to provide are:

- Blank paper for cover sheets;
- Any coloring materials that are housed in the music room; and
- Items donated by former students that are useful (e.g., writing materials, binders, etc.).

The items donated by former students are given to students who are missing items and/or unable to obtain or purchase portfolio-building materials. These donated items are simply left at the end of each academic year by students who have the means to provide additional binders, index dividers, coloring materials, and page protectors. Other places for teachers to find additional supplies are local businesses and office supply stores, who may make a donation to the school. Sometimes large corporations will "clear out" their office supplies that are no longer needed (this is a great way to obtain ring binders), and they are often quite happy to share these with local schools.

In cases where there are not enough binders for every student, the file folder can be converted into a portfolio "binder" by punching holes near the fold to match the holes in the page protectors or papers being filed. These can then be fastened together with prong-type paper fasteners. Another option is to have students use a much less expensive paper folder, often available in the school bookstore, which already has two or three prong-type fasteners built in.

Organizing the Portfolio

There are two primary designs for portfolio building in general music. Both approaches can be used regardless of the number of years of materials to be organized. The *serial design* involves the organization of each year's materials according to a specific format for that year. The *sectional design* involves the chronological organization of the materials within a designated category or learning area together into sections, and there are materials from several grade levels within each section.

Both designs share common steps to begin the portfolio project:

1. Students should gather their materials into three general categories: (a) *school,* (b) *home,* and (c) *community. School* musical materials are those that have been gathered in the file folder over the year or years in the music room. *Home* music evidence is that which shows the student's musical activity at home, such as singing with the family, practicing an instrument, or listening to music. *Community* music evidence shows musical activity outside of home and outside of school—in church, private lessons, and community music groups.

2. These materials should be reviewed and organized before placing them in the portfolio. *School* materials should be organized into chronological order by learning area. For example, writing samples should be organized by date and year within grade levels, compositions by grade levels, etc. *Home* musical evidence should be organized in the most sensible manner—chronologically, or by event (for example, some students may have photos of singing at family gatherings, etc.). *Community* musical evidence should be organized in a similar manner. Once this is done, the organization within the preferred design can begin.

3. Teachers may also ask students to select a certain number of representative entries, or a minimum number if desired. For example, students may have forty or fifty writing samples in a file that has been developed over a two- or three-year period, and it may not be feasible to include all of these in the final portfolio. In this case, the instruction may be given for the students to select at least three writing samples (or whatever the teacher deems important), one each from the beginning, middle, and end of each school year, that the student feels show his or her improvement in writing about music. The same may apply for any category of materials that students may have in their files, and teacher discretion is advised in these situations.

4. When the final selection of materials is completed, the materials are carefully placed within the clear page protectors. Audio- and videotapes can also be placed within the page protectors and stored in the portfolio notebook. Another alternative for storing tapes in the notebook is to place them in a larger, freezer-type, sealable storage bag, punch holes in the edge for the three rings of the binder, and insert the bag in the notebook. Freezer bags are heavier in weight and still have a sealed top, which will help prevent the tapes from falling out of the notebook.

The Reflective Essay as Part of the Portfolio

One of the benefits of having students complete the portfolio process is the opportunity for them to realize their musical progress in deep and profound ways. Through the examination of musical work across the grade levels, they see tangible evidence of their growth in musical knowledge, composing and notating music, writing about music, and performing music.

To help students realize fully their own musical growth, each portfolio should require reflective essays on the student's musical progress in particular areas. These can range from specific topical essays that refer to projects completed during the year—such as "What I Know About the Business of Music"—to straightforward reflections of musical progress, such as "My Progress in Writing About Music from Fourth to Fifth Grade." The designs presented both in this chapter and in the appendices to this book include such essays as essential parts of the total experience.

The Serial Design Portfolio

Serial literally means *sequential*, so the portfolio organized in this design is organized by consecutive years. The primary divisions of the portfolio are arranged by grade level from earliest to current, and the student marks each division with a page that announces "Music in the (number of grade level) Grade." Within each of these divisions are housed materials that have been deemed important by the teacher, school, and/or school district to be placed in the portfolio. The teacher predetermines the order of these materials, and the portfolio checklist reflects this order. The complete *School* materials portion of a serial design portfolio is reproduced in Appendix A. (The *Community* and *Home* portions are not reproduced due to privacy concerns.)

Once the initial organization of the materials is completed, the student can begin following the "Portfolio Checklist." A sample checklist is shown in Figure 6-2. The checklist is designed for the student to check off each section as it is completed and for the teacher to also check each section as it is assessed (more on the assessment of portfolios later). The "cover pages"—four in all—are hand drawn by the students to reflect their own artistic style and to help personalize the portfolio. In this design, the index dividers are used to separate the school, home, and community sections of the portfolio. The checklist also shows the students that the *Home* and *Community* sections are optional by printing these sections in italics.

The design shown in Figure 6-2 divides the school materials into three subdivisions, which are based on the three artistic processes/assessment response modes: *performing, creating,* and *responding.* For the students, these are "Writing Samples," "Composing and Notating Music," and "Performances." The essays that are required as parts of the project are indicated in bold print on the checklist; they are reflective essays on progress and performances. The "My Future" essay is optional, indicated by italics. The portfolio may contain additional essays if the teacher chooses to include them, and they are relevant to the student's course of study.

Another sample serial portfolio checklist is shown in Figure 6-3. This checklist provides instructions for organizing two years of materials (collected in files from the fourth and fifth grades), and requires additional essays that reflect curricular emphases. Students are instructed that there will be two cover pages for each section of the portfolio, one for the fourth grade and one for the fifth grade. The first five essays are to be written regarding work

Serial Design Portfolio Checklist
(One Year of Materials with Basic Essays)

Portfolio Checklist

Name _____Teacher _____

Please check each section of your portfolio. When you are finished, place a checkmark in the student blank indicating that you have checked that section of your portfolio.
All essays (in bold print) are required.
Sections in italics are optional.   **Due May 18**

Student	*Teacher*	*Section*
_____	_____	Cover page — "Music in the Fifth Grade"
_____	_____	index divider marked "School '96-'97"
_____	_____	Writing Samples cover page
_____	_____	at least three pages of samples, in chronological order
_____	_____	**Essay 1: My Progress in Writing About Music**
_____	_____	Compositions cover page
_____	_____	all written music
_____	_____	**Essay 2: My Progress in Composing and Notating Music**
_____	_____	Performances cover page
_____	_____	**Essay 3: My Performances**
_____	_____	*Optional: index divider—Community*
_____	_____	*Community music evidence*
_____	_____	*Optional: index divider—Home*
_____	_____	*Home music evidence*
_____	_____	*Optional: index divider—My Future*
_____	_____	*Essay 4: My Future in Music*

Teacher Comments

Figure 6-2.

Serial Design Portfolio Checklist
(Two Years of Materials with Basic Essays)

Portfolio Checklist — Fourth and Fifth Grades

Name _____   Teacher _____

You will be organizing two years of materials in this portfolio, from fourth and fifth grades. Organize your fourth grade materials first, following this checklist, leaving out the essays. Place the essays in the fifth grade section. Essays 1-5 should refer to your work in the fifth grade only. When you are finished, place a checkmark in the student blank indicating that you have checked that section of your portfolio for both years.

All essays (in bold print) are required.
Sections in italics are optional.   **Due May 21**

Student Teacher Section

_____ _____   Cover pages—"Music in the Fourth Grade" and "Music in the Fifth Grade"
_____ _____   index dividers marked "School '96-'97" and "School '97-'98"
_____ _____   Writing Samples cover page (for each year)
_____ _____   at least three pages of samples, in chronological order, for each year

_____ _____   **Essay 1: My Progress in Writing About Music in the Fifth Grade**

_____ _____   Compositions and Projects cover pages for each year
_____ _____   all compositions and project logs for each year

_____ _____   **Essay 2: My Progress in Composing and Notating Music in Fifth Grade**

_____ _____   **Essay 3: What I Know About the Business of Music**

_____ _____   Performances cover pages for each year

_____ _____   **Essay 4: My Performances in Fourth and Fifth Grades**

Figure 6-3.

_____ _____ **Essay 5: My Progress in Evaluating Musical Performances in Fifth Grade**

_____ _____ **Essay 6: My Progress from Fourth to Fifth Grade in Music: Writing About Music, Composing and Notating Music, and General Knowledge About Music** (at least one paragraph for each topic)

_____ _____ *Optional: index divider — Community*
_____ _____ *Community music evidence*
_____ _____ *Optional: index divider — Home*
_____ _____ *Home music evidence*
_____ _____ *Essay 7: My Future in Music*

Teacher Comments

Figure 6-3. (continued)

done in the fifth grade, and the sixth essay requires an examination of work in both grades and an assessment of personal progress. Again, the final essay, "My Future," is optional. The additional essays, having to do with the business of music and evaluating musical performances, are related to special units that were covered in that particular year.

Once the serial design format has been started with a particular group of students at a particular grade level, it must be continued in future years. It is not recommended to change designs. A portfolio is always a "work in progress," and such change, if attempted, would be very confusing to the students.

Figure 6-4 shows a sixth grade serial design portfolio checklist for a group of students who organized their files in fifth grade and are now adding their sixth grade materials. This checklist requires only one essay, and the essay is inclusive of the entire year's work. The *Home* and *Community* sections are still optional. In this checklist, all of the required sections are in bold print, not just the essay as was the case in the checklists in Figures 6-2 and 6-3. This prevents the older students from becoming "confused" about what is required and what is not.

Serial Design Portfolio Checklist
(Continuing Year)

Portfolio Checklist — Sixth Grade

Name _____   Teacher _____

Use this checklist as a guide for building your portfolio, and be sure to complete each section of your portfolio. When you are finished, place a checkmark in the student blank indicating that you have checked that section of your portfolio. This checklist and all other pages and papers should be placed in page protectors before being placed in your 1-inch ring binder. You may design the pages on the computer or by hand.

All sections in bold print are required.
Sections in italics are optional.   **Due May 26**

Student   Section/Instructions

_____   **Cover page — "Music in the Sixth Grade"**

_____   **index divider marked "School '98-'99"**

_____   **Writing Samples cover page**

_____   **at least three pages of samples, in chronological order**

_____   **Compositions cover page**

_____   **all written music from sixth grade**

_____   **Projects and Performances cover page**
            You must include evidence of your radio play project —
            your log, a copy of the script, and the other materials you
            may have. **You will also need to include a paragraph**
            describing your sixth grade performances (Peace Awards,
            Advanced Recorder, Choir, radio plays, recording sessions,
            etc.).

_____   **REQUIRED ESSAY: My Progress in Writing About Music,**
            Composing and Notating Music, Performing Music, and
            General Knowledge About Music from Fourth to Sixth
            Grade. Once you have organized your portfolio, look at
            your work and think about your musical progress since
            fourth grade. Do you see improvement? Are you a better
            and more knowledgeable musician now than you were in
            fourth grade? In fifth grade? Since the beginning of sixth
            grade?

Figure 6-4.

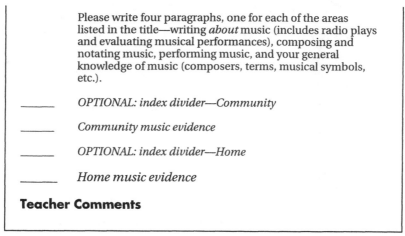

Please write four paragraphs, one for each of the areas listed in the title—writing *about* music (includes radio plays and evaluating musical performances), composing and notating music, performing music, and your general knowledge of music (composers, terms, musical symbols, etc.).

_____ *OPTIONAL: index divider—Community*

_____ *Community music evidence*

_____ *OPTIONAL: index divider—Home*

_____ *Home music evidence*

Teacher Comments

Figure 6-4. (continued)

The serial design works well for teachers who have students organizing only one or two years of materials at a time. For students who have collected three or more years of materials by the time they begin this project, the sectional design is recommended.

The Sectional Design Portfolio

The sectional design portfolio differs from the serial design in that the organization of materials is by category rather than grade level. Within each designated category of materials, the student organizes his or her entries by grade level, in chronological order from earliest to present. In ensuing years, the student simply adds the new year's materials to the section in which it belongs. The organizing pages of a sectional design portfolio are reproduced in Appendix B.

In this design format, the teacher must predetermine the categories for the division of materials. A good rule of thumb is to organize sections according to curricular emphases, by district requirements, or by artistic process/assessment response mode (as discussed earlier). Once this is done, then index dividers can be used to separate the sections. In this design, there is one cover page, hand drawn and designed by the student, that announces the portfolio with the words "My Music Portfolio." This cover page can be replaced yearly if the student desires to do this. Directly following the index divider for each section is a "Table of Contents" for each section. After students organize their materials in chronological order by grade level, they are required to number each page consecutively, placing the page number and grade level on each page. In other words, the first page of any section is the earliest chronologically by date and grade level. Essays can be included either at the end of each section or at the end of the entire portfolio. *Home* and *Community* music sections should remain optional for those students who are interested.

Figure 6-5 shows a sample sectional design portfolio checklist for students who are organizing three years of material. The three sections indicated are "Writing Samples," "Musical Compositions," and "Performances and Projects." Within each of these sections, students are required to number and identify pages by grade level and place a hand-drawn or computer-designed table of contents behind each of the index dividers. The checklist includes specific instructions in some cases, such as the requirement to include evidence of the game project that these students completed in fifth grade. The essay instructions specify that there should be four paragraphs, one for each topic to be covered. The essay is to be placed at the end of the entire portfolio.

Once this design has been started, it must be continued in subsequent years. Figure 6-6 shows a sectional design checklist for a continuing year beyond the organizing year. The format is nearly identical, with instructions to the students to reorganize or redo the cover page and tables of contents should they need or desire to do so. The index dividers remain the same, as do the optional sections.

Sectional Design Portfolio Checklist
(Three Years of Materials)

Fifth Grade Portfolio Checklist

Name _____   Teacher _____

Use this checklist as a guide for building your portfolio, and be sure to complete each section of your portfolio. When you are finished, place a checkmark in the student blank indicating that you have checked that section of your portfolio. **All sections in bold print are required.** This checklist and all other pages and papers should be placed in page protectors before being placed in your 1-inch ring binder. You may design the pages on the computer or by hand.   **Due May 26**

Student   Section/Instructions

_____   **Cover page — "My Music Portfolio"**; design this as you wish, but include your name on the page somewhere.

_____   **index divider marked "Writing Samples"**

_____   **Table of Contents: Writing Samples**; make this page colorful and bright. **Following this page, organize your writing samples by grade level:** third grade, fourth grade, then fifth grade. Write the page number and grade level of the writing sample at the top of each page, starting with "1-third grade." Include these page numbers in the table of contents, such as: "Third Grade...1," "Fourth Grade...5," etc.

_____   **index divider marked "Musical Compositions"**

_____   **Table of Contents: Musical Compositions; follow the same procedures for organizing your musical compositions as you did for Writing Samples**, only in this section include *all* music written and composed by you since third grade, including the draft copies and computer-generated copies if you have them. Use page numbers in the same manner.

_____   **index divider marked "Performances and Projects"**

_____   **Table of Contents: Performances and Projects; in these pages, organize the evidence of your previous performances and projects in music.** You might want to write a paragraph about your performances in third, fourth, and fifth grades at school, or include pictures, or even a tape if you have one. **You must include evidence of your game project—your log, a design sheet, and/or artifacts from the game.**

Figure 6-5. (front)

_____ **REQUIRED ESSAY: My Progress in Writing About Music, Composing and Notating Music, Performing Music, and General Knowledge About Music from Third to Fifth Grade.** Once you have organized your portfolio, look at your work and think about your musical progress since third grade. Do you see improvement? Are you a better and more knowledgeable musician now than you were in third grade? In fourth grade? Since the beginning of fifth grade? Please write four paragraphs, one for each of the areas listed in the title—writing *about* music (includes evaluating musical performances), composing and notating music, performing music, and your general knowledge of music (composers, terms, musical symbols, etc.).

Figure 6-5. (continued)

Continuation of Sectional Design Portfolio Checklist

Fifth Grade Portfolio Checklist

Student   *Section/Instructions*

_____   *OPTIONAL SECTION: index divider— Community*

_____   *Community music evidence — If you are involved in musical activities that are not done at home or at school, then you may include a section here that shows evidence of what you do (sing in church choir, take private lessons, etc.). If you include these materials, include a paragraph about what you do. Evidence includes programs, photos, tapes, etc.*

_____   *OPTIONAL SECTION: index divider — Home*

_____   *Home music evidence — If you are involved in musical activities at home, then you may include a section here that shows evidence of what you do. Organize this section following the instructions given in the Community music section.*

Figure 6-5. (back)

Sectional Portfolio Design

(Continuing Year)

Sixth Grade Portfolio Checklist

Name _____   Teacher _____

Use this checklist as a guide for building your portfolio, and be sure to complete each section of your portfolio. When you are finished, place a checkmark in the student blank indicating that you have checked that section of your portfolio. **All sections in bold print are required.** This checklist and all other pages and papers should be placed in page protectors before being placed in your 1-inch ring binder. You may design the pages on the computer or by hand.   **Due May 25**

Student   Section/Instructions

_____   **Cover page — "My Music Portfolio"**; you may keep what you have or redesign this as you wish; if you redesign, include your name on the page somewhere.

_____   After the index divider marked "Writing Samples," reorganize or redo your **Table of Contents: Writing Samples** to include your sixth grade materials. Organize your writing samples by writing the page number (the next number after your last fifth grade example) and "Sixth Grade" at the top, in the same manner you did last year. Include these page numbers in the table of contents as follows: "Sixth Grade...(page number)."

_____   After the index divider marked "Musical Compositions," reorganize or redo your **Table of Contents: Musical Compositions** to include your sixth grade work. **Follow the same procedures for organizing your musical compositions as you did for the Writing Samples.** Be sure to include *all* music written and composed by you in sixth grade, including draft copies and computer-generated copies if you have them. Use page numbers in the same manner.

_____   After the index divider marked "Performances and Projects," reorganize or redo your **Table of Contents: Performances and Projects** to include your sixth grade work. **In these pages, organize the evidence of your sixth grade performances and projects in music.** You might want to write a paragraph about your performances in sixth grade, or include pictures, or even a tape if you have one. **You must include evidence of your radio play project—your log, a copy of the script, and your self-assessment.**

Figure 6-6.

REQUIRED ESSAY: My Progress in Writing About Music, Composing and Notating Music, Performing Music, and General Knowledge About Music from Third to Sixth Grade. Once you have organized your portfolio, look at your work (and last year's essay) and think about your musical progress since third grade. Do you see improvement? Are you a better and more knowledgeable musician now than you were in third grade? In fourth grade? In fifth grade? Since the beginning of sixth grade? Please write four paragraphs, one for each of the areas listed in the title —writing *about* music (includes evaluating musical performances), composing and notating music, performing music, and your general knowledge of music (composers, terms, musical symbols, etc.).

(over for optional sections, same as in Figure 6-5)

Figure 6-6. (continued)

Assessing the Completed Portfolio

Because a portfolio is a repository for materials and performances that have already been assessed, assessment of the portfolio itself focuses upon its organization and essays. Because the essays are reflections on progress, the thinking direction is metacognitive. Therefore, the essays are best assessed as either being *completed* or *not completed*. Essays may also be assessed for their grammar usage and writing skills if this is desired (refer to chapter 5 regarding the assessment of grammar and writing).

Figure 6-7 presents a sample rubric for assessing portfolios, which is provided to students at the start of the project. There are five levels of achievement in order to accommodate those situations where the portfolio is not submitted (the "0" level). The distinctions among the levels have to do with (1) *completeness of the sections*, (2) *attention to the details of organization* (chronological entries, tables of contents, etc.), and (3) *grammar and writing in the essays*. Because there are metacognitive responses, their content should be assessed only with respect to whether or not they cover the required topics. This sample rubric can also be

Suggested Rubric for Completed Portfolios

Rubric for Portfolios

Level   Description of Portfolio

4   All sections are complete; the required materials are present and organized chronologically, according to instructions (optional sections do not affect this judgment); the essay is well written with correct grammar and spelling, each sentence and paragraph is correctly structured, and the content of the essay covers the assigned topic(s).

3   All sections are complete; the required materials are present and organized chronologically, according to instructions (optional sections do not affect this judgment); the essay is well written with primarily correct grammar and spelling, but a few errors exist; most sentences and paragraphs are correctly structured, and the content of the essay covers the assigned topic(s).

2   Some sections are incomplete; the required materials are neither all present nor organized chronologically, according to instructions (optional sections do not affect this judgment); the essay is poorly written with primarily incorrect grammar and spelling; most sentences and paragraphs are incorrectly structured, and the content of the essay does not cover the assigned topic(s).

1   All sections are incomplete; the required materials are neither all present nor organized chronologically, according to instructions (optional sections do not affect this judgment); the essay is missing and/or poorly written with incorrect grammar and spelling; the sentences and paragraphs are incorrectly structured, and the content of the essay does not cover the assigned topic(s).

0   Portfolio is not submitted.

Figure 6-7.

adapted or expanded to accommodate different or additional music portfolio requirements.

The issue of assigning a grade to a portfolio is a difficult one, and there is no theoretically or philosophically sound solution.

However, a suggested accommodation that can be made in situations where a grade must be given is as follows:

- Level 4 can translate to "A" or "E" (excellent).
- Level 3 can translate to "B" or "S" (satisfactory).
- Level 2 can translate to "C" or "N" (needs improvement).
- Level 1 can translate to "D" or "U" (unsatisfactory).
- Level 0—a portfolio that is not turned in—should be marked "F" or "I" (incomplete).

There will be a longer discussion on grading in the second half of this chapter, when reporting progress to parents is covered.

Planning and Designing a Portfolio Project for Your Teaching Situation

When the decision is made to begin portfolio building with students, several factors influence the *choice of portfolio design*, the *categories for division of materials*, the *number of essays to be included*, and the *essay topics*. There are specific steps that can help teachers make these decisions. An explanation of each step follows:

1. *Determine what is important that you teach for which you have evidence.* This step is crucial in helping to determine the categories of materials that will be used to organize the portfolio. Evidence includes (but is not limited to) (a) *writing*, (b) *musical compositions*, (c) *audio-* and *videotapes*, (d) *photos*, and (e) *computer disks*. Every curriculum offers many opportunities for producing materials and products that can later become portfolio entries. Some school districts may require that specific assignments or assessments be placed in the portfolio.

2. *Determine what is important for your students to reflect upon from their study with you.* These topics form the basis for the essays that the children write and place within the portfolio. Ask yourself: What do I really want my students to know about their year of work in music? The topics should not involve recall of information but instead produce responses that may include specific facts about what was learned in the context of evaluating personal progress. The essay topic should also require students to reflect back on the year's work (or even further back to preceding years).

3. *Decide how you will ask the children to organize the portfolio.* First, *determine the design* that you will employ. A recommended approach is to begin the first- and second-year fifth grade classes with the *serial* design because they will have only one or two years of materials to organize; then begin the third-year fifth grade class with the *sectional* design because the students will have three years of data collected. Then, *determine the materials* that you feel will be necessary for the completion of the project. Suggested (but not required) items are (a) page protectors, (b) index dividers, (c) binders, and (d) coloring materials. Next, *decide what materials you might be able to provide* for those students who may be unable to obtain the basic requirements. Finally, *determine how the materials collected for portfolio entries will be categorized* into sections.

4. *Determine a time line for implementation.* Once the commitment is made to begin portfolio building, it is recommended that the process begin *with the first lesson of the year.* Students should bring their file folders to the initial music lesson, and these should be collected and organized at that time. General music teachers know how important being a member of a higher grade is to their students, and the excitement of their "first music lesson as fourth graders" (or whatever their new grade level may be) can be enhanced by the announcement of a year-long portfolio project at the beginning of the year. In ensuing years, the "old" files from previous grades need to be redistributed to students *during the first lesson* in their "new classes." During this redistribution, students get an opportunity to briefly review their collected work from previous years, reviving their excitement about the portfolio process. Depending on the music teacher's schedule, these files can be updated *monthly* or *at the end of each semester or grading period.* Regardless of how often students formally update their files, it is important that they have the opportunity to add to their files at any time.

The additional materials needed for the organizing year (usually fifth grade) can pose a storage challenge for the music teacher. If students bring in their binders, index dividers, and page protectors at the beginning of the year, the teacher should plan ahead for a place to store these items. Materials should not be stored without clear student identification, and it is best to store them in as secure a place as possible. If space is a problem, then perhaps the classroom teacher will have a closet or small storage area where these can be kept until they are ready to be used. In my own classroom, shelves have been constructed to house the nearly 200 portfolios that my students produce each year.

The recommended time to make the transition from files to portfolios is *at the end of the academic year.* If the school system or state gives achievement tests in the spring, it is best to start the project after these have been completed. The students are more relaxed, less distracted, and ready to devote their full attention to their portfolios.

5. *Determine if this project will be graded and, if so, how it will be graded or assessed.* It is imperative that students understand from the beginning of the project how their work on this project will be assessed and reported to their parents. It is recommended that the rubric be published on the same page as the portfolio checklist, perhaps on the back. Design the rubric carefully so that it covers the required elements of the portfolio, because students will use the rubric as their guide to attaining their highest level of achievement.

6. *Set a due date and a collection/return plan.* Students will need to know exactly when the portfolio is due, and this date should be published on the portfolio checklist (as shown in Figures 6-2 through 6-6). *The minimum recommended time for completion of the project is two weeks; three or four weeks are best.* Students should be allowed to work on their portfolios during music class time as well as at home. It is recommended to assign four or five students per class as the portfolio "collectors," whose job it is to bring the portfolios to the music room on the due date. If the students are leaving the school to move on to a higher grade, the "collectors" can return the portfolios when they have been assessed. For students who are returning the following year, the "collectors" can assist in placing the portfolios in the designated storage area for the summer. They will then be ready to access at the beginning of the next year.

7. *Design a portfolio checklist for your students*. This is the final step. The checklist is an invaluable tool, especially if your students wish to work on this at home. Use the examples in Figures 6-2 through 6-6 as models, or create your own.

Portfolios and the "Traveling Teacher"

The reality of the music teaching profession is that there are a number of music specialists who "travel" as part of their duties. The word "traveling" describes two types of teaching situations: (1) when the teacher travels to more than one school (some as many as five) and (2) when the school building is so overcrowded that there is no assigned music classroom, making it necessary for the music specialist to travel (carrying everything to teach music on a cart) from room to room. Many general music teachers have had to face "traveling" at some point in their careers, and this type of situation has an impact on the extent to which certain musical activities can be undertaken.

A music specialist's first duty is to instruct students, assess their progress, and report this progress to parents. This can all be accomplished effectively by the traveling teacher. Portfolio building can also be accomplished, but it takes some additional planning and teamwork. Some suggestions for the traveling teacher follow:

1. *After reading the steps presented in this chapter on designing a portfolio project, determine and list the aspects of your teaching situation that pose constraints on the portfolio-building process.* These constraints may include (but not be limited to) storage room for files and the finished portfolios, managing the materials needed for the project, and the willingness of some classroom teachers to actively assist you with management issues.

2. *Discuss your interest in portfolio building with the school administrators.* Review the opening of this chapter and prepare yourself to present a plan for beginning portfolio building in your school(s). On one page, write a brief summary of the following aspects of the project: (a) why this is important to you and your students, (b) the positive aspects of your teaching situation that will facilitate portfolio construction, and (c) any constraints you can foresee in the process. Be sure to identify this with your name, especially if you are in a school for only a few classes per week. Leave this with the principal to read, then set up an appointment to meet within the next week.

During the meeting with the administrator, be prepared to support your plan. Most principals, especially in light of the educational reforms that are taking place across the country at the start of the twenty-first century, are going to be very supportive of this effort. Once the support of the administrator is gained, then work together to find solutions for the constraints you have listed. Administrative support is also essential for meeting any future challenges that might arise.

In a situation where an administrator is not supportive, there are still a few options for the music specialist. First, gather some recent materials (including this book!) that define and describe portfolios in music and their educational benefits. Second, search the school's mission and vision for statements that support portfolio building in all school disciplines. Third, link the portfolio process to real life and the development of skills necessary to become a productive citizen in the twenty-first century. Any principal who is truly interested in providing the highest quality education for students will eventually be convinced.

3. *Discuss your interest in portfolio building with the classroom teachers.* Once you have obtained the support of your administration, prepare a short note for the classroom teachers with whom you work that explains your goals and what you would like their part to be in the process. In most situations, all the classroom teacher will need to do is provide some storage space for files (twenty-five or so file folders require very little room) and finished portfolios. Because finished portfolios are usually in one-inch ring binders, and each of these takes up approximately one and one-half inches of shelf space, a simple calculation is all that is necessary to determine the amount of shelf space needed. If the classroom teacher does not have additional bookends to hold up the portfolios, these can usually be obtained from the school media specialist. Other storage options include stackable crates or lidded boxes. To reduce storage space, traveling teachers may want to have students organize their portfolios in pocket folders with built-in, prong-type paper fasteners rather than in binders. These types of decisions can be made with the classroom teacher.

Portfolios in Schools with Transient Populations

Another reality of today's schools has to do with student transience. Families move now more than ever before, and this often results in students changing schools. Transient enrollment is a particular concern to the music specialist, who may find class rosters changing nearly every week in some schools. This type of situation poses challenges to the continuity of instruction and, in particular, the portfolio process because of its long-term nature.

Even in schools where transience is expected, there is usually a *core body* of students who remain at the school for most or all of their grade levels. Most classrooms house some of these non-transient students. It is recommended that the music specialist assign two or three of these students as "student assistants," or "peer mentors." It is best to have two or three (or a few more if they are available) in case of absenteeism on the day(s) they are needed. The student assistant/peer mentor's primary job is to guide new students through the first few music lessons. This can include setting up a file folder for collecting portfolio materials and helping new students obtain the supply list for the class. Assigning students this important job not only builds their self-esteem but also saves the teacher valuable instructional time.

It is advisable to have some file folders on hand for new students. When students leave the school, they should take their portfolio materials with them.

Looking Toward the Future: The Digital Music Portfolio

Currently available digital recording technologies hold promise for the future of music portfolio building at all levels. While most schools do not yet possess this type of technology, it is definitely on the horizon and will likely help to revolutionize record keeping and portfolio building across the school disciplines.

Digital video and audio recordings, unlike traditional analog recording, can be downloaded to computers and saved on diskette or CD. New CD read-and-write drives allow users to save computer files on recordable CDs. Combined with scanning technology (scanners convert still pictures and text into digital form), this has the potential to reduce the paper-and-analog-tape music portfolio to a single CD. Eventually, students will be able to include all of their assessments—performances, created works, and written pages—in a digital portfolio. New software programs can also be used to provide a format for these; *Hyperstudio* is one that is particularly well suited.

Additionally, digital recordings can be edited. This provides flexibility in storage and playback that is not possible with analog technology. For example, the teacher can videotape an entire class of vocal solos (such as a group of third graders playing "The Closet Key" singing game for assessment), extract each child's individual solo footage, copy it, and save it to the child's digital portfolio CD. The digital audio track produced from the video can be further analyzed (if desired) using any good sequencing software (*FreeStyle* and *Cakewalk* are two well-known names).

While music specialists can certainly look forward to this "digital future" in schools, this transformation will undoubtedly take years to complete. Most music portfolios will continue to be constructed with paper evidence and analog tapes, and organized by students in notebook binders for many years to come.

Reporting Musical Progress to Parents: The Developmental Profile

"Grading" and Musical Progress

Every school district prescribes a method of reporting student educational progress to parents. One widely used and relatively standard system reports student progress in the form of letter grades on a periodic report card, with the range of highest to lowest represented by the letters A, B, C, D, and F. Other systems use similar nomenclature, such as E, S, N, and U (excellent, satisfactory, needs improvement, and unsatisfactory), or O, S, N, and U, with "O" representing the word "outstanding." Exactly how these grades are assigned and what they represent as far as student achievement is concerned is determined at either the school or district level. In most instances, individual teachers possess a fair amount of autonomy to decide the parameters that determine what level of progress receives an "A" or similar grade in their class and, more importantly, what does not.

This entire book has been devoted to helping music teachers gain an understanding of the assessment process and what it can reveal about students' musical progress. As part of their regular duties, *music specialists are expected to report student progress in music to parents.* Most often this is required to be reported in the same format as other subject areas, which for most teachers means that a standard letter grade must be provided for each student. Ideally, this grade should clearly reflect the musical progress of students, free from the influence of social and personal factors (student attitude, behavior, attendance in class/rehearsals, effort, etc.).

The first chapter of this book discussed the constructivist nature of music learning. During the learning process, existing musical knowledge is reconstructed in new ways to solve new musical problems. Because the domain of musical knowledge consists of a number of learning areas and skills, reporting students' musical progress requires that these be addressed as thoroughly as possible.

Each student possesses a unique constellation of musical abilities. For example, a teacher may find that a student who is a particularly good singer may have difficulty with rhythm reading, playing the recorder, or analysis. Furthermore, these differences may vary across the spectrum of musical skills and knowledge. Because students do not develop uniformly throughout their general music experience, a *single letter grade* is an inadequate way to report this development to parents. A single letter grade is not representative of the wide variety of musical learning experiences that teachers provide, nor does it convey the variability of individual development indicated by the assessment data collected by the music teacher.

Presenting Musical Progress to Parents

While the "best" method of reporting musical progress to parents has not yet been determined, a recommended alternative to letter grades is the *developmental profile progress report.* This report profiles a student's development in music across a variety of skills and knowledge, and is designed to reflect what is expected at each grade level and communicate a student's individual progress within each expectation. The developmental profile replaces the standard letter grade and is included in the student's regular periodic progress report as an insert.

The profile can assume several forms and can represent varying levels of detail. This type of progress report follows a basic design that can be adapted to any curriculum. A diagram of the general design is shown in Figure 6-8, and the parts of this design are described below, including their purpose and function.

> **1.** *Introduction and Scoring Key.* This section should contain *identifying information* such as the name of the student, classroom or homeroom teacher, music teacher, and school year, as well as introductory information if desired. For many parents, this type of report will be new and will require explanation. While the report is somewhat self-explanatory, it is recommended that a note or letter of explanation be included with the first distribution. Figure 6-9 presents a sample letter to parents.
>
> An explanation of the *scoring key* for the report should also be included in the top section. Most profiles will report three levels of progress or four levels of development in each listed area. The three levels of progress and some suggested verbal descriptors are:
>
> > 1 = beginning, exposed, novice
> > 2 = developing, progressing normally
> > 3 = has achieved mastery, competent
>
> If four developmental levels are used, the following are recommended:

General Diagram of the Developmental Progress Report

Introduction and Scoring Key	
Statements of Accomplishment	**Marking Grid**
Comment Area	

Figure 6-8.

1 = no development observed
2 = development is below expectations
3 = developing as expected
4 = exceeds developmental expectations

Additional markings may be used if desired. For example, to indicate learning areas or indicators that have not yet been addressed at the time of the report (it may be too early in the year), one can use the letters "IP" to indicate that this is "in progress."

2. *Statements of Accomplishment: Standards, Expectations, Indicators, and Objectives.* This section is devoted to listing the statements of accomplishment that represent the significant musical goals for the year. These statements are developed from:

a. *Standards*—broad statements that define the significant skills and content that every student should obtain (see MENC, 1994);

b. *Expectations*—what a student is expected to do or produce in reference to that standard at his or her level of development or training;

c. *Performance indicators*—what the student can actually do (or perform) in order to demonstrate that the expectation has been met; and

d. *Objectives*—the specific steps that help students obtain the skills and knowledge that will enable them to execute the performance indicators.

Statements of accomplishment should be written in simple, clear language that minimizes confusion and misinterpretation. They should also be sensibly measurable using the scoring key that has been chosen, and they should be supported by actual assessment data that has been collected throughout the academic year. Parents should be able to read a statement, understand what it means, and then make sense of what the given rating means in relation to that statement. A good way to facilitate this is to write some statements and ask

Sample Letter to Parents Introducing the Developmental Profile Progress Report

12/15/99

Dear Parents,

   With this report card you are receiving a newly designed *Developmental Profile Progress Report* that replaces your child's music grade. Your child will receive this report twice a year, at the end of each semester. These reports are designed to reflect the National Standards for the Arts and our local school district standards for music. On the back of each report you will find an outline of these standards; I encourage you to familiarize yourself with them.

   These reports are designed to provide you with progress information in each of five learning areas in music: skills, literacy, analysis and preference, history and literature, and the related arts. Each learning area lists specific performance indicators that your child should be able to demonstrate in order to achieve proficiency at his/her grade level. At this point in the year, your child has had 18 music lessons and is well on the way to achieving these indicators.

   The progress reports also have a designated area where I can write specific remarks to you regarding your child's work in the music room. If there are no comments, then you may assume that everything is going well. If comments are written, please read them carefully and respond if necessary. There is a place on the report for you to respond back to me in writing, *but this is at your own discretion*. It is not necessary for you to return this report to me.

   If you have any questions or comments regarding this type of progress reporting, please do not hesitate to contact me at school by letter or phone. Thank you for your continued support of our music program.

Sincerely,

Figure 6-9.

your administrator as well as a few fellow teachers and parents to review them for their clarity, measurability, possible interpretations, and understandability. After making any recommended adjustments, the statements should be ready for distribution.

The organization of the statements on the progress report is dependent upon the curriculum and the teacher's preference. These can be arranged as a single list of behaviors or standards, or as several shorter lists grouped by learning areas or some other organizing criterion.

3. *Marking Grid.* This area of the report is where the marks indicating the student's level of achievement for the statements of accomplishment are placed. If desired, the symbols representing the various levels of achievement may be written across the top of the grid. To form the grid, lines are first drawn underneath each statement or group list from the left edge of the statement list to the right edge of the marking grid. Drawing lines from top to bottom within the grid area completes the grid. The grid boxes need to be large enough to hold the necessary markings. The markings may be checkmarks (√), "plus" or "minus" symbols (+ or –), numbers, letters, or whatever is indicated in the scoring key.

4. *Comment Area.* This section is reserved for teacher and parent comments. This is where the teacher can write comments about those characteristics of a student's behavior that may impede musical progress. There should be designated space for each period during which the report is given. It is important to leave as much space as possible in the comment area. If parent signatures are desired, these can also go in this area.

Sample Reports

This design scheme is best illustrated in the fourth grade examples shown in Figures 6-10 through 6-13.

A sample report designed by Paul Lehman is shown in Figure 6-10 (Lehman, 1998). In this report, the statements of

Sample Fourth Grade Music Report

Report to Parents Music – Grade 4				

Child's Name: **Music Instructor:**

School Year: **Grading Period (circle):**
   1   2   3   4

Explanation of symbols

A = **Advanced Level** Your child's achievement is significantly above the level of skill desired at this stage.

P = **Proficient Level** Your child has achieved the level of skill desired at this stage.

B = **Basic Level** Your child has made distinct progress but has not yet achieved the level of skill desired at this stage.

N = **Needs Improvement** Your child needs further work to demonstrate the level of skill desired at this stage.

	A	P	B	N
1. Singing				
2. Performing on instruments				
3. Improvising melodies, variations, and accompaniments				
4. Composing and arranging music				
5. Reading and notating music				
6. Listening to, analyzing, and describing music				
7. Evaluating music and music performances				
8. Understanding relationships between music and other disciplines				
9. Understanding music in relation to history and culture				

Teacher's comments (first grading period)

Teacher's comments (second grading period)

Teacher's comments (third grading period)

Teacher's comments (fourth grading period)

Parents' comments for each grading period are invited on the reverse side.

Figure 6-10.

Sample Fourth Grade Music Objectives Report

Child's Name_____Classroom Teacher_____

Music Objectives – Fourth Grade

The following objectives are those that your fourth grade child will be working toward this year in music. Next to each objective I have checked your child's progress in attaining that objective. If there is no check, the concept has not yet been introduced.

To the best of his/her ability, your child can:

E = Exposed P = Progress M = Mastery	E	P	M
1. Recognize that music is an important part of life.			
2. Perform and notate rhythm patterns of increasing complexity.			
3. Perform movements to simple folk dances.			
4. Play I, IV, or V chords to accompany a two-chord melody.			
5. Sing in a group performing songs in simple harmony.			
6. Identify orchestral instruments from aural and visual examples.			
7. Distinguish among short melodic patterns which consist principally of one of the following: a series of repeated tones, scale-wise tones (steps), or tones which move by leaps (skips).			
8. Distinguish between major and minor tonality.			
9. Recognize beat patterns (meter) of 2, 3, or 4 beats per measure.			
10. Identify dynamic markings and interpret them in performance.			
11. Read short scale-wise melodic patterns written on the treble staff by finding pitches on a simple classroom instrument.			
12. Identify career opportunities available to music performers.			
Comments:			

Figure 6-11.

Sample Fourth Grade Music Progress Report

Music Progress Report – Fourth Grade

Child's Name_____Music Instructor_____School Year_____

Guide:

(B)eginning Your child has been exposed to this area of learning.

(D)eveloping Your child is presently developing an understanding of this area through direct instruction.

(C)ompetent Your child has demonstrated, through assessment, competency in this learning area.

Not marked This area has not been approached at the time of this report.

Learning Area:	Progress Level:		
	B	**D**	**C**
Musical Skills *(singing, playing instruments, improvising)*			
1. Demonstrates basic understanding of score reading, can point out clefs, meter and key signatures, staves, and notes			
2. Sings in tune from middle C to C an octave above			
3. Sings with correct technique and proper expression			
4. Performs on classroom instruments with correct technique and proper expression			
5. Improvises freely on a variety of instruments			
6. Composes in a pentatonic scale (i.e., D, F, or G) and creates a melody with balanced phrases			
Literacy *(reading and writing music)*			
1. Interprets whole, half, quarter, and eighth notes and rests in 2/4, 3/4, and 4/4 meters			
2. Reads and understands 3- to 5-note melodies in simple rhythms on the treble clef			
3. Identifies and interprets clefs, meter and key signatures, dynamic and tempo markings in performance			
4. Correctly notates his/her own melodies on the treble clef, using standard music notation with proper stem directions and note groupings			

Figure 6-12.

History and Literature *(appreciation and listening)* **1.** Identifies different types and styles of music			
2. Demonstrates appreciation for various masterworks from the Medieval, Renaissance, Baroque, Classical, Romantic, and twentieth century musical periods			
Analysis and Preference *(analyzing music and reactions to music)* **1.** Uses appropriate terminology in describing and explaining music			
2. Aurally identifies various instrument timbres			
3. Understands personal preferences and the preferences of others for certain musical works and styles			
Related Arts and Humanities *(culture, society, and other art forms)* **1.** Demonstrates a basic understanding of how music reflects society and culture, historical influences on musical works, and primary interrelationships among the arts (dance, visual arts, drama, and music) and disciplines outside the arts			

Teacher Comments (first grading period)	Parent Comments (first grading period)
Teacher Comments (second grading period)	Parent Comments (second grading period)
Teacher Comments (third grading period)	Parent Comments (third grading period)
Teacher Comments (fourth grading period)	Parent Comments (fourth grading period)

Figure 6-12. (continued)

Sample Fourth Grade Musical Development
Progress Report

Musical Development – Fourth Grade Progress Report

Child's Name_____Music Instructor_____School Year_____

Key
Your child's progress toward achieving the school district's standards
for music is assessed regularly through tasks based within the three
artistic response modes: performing, creating, and responding. Below is
a report of your child's musical development as observed through these
assessments. The following scale is used: **4** = development exceeds
expectations; **3** = development is appropriate; **2** = development is
below expectations; **1** = no development has been observed; **IP** =
further instruction in this area is planned or in progress.

Music Learning Area:	Reporting Period: 1	2
Musical Skills *(singing, playing instruments, improvising;* *District Standards #1 and #2)*		
Literacy *(reading and writing music;* *District Standards #1 and #2)*		

Musical Skills
(singing, playing instruments, improvising;
District Standards #1 and #2)

- Sings in tune within the C and D major scales
- Sings with correct technique in both light and heavy registers
- Performs on classroom instruments with correct technique and
  proper expression
- Performs an independent part while singing or playing an instrument
- Composes original melodies within given rhythmic and melodic
  guidelines
- Improvises within a structured context

Literacy
(reading and writing music;
District Standards #1 and #2)

- Interprets eighth, quarter, half, and whole notes and rests in 2/4, 3/4,
  and 4/4 meter
- Visually recognizes and notates simple pitch patterns in the C, F, and
  G pentatonic scales
- Reads and correctly performs 3- to 5-note melodies
- Correctly notates original compositions in the treble clef
- Demonstrates basic score reading skills

Figure 6-13.

Analysis and Preference
(analyzing music and reactions to music;
District Standard #3)

- Identifies basic musical structures: measure, phrase, melodic direction, and form
- Aurally identifies orchestral instruments, individually and in groups
- Evaluates musical performances and works using given criteria
- Develops reasonable criteria for evaluating musical performances and works
- Writes reasoned explanations of personal musical preferences
- Can self-assess own musical works and performances

History and Literature
(appreciation and listening;
District Standard #4)

- Distinguishes between different musical types and styles
- Appreciates musical masterworks from various historical periods
- Critiques musical works within given guidelines using appropriate terminology

Related Arts and Humanities
(culture, society, and other art forms,
District Standard #5)

- Demonstrates through verbal and written descriptions a basic understanding of how world musics reflect their respective cultures
- Identifies simple common structural attributes between visual art, music, dance, and drama, and simple relationships between music and other nonmusic disciplines

Teacher Comments (first report)	Parent Comments (first report)
Teacher Comments (second report)	Parent Comments (second report)

Figure 6-13. (continued)

accomplishment are the *nine National Standards.* The scoring key is taken from the book *Performance Standards for Music, Grades PreK-12: Strategies and Benchmarks for Assessing Progress Toward the National Standards* (MENC, 1996). The scoring key is an adaptation of the *four levels of development* described earlier, using the terms *advanced* (A), *proficient* (P), *basic* (B), and *needs improvement* (N). Because the statements of accomplishment are the nine National Standards, it is advised to add to the scoring key, "Areas not yet covered are left blank," in order to accommodate the early marking periods where all of the Standards may not yet have been addressed. The marking grid is a single box for each Standard, in which the letter representing the level of assessed achievement is placed. There is room for comments at the bottom from the teacher, and parents are invited to respond on the back of the report.

The report shown in Figure 6-11 uses a *list of objectives for fourth grade music* as the statements of accomplishment. The scoring key (shown in the Comments area of the report) is an adaptation of the *three levels* of progress described earlier, using the terms *exposed* (E) to represent the beginning level, *progress* (P), and *mastery* (M). The comment area is adequate for the teacher's comments, but does not invite parental written responses. The marking grid is clear and easy to read.

Figure 6-12 shows a fourth grade progress report that organizes performance indicators by the *five musical learning areas* as presented in chapter 2. Each learning area is followed by a brief parenthetical description to help parents understand exactly what each area covers. For example, "Literacy" is followed by the four-word description "reading and writing music." The scoring key employs *three levels* of progress. The marking grid is separated into sections that correspond with the learning areas, and there are three grid boxes for each performance indicator. Each performance indicator is marked with a checkmark (√) in the box that corresponds to the assessed level of progress. There is a comment area for both the teacher and the parents, but these could be enlarged to encourage parental responses.

Figure 6-13 shows a fourth grade report that reflects a local district's standards for music. This report employs a *four-level* developmental scoring key and organizes performance indicators by *learning area*. In addition to the brief description of the learning areas (as discussed with Figure 6-12), the related local school standards are mentioned. The marking system is slightly different in that there is one mark given per *learning area*, regardless of the number of performance indicators within that learning area. There are two grid boxes per learning area, indicating that this report is completed twice yearly. Development is indicated to parents through a number that corresponds to the appropriate level of achievement in each learning area. The comment areas at the bottom of the report provide space for both the teacher and the parents to write at both distributions.

Figures 6-14, 6-15, and 6-16 show progress reports for third, fifth, and sixth grades, respectively, that are designed in the same manner.

Advantages and Challenges of Developmental Progress Reporting

The use of developmental musical progress reports over a period of years results in a *reasonably complete profile of a student's individual musical growth.* The developmental profile should contain multiple copies, an original and one for each reporting period to send home to parents. The original reports can be filed in each student's accumulative folder at the end of each school year so that when students leave the elementary school and go to the middle or junior high school, these reports can combine to give the music specialist at that level a thorough and meaningful view of each student's musical strengths and weaknesses. Additionally, if a student leaves one district and travels to another, the music specialist in the new district can access these reports to determine a child's level of musical progress.

Another advantage of this type of reporting is *advocacy for the music program.* Parents, who are often not aware of what goes on

Sample Third Grade Musical Development
Progress Report

Musical Development – Third Grade Progress Report

Child's Name_____Music Instructor_____School Year_____

Key

Your child's progress toward achieving the school district's standards for music is assessed regularly through tasks based within the three artistic response modes: performing, creating, and responding. Below is a report of your child's musical development as observed through these assessments. The following scale is used: **4** = development exceeds expectations; **3** = development is appropriate; **2** = development is below expectations; **1** = no development has been observed; **IP** = further instruction in this area is planned or in progress.

Music Learning Area:	Reporting Period:	
	1	2
Musical Skills *(singing, playing instruments, improvising; District Standards #1 and #2)*		

- Sings in tune within the D and F pentatonic scales
- Plays mallet instruments with correct technique
- Plays rhythm instruments with correct technique
- Improvises within a structured context
- Aurally identifies and performs simple pitch patterns in the pentatonic scale

Literacy *(reading and writing music; District Standards #1 and #2)*		

- Interprets eighth, quarter, and half notes and rests in duple/simple meter
- Visually recognizes and notates simple pitch patterns in the pentatonic scale
- Composes original melodies within given rhythmic and melodic guidelines
- Correctly notates original compositions in the treble clef

Figure 6-14.

Analysis and Preference
(analyzing music and reactions to music;
District Standard #3)

- Identifies simple musical forms, such as ABA
- Aurally identifies the four orchestral instrument families
- Aurally identifies musical phrases
- Verbally describes and physically demonstrates melodic direction in given works
- Evaluates musical performance and works using simple criteria
- Develops reasonable criteria for evaluating musical performances and works
- Writes reasoned explanations of personal musical preferences
- Can self-assess own musical works and performances

History and Literature
(appreciation and listening;
District Standard #4)

- Distinguishes between different musical styles
- Appreciates musical masterworks from various historical periods
- Critiques musical works within given guidelines using appropriate terminology

Related Arts and Humanities
(culture, society, and other art forms,
District Standard #5)

- Demonstrates through verbal descriptions an understanding of the basic connections between the music of various societies and their respective cultures
- Identifies basic common attributes between visual art, music, dance, and drama, and disciplines outside the arts

Teacher Comments (first report)	Parent Comments (first report)
Teacher Comments (second report)	Parent Comments (second report)

Figure 6-14. (continued)

Sample Fifth Grade Musical Development
Progress Report

Musical Development – Fifth Grade Progress Report

Child's Name_____Music Instructor_____School Year_____

Key

Your child's progress toward achieving the school district's standards for music is assessed regularly through tasks based within the three artistic response modes: performing, creating, and responding. Below is a report of your child's musical development as observed through these assessments. The following scale is used: **4** = development exceeds expectations; **3** = development is appropriate; **2** = development is below expectations; **1** = no development has been observed; **IP** = further instruction in this area is planned or in progress.

Music Learning Area:	Reporting Period:	
	1	2
Musical Skills *(singing, playing instruments, improvising;* *District Standards #1 and #2)*		

- Sings in tune within the range A-flat below middle C to E an octave above
- Sings with correct technique and expression across the vocal range
- Sings simple harmonic parts to familiar melodies
- Aurally identifies major and minor tonality
- Performs independently within multi-level musical textures
- Independently composes original melodies and accompaniments in the C, F, or G pentatonic scales
- Improvisations demonstrate attention to structure and product

Literacy *(reading and writing music;* *District Standards #1 and #2)*		

- Interprets sixteenth, eighth, quarter, half, and whole notes and rests in 2/4, 3/4, and 4/4 meter
- Visually recognizes/notates simple melodies in C and G major scales
- Reads and correctly performs two-measure rhythms and melodies
- Correctly notates original compositions and accompaniments using two clefs
- Interprets simple dynamic, tempo, and structural markings in musical scores

---

Figure 6-15.

Analysis and Preference
(analyzing music and reactions to music;
District Standard #3)

- Identifies imitative and developmental musical forms (e.g., canon, fugue, sonata)
- Aurally and visually identifies individual orchestral instruments
- Evaluates musical performances and works using multiple criteria
- Develops reasonable criteria for evaluating musical performances and works
- Writes/develops sound musical arguments supporting personal musical preferences
- Can self-assess own musical works and performances
- Successfully assesses the musical works and performances of peers

History and Literature
(appreciation and listening;
District Standard #4)

- Distinguishes between different musical types and styles
- Identifies selected musical masterworks from various historical periods
- Critiques musical works employing multiple criteria and appropriate terminology

Related Arts and Humanities
(culture, society, and other art forms,
District Standard #5)

- Demonstrates through verbal and written descriptions a basic understanding of how world musics reflect their respective cultures
- Recognizes and describes common terms in the arts and describes simple relationships between music and nonmusic disciplines

Teacher Comments (first report)	Parent Comments (first report)
Teacher Comments (second report)	Parent Comments (second report)

Figure 6-15. (continued)

Sample Sixth Grade Musical Development Progress Report

Musical Development – Sixth Grade Progress Report

Child's Name_____Music Instructor_____School Year_____

Key

Your child's progress toward achieving the school district's standards for music is assessed regularly through tasks based within the three artistic response modes: performing, creating, and responding. Below is a report of your child's musical development as observed through these assessments. The following scale is used: **4** = development exceeds expectations; **3** = development is appropriate; **2** = development is below expectations; **1** = no development has been observed; **IP** = further instruction in this area is planned or in progress.

Music Learning Area:	Reporting Period:	
	1	2
Musical Skills *(singing, playing instruments, improvising; District Standards #1 and #2)*		

- Sings in tune and with correct technique across the entire vocal range
- Sings in two- and three-part harmony
- Aurally identifies tonic, dominant, and sub-dominant harmonic relationships
- Performs advanced instrumental techniques (e.g., 3-mallet playing, recorder above high E)
- Performs independently within multi-level musical textures
- Independently composes melodies and accompaniments in a major scale
- Composes works that demonstrate a harmonic change
- Improvisations exhibit attention to structure and product

Literacy *(reading and writing music; District Standards #1 and #2)*		

- Interprets sixteenth, eighth, quarter, half, and whole notes and rests in 2/4, 3/4, and 4/4 meter
- Recognizes and notates melodies and harmonic changes in the C, F, and G major scales
- Reads and correctly performs four-measure rhythms and melodies
- Correctly notates original compositions and accompaniments using two or more staves
- Interprets simple dynamic, tempo, and structural markings in musical scores

Figure 6-16.

Analysis and Preference
(analyzing music and reactions to music;
District Standard #3)

- Identifies and describes multiple-part musical forms (e.g., march, rondo, song)
- Identifies the make-up of the orchestra in different historical periods
- Evaluates and reviews musical performances and works using multiple criteria
- Develops reasonable criteria for evaluating musical performances and works
- Writes/develops sound musical arguments supporting personal musical preferences
- Can self-assess own musical works and performances
- Successfully assesses the musical works and performances of peers

History and Literature
(appreciation and listening;
District Standard #4)

- Distinguishes between different musical types, styles, and interpretations
- Identifies musical masterworks from various historical periods by their musical traits
- Critiques musical works employing multiple criteria and appropriate terminology

Related Arts and Humanities
(culture, society, and other art forms,
District Standard #5)

- Demonstrates through verbal and written descriptions a basic understanding of how American music reflects American history
- Recognizes and describes common forms in the arts and interrelationships among the subject matter learned in music and nonmusic disciplines

Teacher Comments (first report)	Parent Comments (first report)
Teacher Comments (second report)	Parent Comments (second report)

Figure 6-16. (continued)

in the school music classroom, are most often genuinely impressed with the scope of the music program as outlined on the report. They come to realize in an important way that there is much more to the general music program than the December and Spring concerts.

The primary challenge to the use of developmental profile reporting is *time*. Each school or district that adopts this type of reporting system will need to provide music teachers the necessary release time for their completion and distribution. Teachers who wish to employ this type of reporting system must become advocates for an appropriate amount of time to complete the reports and accept the challenge of convincing those in charge that this type of reporting is valuable to both students and parents. Because of the time involved, the teacher must decide how often this report will be distributed; twice yearly is reasonable.

Another challenge relates to the *amount of paper and copying necessary to produce these reports*. There should be two reports per student—one for the teacher and one to be sent home in the report card—for each marking period. If this is sent home twice a year to 500 students, four reams of paper (2,000 sheets) will be needed, along with the copier supplies (toner, etc.). Preplanning for these printing costs can avoid any confusion over this matter, especially in schools where supply budgets are low.

Managing the reports is a simple matter of filing them by teacher each year in the music room or, for traveling teachers, in an additional file that is kept with the portfolio files. It is not necessary to keep copies of these reports past the beginning of the following academic year. These reports can come in very handy should a dispute or question arise regarding the report. By having the copies on hand at the beginning of the following year, any disputes that arise over the summer can be quickly resolved before the next year begins.

Placing the names on 500 to 600 reports can also be a challenge. This can be managed in one of two ways. The easiest and most efficient method is to hand out the reports during the first music lesson (the same lesson in which the assessment files and portfolios are redistributed), explain and discuss them, and then have the students place their names and their new classroom teacher's name at the top. This job can also be part of the responsibilities of the student assistants/peer mentors for students who enter the class new throughout the year. The second method involves asking the teacher assistants to write the names at the top for you, which they may or may not have time to do. If the assistants cannot do them all, they can be most helpful by completing the names of as many students as they can.

The Self-Assessment Progress Report

In certain circumstances, music teachers may want to allow students the opportunity to report their own progress to their parents. This is best done with older students, and in conjunction with specific projects or works. The design of a self-assessment progress report follows the same format as the profile progress report with two important exceptions. First, *the statements of accomplishment are replaced by criteria for self-assessment,* designed in the same manner discussed in chapter 5. Second, *both the marking grid and the comment area are optional.*

Figure 6-17 is a sample self-assessment, designed for sixth graders to complete at the end of a marking period while they were in the middle of a radio play project (this project is presented in Figure 2-6). The format is very similar to the profile progress report, except that the letters replace the marking grid and there is no designated area for comments. The scoring key is based on the four levels of development model and represents those levels with the letter grades E, S, N, and U instead of numbers.

Sample Self-Assessment as a Progress Report

Sixth Grade Self-Evaluation – Music

Student Name_____Classroom Teacher_____

Dear Parents,

This form is your child's self-evaluation of his/her progress in our Radio Play music lesson project. Your child has also graded himself/herself for the six-week reporting period, and if this grade is consistent with my assessment of your child's work, this grade is the same as that on the report card.

Sincerely,

> **Key** E = expectations exceeded
> S = expectations met
> N = expectations partially met
> U = expectations not met

Project Title_____Project Topic_____

Circle the letter that indicates your progress towards each item.

1. I contributed to the selection of a topic for my group's project.
E S N U

2. I contributed to the research of the topic we chose.
E S N U

3. I helped determine the plot in which our play takes place.
E S N U

4. I contributed to the selection of the characters in our play.
E S N U

5. I contributed to the selection of sound effects and standard repertory selections for our play.
E S N U

6. I am contributing to the development of our script.
E S N U

7. I am contributing to the rehearsal of our script.
E S N U

Because of my overall performance and contribution to our project, my six-week grade should be (circle one):

(E)xcellent **(S)**atisfactory **(N)**eeds improvement **(U)**nsatisfactory

---

Figure 6-17.

It is recommended that when children are given this opportunity, it be given fully and without reservation. However, students need to know that if their self-evaluation results in a report that is deliberately false, the report will be altered to reflect the truth and parents will be informed of the student's attempt to misrepresent his or her progress.

What If a Grade Must Be Given?

Despite the incongruity of grading as a representation of musical progress, there are still many school systems that require a single letter grade as the sole indicator of progress in each school discipline. As discussed earlier, there are many grading practices, the most common being the "A through F" and "E through U" systems. These number-based systems rank order achievement based on mean scores, and therefore, students who obtain "higher grades" are perceived as "better" or "smarter" than those who receive "lower grades." The nuances of musical development are not accounted for or reported to parents in such systems.

Yet, the reality of many teaching situations is that a single letter grade is required. Therefore, fully aware of the theoretical and philosophical lack of fit between the rich assessment data collected in music class and single-grade progress reporting, there are some suggestions that can be made for grading:

1. Even though converting authentic data to ranked grades is mathematically unsupported, the teacher can review the assessment results for the grading period and assign a grade based on *consistency* or *inconsistency* of performance. For example, simply because there may be five letter grades available—A, B, C, D, and F—does not mean that the music specialist must assign each of those grades. It is quite appropriate for a teacher to assign "A" or "B" to those students whose assessments reveal exceptional or consistent progress, and lower grades to those whose progress is inconsistent for reasons *other than natural development.* It is important that the music specialist set some criteria to help distinguish developmentally rooted skill or knowledge problems from those that are deliberate attempts to diminish performance outcomes.

2. Some teachers prefer to give every student the same grade—A, or E—and then send out a letter of explanation about the grades and a profile progress report. In this procedure, the profile is given as *additional information to the grade.*

3. Another approach is to send a brief note of explanation as to what was accomplished in music during the previous marking period, along with a scoring key that explains what the grades mean for *music.* This explanation may be completely different than what the grades mean in other core subjects.

4. A fourth way to bridge the gap between musical performance data and grades that are based on point systems (e.g., A = 93-100, B = 85-92, etc.) is to develop specialized rubrics that give points as levels of achievement. These rubrics are called *point-system rubrics.* That is, in lieu of the usual two to five levels of achievement for each criterion, a range of points, such as 0-20, may be substituted. When using this type of rubric, the teacher first assigns a number of points for the criteria assessed, then determines the number of points the performance earned for that criterion, then adds the points together to make a total score.

An example is shown in Figure 6-18. (Figure 5-10 is another example of a rubric where the levels of achievement represent a number of points.) In this example, the teacher is assessing five criteria for a student's performance of a recorder piece. Each of the five criteria is worth a possible twenty points, and the teacher assigns a number of points he/she feels represents the level of achievement of each criterion based on the performance. The points take the place of levels of achievement, with a higher number of points representing a higher level of achievement. The difficulty with this approach lies in the assignment of points; since there are twenty-one possible point values between zero and twenty, does this mean that there are twenty-one levels of possible achievement? The teacher must predetermine exactly *how many points* will be assigned to certain types of performances so that students can better understand the teacher's point assignments. Therefore, an additional step is recommended to make this type of scoring system absolutely clear to students.

To help students (and teachers) with this approach, it is recommended that levels of achievement be identified and specific numbers of points assigned to these levels of achievement. Referring to the example in Figure 6-18, if the first criterion is worth a total of twenty points, then it is helpful to examine the possible outcomes of that criterion (as discussed in chapter 2) in order to determine a possible number of levels of achievement for the criterion and how those twenty points might represent those levels of achievement. There are three possible levels of achievement for "hand position" on the recorder. In a standard scoring guide, the levels might be:

Level 3 correct hand position

Level 2 inconsistent hand position (position changes during the piece)

Level 1 incorrect hand position

In this case, the teacher might choose to assign the full twenty points for correct hand position, ten points for inconsistent hand position, and zero points for incorrect hand position. Point assignments and levels of achievement can be designed in any way the teacher chooses, as long as the teacher can defend his/her decisions with respect to the assignment of points should a question arise later.

Additionally, numbers of points and how levels of achievement are assigned points is at the teacher's discretion. Certain

Example of a Point-System Rubric

**Event:
Performance of Instrumental Piece – Recorder**

Criterion	Points Possible	Points Earned
1 **Hand position**	20	_____
2 **Fingerings**	20	_____
3 **Accuracy**	20	_____
4 **Phrasing**	20	_____
5 **Use of dynamics**	20	_____
Total	100	_____

Figure 6-18.

assessment criteria may be considered to be more important than others; if so, then the teacher can assign these criteria more points and assign less important criteria fewer points. This practice is called *weighting* the criteria. When score weighting is employed, certain criteria have a greater or lesser effect on the final score (and the final grade) obtained by a student. This can be effective if a teacher wishes to allow more emphasis on certain criteria in the assessment/grading process.

For example, Figure 6-19 displays a weighted version of the rubric shown in Figure 6-18. In this rubric, the teacher has given more points for fingerings and accuracy than for hand position, phrasing, and use of dynamics. This has the effect of giving the scores for fingerings and accuracy more weight in the overall score and final grading. This also implies that the teacher places more emphasis on the students' correct fingerings and the accuracy of the piece rather than the other criteria *for this assessment.* The students who see this rubric before they are assessed also know this; from their viewpoint, fingering and accuracy are worth seventy percent of the total grade, and they will work to get as many of those points as they can. It is important that the teacher stress the other criteria as well (these are very important aspects of a good, total musical performance) because students may focus on the more heavily weighted criteria to the exclusion of the less-weighted criteria.

Example of a Weighted Point-System Rubric

Event: Performance of Instrumental Piece – Recorder		
Criterion	*Points Possible*	*Points Earned*
1 Hand position	10	_____
2 Fingerings	40	_____
3 Accuracy	30	_____
4 Phrasing	10	_____
5 Use of dynamics	10	_____
Total	100	_____

Figure 6-19.

Summary

- As students complete assessment tasks in music, they produce results that can be stored and saved in a portfolio, which is a collection of a student's works that he or she feels best represents his or her progress in a particular school discipline.

- Started as a file in the primary grades, a student's collected musical works can be transformed into a portfolio in the fourth or fifth grade.

- Portfolios may contain written work, tapes, compositions, photos, diskettes, and other items.

- There are two primary portfolio designs: (1) *serial* and (2) *sectional.* The *serial* portfolio is organized by consecutive years. The *sectional* portfolio is organized by a selected criterion, usually the assessment response modes.

- Because of the constructivist nature of music learning, the assessment data collected in music class is rich and varied. More importantly, it represents the efforts of only one student, and this unique data cannot be used for comparing a student's progress with other individuals. Therefore, the *developmental profile progress report* is recommended for reporting musical progress to parents. This report provides parents a set of statements of accomplishment in music that are marked according to a predetermined scoring key. The report also provides space for teacher and parent comments.

- If a grade must be given for music, the teacher should approach this carefully so the proper message is given to parents. This can be handled through written communication with parents at reporting times or through point-system rubrics.

Questions for Clarification

1) Unlike other assessments, portfolios are developed over a period of _____.

2) The music portfolio is a _____ of a student's work that represents his/her musical progress and development.

3) Data collection for portfolio development can begin in the primary grades using _____ _____.

4) Files can be converted into portfolios at the end of _____ or _____ grade.

5) The _____ portfolio design organizes materials by the academic year in which they were produced.

6) The _____ portfolio design organizes materials by category or criterion.

7) Because each student develops musically at a unique pace, reporting musical progress to parents is more effective with the _____ _____ _____ _____.

8) The recommended scoring keys for profile progress reports involve either _____ levels of musical progress or _____ levels of musical development.

9) The profile report's Statements of Accomplishment are based on the school district's _____, _____, _____ _____, and/or _____.

10) Behavioral information that may be affecting a student's progress belongs in the _____ section of the progress report.

11) When a profile report's Statements of Accomplishment are metacognitive criteria, then the profile is actually a _____ - _____ progress report.

Questions for Discussion

1) Do you feel that music portfolios are worth the time and effort to complete? Do you believe that your students would benefit from such a project?

2) How might you begin the portfolio process (with files) in your teaching situation? With what grade level? When would you plan to have the students convert their files to portfolios?

3) Of the two portfolio designs discussed in this chapter, which do you feel would work best in your situation? Why? Are reflective essays an important part of a child's music education?

4) In your opinion, should portfolios be assessed? Support your response.

5) Do you have access to any technological resources that might help you streamline the portfolio process in your teaching situation? Describe these and how they might help.

6) How do you feel about giving grades in music? Why do you feel this way?

7) What are some of the ways you report student musical progress to parents other than the report card?

8) Is the developmental profile progress report feasible? Why or why not?

9) If you are currently teaching (or might be in the future) in a school system that requires a single letter grade for music, how do you (or would you) approach this? Do any of the approaches suggested in this book seem feasible to you?

Assessment Practice

Assessment Practice 1

Using the steps outlined in this chapter, design a portfolio project that will suit your particular teaching situation or one that you anticipate. Present the final project outline to the class, your supervisor, or your administrator for comment.

Step 1: Determine what is important that you teach for which you have evidence.

Step 2: Determine what is important for your students to reflect upon from their study with you, and formulate the topics of the reflective essays.

Step 3: Determine a portfolio design (serial or sectional), and determine what materials students will need.
- Materials needed
- What I can provide
- Organizing scheme

Step 4: Determine a time line for implementation.

- When is a good time to start?
- How will I start? (with one class, grade level, entire student body, etc.)

Step 5: Determine if the portfolio will be assessed and, if so, the rubric and/or grading scale to be used.

Step 6:   Set a due date; give at least two weeks for completion.

- Due date (projected)
- How will these be collected and returned?
- Will these be housed in the music room? How?

Step 7:   Design a portfolio checklist for your students.

Assessment Practice 2

Choose a grade level and design a developmental profile progress report, using the guidelines presented in this chapter for the sections. Use your computer word processing program to assist in the formatting.

Step 1:   Determine the introductory statements (if any) and the scoring key. If beneficial, plan and write an introductory letter to parents announcing this type of reporting.

Step 2:   Develop a set of (eight to ten) clear Statements of Accomplishment.

Step 3:   Design and draw the marking grid, and add the comment area.

Assessment Practice 3

Appendix A (in the back of this book) contains a reproduction of Whitney's serial design music portfolio, with materials from three years (grades 4, 5, and 6). (The optional sections and the entire radio play, though, are not reproduced because of space limitations.) Whitney organized this portfolio using the following checklists:

- Fourth and fifth grade materials—checklist in Figure 6-3
- Sixth grade materials—checklist in Figure 6-4

First, examine this portfolio carefully and determine if the checklists were followed. Then, using the rubric in Figure 6-7, assess the portfolio itself. How did you rate this portfolio? Do you need to adjust the rubric?

Assessment Practice 4

Appendix B presents the organizing pages only from Pooja's sectional design portfolio. Is the organization clear? What is your opinion of this organizing scheme as compared to the serial design?

Pooja organized this using the checklist in Figure 6-5. Did she follow the checklist?

Chapter 7

Implementing a Total Assessment Program

This final chapter focuses upon the issues involved in implementing a teacher-designed assessment component in the music classroom. These issues—*administering tasks, piloting and benchmarking tasks, making a plan for implementation*—have been brought up throughout this book. This chapter seeks to help the music specialist understand and deal with these issues in ways that will provide maximum benefit to the music program.

Administering Tasks

Teachers who write assessment tasks for their classes also need to administer them properly. Appropriate and consistent administrative procedures help ensure that the task is fair to students and will yield reliable results. While each task developed by the music teacher is different, there is a standard procedure that should be followed for implementing all types of assessments (see Figure 7-1). The following is a description of these steps:

1. *Pre-task issues.* Inform students at least a week in advance (if possible) that the assessment task will be administered. As part of this advance notice, provide a review or list of specific knowledge and/or skills to be covered. It is also good practice to assign the student assistants or other reliable individuals the job of providing this information to any absentees.

2. *Present the task.* It is recommended that the task be presented in several different ways to help ensure that all

Steps for Administering Assessment Tasks

1. **Pre-task issues** — inform students at least a week in advance (if possible) that the assessment task will be administered

2. **Present the task** — provide a thorough verbal explanation and back this up in writing either on the board, a chart, individual task sheets, or the computer video monitor; allow questions regarding the procedures

3. **Check for materials and supplies** — make sure all students have the proper materials and supplies before the task begins; instrument preparations should also be completed at this time

4. **Discuss the room arrangement for the task** — single student, student pairs, or small groups

5. **Present the scoring guide and discuss the time allowed for completion** — explain and post the scoring guide for the task, either on the board, video monitor, chart, or individual papers; then, inform students of the amount of time allotted for completion of the task

6. **Present sample responses representative of each level of achievement in the scoring guide** — show students sample responses that reflect the levels of achievement in the scoring guide

7. **Set the protocol for student behavior during the task** — talking, restroom breaks, procedure for asking questions, as well as consequences for not following the protocol

8. **Start the task, monitor the students, end the task, and collect the responses**

Figure 7-1.

students understand what needs to be done once the task begins. The teacher should provide a thorough verbal explanation and back this up in writing either on the board, a chart, individual task sheets, or the computer video monitor (if the classroom is equipped with a television/video monitor, most

TVs can be connected to the classroom computer in order to display the computer monitor on the TV screen). If the task involves a specific order of steps, then explain each of these steps in the order in which they must be completed. Allow students to ask questions regarding the procedures during this presentation period.

3. *Check for materials and supplies.* If the task requires specific materials and/or supplies, check to make sure these are available to all students before the task begins. This is the time to check the readiness of musical instruments and prepare them.

4. *Discuss the room arrangement for the task.* If the task requires that students be placed in a specific arrangement, do this at this time. There are three primary task arrangements for students: (a) *single student,* (b) *student pairs,* and (c) *cooperative groups.*

5. *Present the scoring guide and discuss the time allowed for completion.* It is imperative that students understand at the outset of any task exactly how they will be assessed and what they need to do to achieve at a high level on any task. Explain the scoring guide fully, going over each criterion and its levels of achievement thoroughly. Posting the scoring guide for the task, either on the board, video monitor, chart, or individual papers, will provide students a frame of reference as they work on the task and will ensure that no student can later claim that he or she didn't know what was expected. Then, set the amount of time allotted for completion of the task.

6. *Present sample responses at each level of achievement in the scoring guide.* If they are available (assuming this is not the first time the task has been administered), show students sample responses that reflect the levels of achievement in the scoring guide. These include (but are not limited to) audio- and videotapes of performances, sample compositions, and sample written work. It is also effective to show students samples that reflect only the highest and lowest levels of achievement; the students can then view what they should aspire to achieve (the top level) and what they should not achieve (the lowest level). The *only* time this step should be omitted is the first time that any task is given because sample responses don't exist until after the first administration. Of course, this should only be done for tasks in which there are many possible good responses. If the assessment is a quiz or other test with right or wrong answers, sample responses would not be shown.

It is important that any teacher who uses student work as a classroom sample obtain permission from the student and parent to do so. A phone call or brief discussion is all that is necessary to take care of this. Samples should also remain anonymous, so the student's name should be removed from any identifying section.

7. *Set the protocol for behavior during the task.* Set the parameters of acceptable behavior during task completion. This includes procedures for asking questions, using the restroom, and communicating with other members of the class (when working in pairs or small groups). Outline clear consequences for not following the set protocol, the strongest of which can be confiscation of the response before it is completed.

8. *Start the task, monitor the students, end the task, and collect the responses.* Once the task begins, enforce the behavior protocol throughout the task. When the task is completed, collect the responses.

When the task is complex and is planned to last for more than one music lesson, follow steps 2 through 6 of this general procedure at the start of each subsequent lesson. Authentic tasks and integrated projects are also learning experiences, and the line of demarcation between "task" and "lesson" can become difficult to ascertain. As long as the general steps above are followed, the responses and products of the tasks will be both valid and reliable for use as assessment data.

Post-Task Adjustments

To devise initial assessment criteria, teachers often make assumptions about the actual outcomes of an assessment task. However, when the students complete and turn in their responses, the responses may not match what was predicted. Even though a great deal of thought may have gone into the task, its criteria, and its scoring procedures, there are times when the actual responses to an assessment task are so different from the original projections that the scoring procedure requires *post-task adjustment*. These situations are almost always a result of errors in judgment and can occur for a number of reasons:

1. The teacher may have made the task too simple, in which case the students all reached the highest level of achievement. In other words, the task did not discriminate among the levels of achievement. There is not much that can be done about this after the task except for the teacher to reexamine and revise the task for its next administration.

2. The opposite may have occurred—the task was too difficult, and all students achieved at the lowest level. In this case, the teacher should first examine the responses with respect to the pre-established criteria to check if there are levels of achievement that are evident. If levels of achievement can be determined, then the scoring guides can be adjusted to accommodate those levels. Otherwise, the task should be revised and administered again.

3. Least common—the responses are all at the same level, but the level is neither the highest nor the lowest. There is little that can be done at this point to change the scoring procedures in a meaningful and fair way. If this occurs, the teacher should redesign the task to be more difficult for the next administration. It is also appropriate to discuss the results with the students and to uncover what they were thinking during the task. Many times the changes necessary for strengthening the task will come from the children themselves.

While it may be appropriate in certain circumstances to adjust the predetermined scoring procedures to accommodate the actual responses received, it is never appropriate to adjust the criteria used for assessment post-task. If the criteria are not met by most or all of the responses, then these results should be disregarded and a new task devised that presents more realistic criteria. Altering the criteria post-task would damage the validity and fairness of the task since the responses were written to meet the original criteria.

Administering Pilot Tasks and Benchmarking

Piloting Assessment Tasks

One way to lessen the necessity for post-task adjustments is to first pilot an assessment task. A *pilot task* is no different than other assessment tasks in design or difficulty. However, the purpose of a pilot task is to *"try out" the task with a small group of students in order to check its effectiveness.* Pilot tasks are usually completed with a "sample group" that is representative of the larger group that will be given the final task. For most music teachers, tasks can be successfully piloted with one class. The class chosen for piloting a task should be representative of all the classes that will eventually complete the task. Tasks within all response modes can be piloted before they are more widely administered.

Once the task is administered (following the above steps), the responses should be collected and examined in relation to the predetermined assessment criteria. Because the results of a pilot task are not used for official progress reporting, the criteria and scoring guides can be adjusted to better reflect the actual responses to strengthen the task's validity, reliability, and ability to discriminate among the levels of achievement in the scoring guide. The task can be redesigned or revised, then administered in its new form.

The Benchmarking Process

Once a task has been piloted and revised, it can be administered for benchmarking. A *benchmark response is one that reflects a task's assessment criteria at a particular level of achievement* and could be considered *representative* or *typical*. Benchmarks are general examples of what a response should *look like* or *sound like* at a particular level of achievement. The benchmarking process involves the examination of task responses, followed by the selection of those that best represent the meaning of the different levels of the assessment criteria. These "benchmarks" can then be used as examples for students to preview and as guides for assessing the other responses. The benchmarking process is valuable for tasks in all of the assessment response modes. Here are some recommended steps for proceeding through the benchmarking process:

1. *Assess the responses and arrange them by achievement level.* The first step in the process is to assess the responses. The assessed responses then need to be compiled into achievement levels. For example, if the responses were scored using a four-level rubric, there would be four compilations of responses, one for each rubric level.

2. *Review each compilation of responses and select two or three typical examples.* The next step is to review all of the responses at one level and select two or three that are the most typical. This decision is a judgment made by the teacher after comparing the responses or products to the assessment criteria. The most typical responses will be those that express what the teacher feels is indicative of the level of achievement that it represents.

3. *Select one response from the two or three as a benchmark.* This is another judgment call made by the teacher. The two or three responses that were selected in step 2 should be reviewed again, then one should be selected as the best example of each level of achievement. These responses become the benchmarks that can serve as "model responses" for future assessment of the benchmarked task. Benchmarks can also be used as samples during the presentation of a task, but like any sample, they must be anonymous, used only with student and parental permission. These steps are summarized in Figure 7-2.

The Benchmarking Process

When the assessment task is completed:

1. **Arrange** the assessed responses by achievement level.

2. **Review** each compilation of responses and select two or three typical examples.

3. **Select** one response from the two or three as a benchmark.

Figure 7-2.

The piloting and benchmarking processes are also valuable for other reasons:

1. They provide students an opportunity to participate in "practice" assessment tasks that provide experience with the assessment process.

2. Teachers can write and administer pilot tasks to sharpen their skills at task design and to gain experience with criteria building and revision.

3. The benchmarking process streamlines future assessment of the task by providing response samples that can be used as models of the typical response at each level of achievement.

Making a Plan for Implementing Assessment in the Classroom

The music specialist who is ready to develop an assessment program for the classroom—designing tasks, administering tasks, benchmarking responses, managing assessment data, gathering assessment files, building portfolios, reporting musical progress to parents—may find the idea of beginning and developing an assessment program with 500 or 600+ students an overwhelming task. Introducing assessment components and the management of large amounts of student data into an already busy or full schedule can seem impossible. However, if approached carefully and systematically, all music teachers can become proficient task designers and data managers. There are two approaches that will be presented here—the *grade-selective model* and the *grade-inclusive model*—both of which permit the gradual introduction of assessment techniques into the teacher's work.

The *grade-selective* model involves introducing a planned assessment program with a selected grade level or class. This is recommended to begin with a primary grade level or class for elementary generalists, and the lowest grade level served by the middle and high school general music teacher, in a similar manner as the approach presented for starting portfolios in chapter 6. Teachers should select a grade level (the youngest appropriate grade level is recommended) at which they feel most comfortable introducing assessment strategies and techniques, plan ahead, and begin at that level for one year. The assessment tasks designed for the grade level would be piloted, revised, implemented, and benchmarked for future years. As the class or grade level "moves up" to the next grade level, the teacher begins the assessment component with the current students in the grade level and continues with the grade level begun the year before. This process continues until the teacher's entire class load is being assessed and managed successfully. This approach takes several years to implement and permits teachers to develop the assessment program gradually.

For example, a teacher opting for the grade-selective approach to assessment program development might decide to begin an assessment program with the current year's first grade class. A series of planned strategies would be administered throughout the year, their data collected and managed, and student progress reported with profiles. When these students progress to the second grade, the assessment program is developed for the second grade as a continuation of what was done in the first grade, and assessment files are started for portfolios. In addition, the first grade assessment component is engaged with the new academic year's first grade students. This process should continue through-out the remainder of the student's years in the school. When the original students are ready to move to their next level of schooling (usually around the fifth grade in elementary schools), the assess-ment program will be fully developed and in practice.

Figure 7-3 illustrates an example of the grade-selective model that starts at the first grade. The example includes three assess-ments per year within each assessment response mode, a total of nine assessments each year. The assessments should be placed near the beginning of the year, the middle of the year, and the end of the year so progress can be adequately gauged. Teachers may certainly administer more or fewer tasks to suit their personal interests or their district's requirements.

The *grade-inclusive* model is the approach used by teachers who wish to begin with all of their students and grade levels in the same year. This model is, by its nature, more challenging to imple-ment because of its scope. To keep this approach manageable, it is recommended that teachers implement fewer assessments in the first year. In this model, because the teacher is starting an assess-ment program with *all* students, the program develops over the years through the addition of assessment tasks until there are suf-ficient data to support confident progress reporting in all learning

The Grade-Selective Model for Introducing Assessment in the General Music Classroom

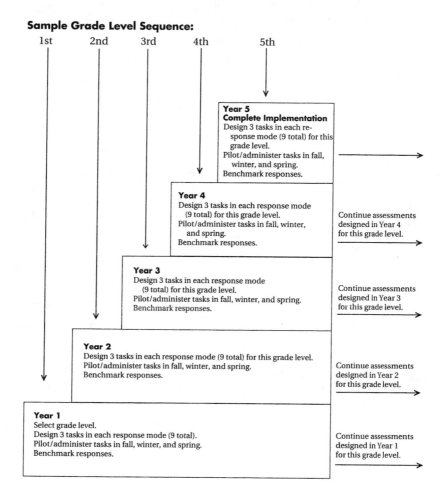

Figure 7-3.

areas pertinent to the curriculum. The recommended sequence of increasing tasks is as follows:

1. For the first year, one task in each response mode should be designed, piloted, revised, implemented, and bench-marked. For example, in the situation where a music teacher serves twenty-four classes, four each from kindergarten through fifth grade, the grade-inclusive model suggests that three assessment tasks be designed and implemented for each class and/or grade level during the first year. The three tasks can be designed in the same response mode, or there can be one task designed in each of the three response modes.

2. During the second year, three additional tasks can be devised and added to the program.

3. In the third year, this can be expanded again by three tasks.

4. At the end of the third year, all classes should be experiencing three assessments per year in each of the response modes.

This model, which is shown in Figure 7-4, demonstrates the two options that teachers have with respect to task development. If three tasks are devised within one response mode, these are implemented at the beginning, middle, and end of the academic year. If one task is developed within each response mode, then these can be placed near the middle or end of the academic year, or wherever the teacher feels that they will best serve his or her needs.

These models are presented not as prescriptions for practice but as general frameworks within which music teachers can work in order to gradually add an assessment component to their teaching. Teachers should feel free to add and design as many tasks as they desire; three is a number that has been chosen only for modeling purposes. By designing and implementing at least one assessment task in the performing, creating, and responding modes at the beginning, middle, and end (fall, winter, and spring for most teachers) of the academic year, teachers have a foundation upon which to build. There is no prescribed number of tasks that teachers ought to give in order to be doing a "good job." Some teachers gather assessment data nearly every music lesson, while others will assess less frequently. It seems, though, that if a teacher

The Grade-Inclusive Model for Introducing Assessment in the General Music Classroom

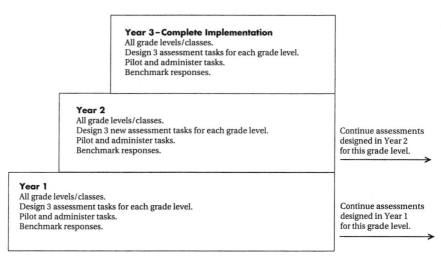

Year 3 – Complete Implementation
All grade levels/classes.
Design 3 assessment tasks for each grade level.
Pilot and administer tasks.
Benchmark responses.

Year 2
All grade levels/classes.
Design 3 new assessment tasks for each grade level.
Pilot and administer tasks.
Benchmark responses.

Continue assessments
designed in Year 2
for this grade level.
⟶

Year 1
All grade levels/classes.
Design 3 assessment tasks for each grade level.
Pilot and administer tasks.
Benchmark responses.

Continue assessments
designed in Year 1
for this grade level.
⟶

Figure 7-4.

is going to keep track of student progress and report this progress to parents with confidence, an assessment in each response mode three times per year is the minimum.

The models do not specifically mention the implementation of developmental progress reports or the collection of data for portfolios. A suggested time line for implementing these practices was presented in chapter 6. However, the teacher who wants to include these practices in the development of the total program will find the grade-selective model the most efficient. Both assessment files and profile progress reports can begin in year one with the selected grade level, and each year another grade level can be added.

Pitfalls to Avoid

To effectively and reliably assess children's musical growth and progress, teachers must maintain their objectivity. By remaining objective, music teachers ensure that they are being fair to the students and the parents by gathering correct data. This issue is important for all music teachers, especially those in the elementary schools, who are genuinely caring and loving individuals who want their students to not be harmed by a less-than-positive assessment result. One of the most important changes that a teacher can make in music education is the implementation of objective but positive assessment reporting. Inaccurate reporting of assessment results is detrimental to a child's progress. It is not helpful to tell children that an inaccurate response is correct; instead, it is better to point out the strengths of their work, then explain that you know they did their best job, but "we're going to work on that some more." After that, the teacher should talk about what needs more attention. For example, a third grader who has sung a solo below the pitch might be told: "You have such a pleasant voice, and you stand so nicely when you sing. However, we need to work on helping you sing with a lighter tone so you can hear the pitch you are supposed to match; that time your voice was a little below the pitch." This is but one of many ways to accurately report results to students while still maintaining their self-esteem.

The second pitfall to avoid is being pressured to do more with assessment than you feel you can comfortably handle. If you sense that your administrator is expecting more from your assessment program than you can do thoroughly, show your administrator the model (from this book) that you have chosen for implementation of your program and discuss this issue openly. Good administrators know that music specialists serve large numbers of students, and they should understand when you are feeling as though they are expecting more than you can provide. If this approach is not as effective as you like, then simply explain that you want what is best for your students, which is a well-designed, properly planned, and effective assessment program, and that his or her expectations will not allow this to happen. It is essential that the music specialist not feel pressured by any level of administration to do more with assessment implementation than can be effective in the classroom at the teacher's level of assessment expertise.

Finally, teachers must remember that the strongest evidence of musical progress is obtained through an ensemble of assessments designed in all three response modes, as well as occasional objectivist-based tests and quizzes. It is important to avoid the pitfall of limiting musical assessment to performance only; valuable and necessary musical information is evidenced in creating and response mode assessments. Additionally, by involving students in these three response modes, we are ensuring that they are given opportunities to be engaged in the three artistic processes. Through a balanced series of assessments that are developed within a high-quality, sequential music education program, music students can demonstrate their musical knowledge and growth in a thorough, valid, and reliable manner.

Conclusion: Maintaining the Momentum

This book opened with a discussion on the importance of assessment in general music. Each of the reasons for the importance of assessment has found explanation and illumination in the chapters since. This book has shown how assessment provides the opportunity to obtain evidence of the musical growth and progress of students so teachers can support their everyday musical decisions. It should be clear now that the data teachers obtain from student assessments can guide instruction and choice of teaching strategies. This book adopts the position that a thorough assessment program and parental reporting procedures can only further validate the general music program. It has been shown that through a well-structured assessment program, students also gain a sense of their own learning and progress.

The general music class should be a place where there is creativity, joy, and a high level of displayed musical skill as well as a place of rigorous musical learning. It is up to the music specialist to ensure that such an environment is maintained. With good lessons and effective, rigorous, and thorough assessment procedures, students can attain levels of musicianship that might have never been imagined before. Musicians become music educators because they want to share their love and knowledge of music with the coming generations. Through a well-designed assessment program, teachers can ensure their students receive the very best music education they can provide.

The purpose of this book is to empower music teachers at all levels of expertise with the skills and knowledge to confidently improve upon their current assessment practices. This book has addressed task design, task administration, piloting and benchmarking, data management, portfolio building, progress reporting to parents, and classroom-level assessment program development.

It's time to get started.

Questions for Clarification

1) To be fair to students, it is important that the music teacher post the _____ _____ for an assessment task for students to refer to during task administration.

2) As part of the explanation of a task, sample _____ that represent different levels of achievement should be shown to students.

3) When the predicted responses do not match the actual responses to a task, it is possible in some cases to make _____ - _____ _____.

4) A task given to a sample group for the purpose of investigating its effectiveness is a _____ _____.

5) The process of selecting "typical" responses from a given set of responses is called _____.

6) There are two models presented in this book for implementing a classroom-level assessment program. The _____ - _____ model begins with a selected grade or class of students and adds a grade each year until the entire program is in place.

7) The _____ - _____ model begins with a few tasks at all grade levels and adds more tasks each year until the entire program is in place.

8) To remain an effective assessor of student work, music teachers must maintain their _____.

Questions for Discussion

1) Using one of the tasks you devised in an earlier chapter, discuss the procedure for administering the task in terms of the steps presented in this chapter. Would you change the administrative procedure in any way to accommodate your task or teaching situation? How and why?

2) Using the same task or another one, discuss whether or not this would be something you would pilot. Is piloting a task worth the time? Discuss the benchmarking process. Do you think benchmarking is a worthwhile procedure?

3) Have you ever had an experience with an assessment, as a teacher or a student, where a post-task adjustment had to take place? Can you think of a possible situation in which this might need to happen?

4) · If you are just beginning a classroom-level assessment program, discuss the models presented in this chapter for developing a program. Which model do you think would be best for you? If you are an experienced teacher and you are already involved with assessment, can you determine where you "are" in either model? Do the models apply to you or your situation?

5) Now that you have finished this book, discuss your thoughts on assessment in general music. How have your thoughts changed? Or have they?

Appendix A
Whitney's Portfolio

Portfolio Figure A-1.

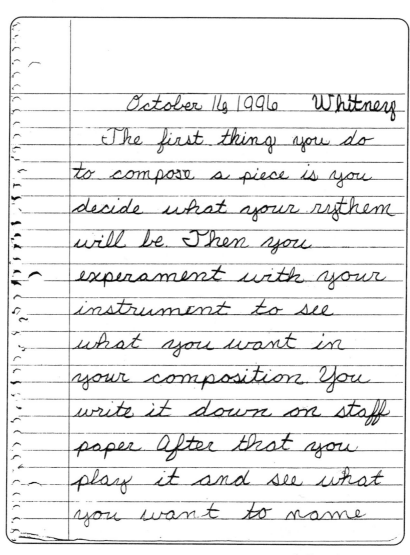

October 16 1996   Whitney

The first thing you do to compose a piece is you decide what your rythem will be. Then you experament with your instrument to see what you want in your composition. You write it down on staff paper After that you play it and see what you want to name

Portfolio Figure A-2.

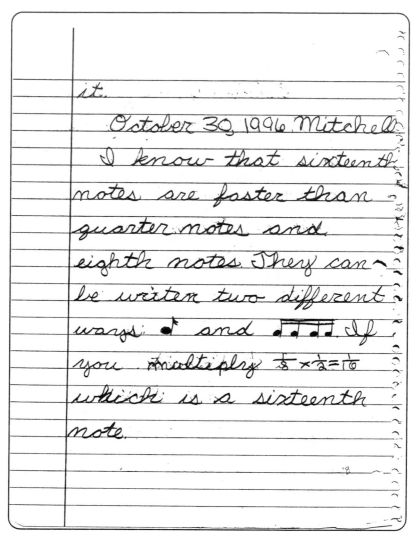

it.

October 30, 1996 Mitchell
I know that sixteenth
notes are faster than
quarter notes and
eighth notes. They can
be written two different
ways: ♪ and ♫ If
you multiply $\frac{1}{8} \times \frac{1}{2} = \frac{1}{16}$
which is a sixteenth
note.

Portfolio Figure A-3.

Music
September 4, 1996
Today I learned what a pentatonic scale is. It is a scale with five tones. I also learned how to play a new song on a glockenspiel.

September 25, 1996
Today I learned how to compose a piece. I also learned what rhythm means. I reviewed and demonstrated the music

Portfolio Figure A-4.

room rules. We also practiced "Music Means the World to Me."

October 2, 1996

Today I demonstrated the music room rules and completed composing from last week. I learned that the measure lines should not go off the staff. I also learned how to draw beams on notes. I

Portfolio Figure A-5.

Portfolio Figure A-6.

Portfolio Figure A-7.

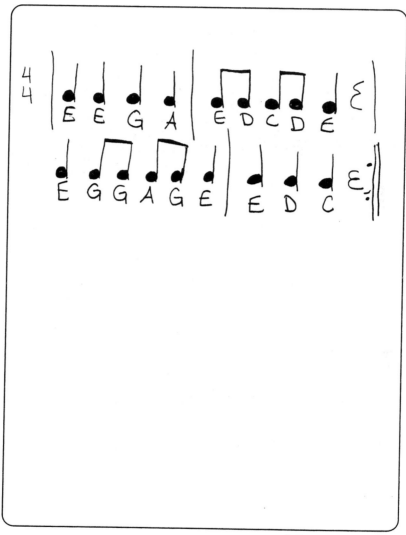

Portfolio Figure A-8.

Portfolio Figure A-9.

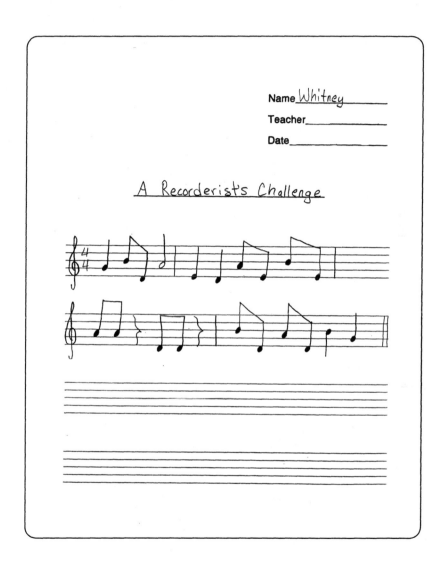

Portfolio Figure A-10.

Portfolio Figure A-11.

I had flute parts in the Christmas and end of the year programs.

Portfolio Figure A-12.

Portfolio Figure A-13.

Portfolio Figure A-14.

Music   Whitney

9-12-97

Tempo = speed of the beat

Fast = allegro
       vivace

Slow = andante
       adagio

Medium = moderato

1. allegro

2. moderato

3. andante moderato

4. allegro

5. allegro

6. moderato

7. allegro

8. adagio

Portfolio Figure A-15.

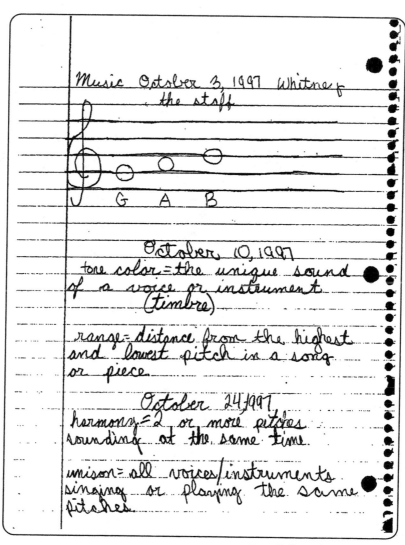

Portfolio Figure A-16.

Whitney   Music 10-31-97

1 beat of silence = 𝄽 = quarter rest

2 sounds/beat = ♫ = eighth

1 sound/beat = ♩ = quarter

2 beats/sound = 𝅗𝅥 = half

meter signature tells the number of beats in one measure.

bar lines separate sets of beats into measures.

a double bar shows the end of a piece.

1-9-98   test notes

singing and vocal production
need good posture, open your mouth,
registers, breath support.

Portfolio Figure A-17.

Instruments:
- how to handle mallets
- where to strike instrument
- which hand goes on top of recorder
- recorder notes
- make fingering chart

Literacy
- identify treble clef, staff, meter signature, measures, and bar lines
- identify Beetoven no.s 5, 9 and Mozart's *Eine Kleine Nachtmusik*
- identify the composer- Bach, Mozart, or Beetoven in pieces.

Rhythum
- identify eighth, quarter, and half notes and rests
- know the division of the beat
- know beats per sound

Portfolio Figure A-18.

My Progress in Writing About Music in Fifth Grade

When I look at my journal entries from the beginning of the year, the things I was just learning are very familar to me now. My later writing was more detailed therefore I had a more complete understanding of music. Once I started learning, the harder things made more sense As I learned more, it was easier to remember the things I learned by writing them down.

Portfolio Figure A-19.

Coda Compositions 𝆑

and

Projects

Portfolio Figure A-20.

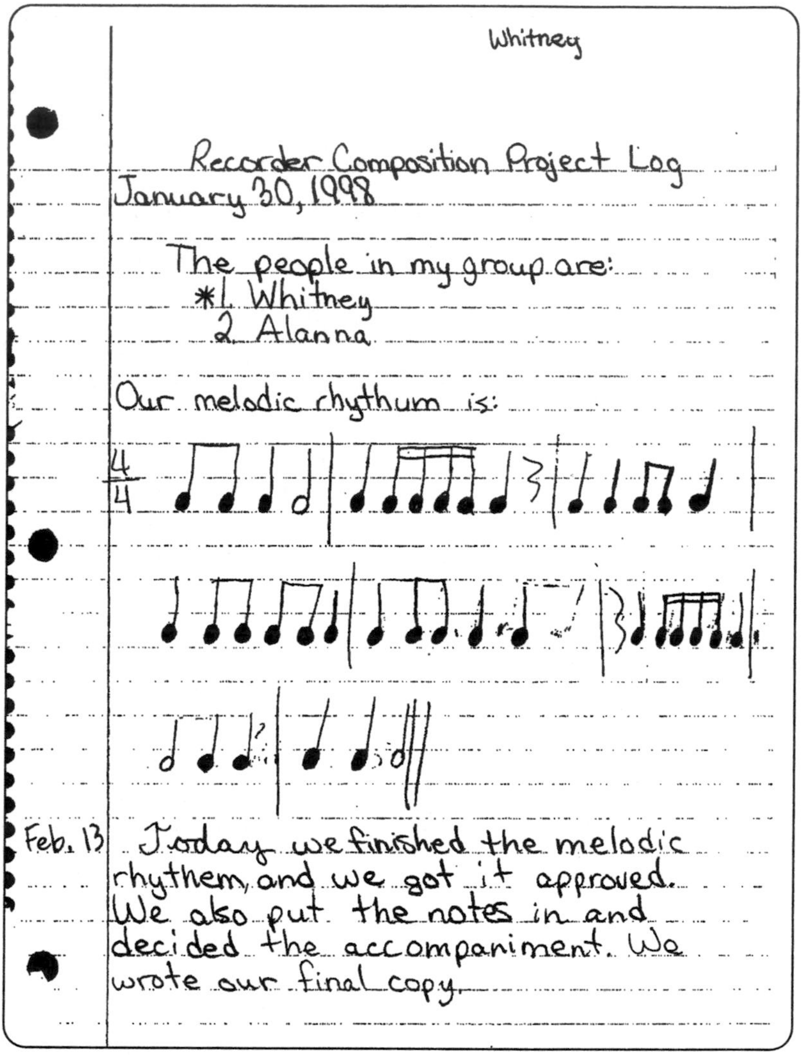

Whitney

Recorder Composition Project Log

January 30, 1998

The people in my group are:
*1. Whitney
2 Alanna

Our melodic rhythum is:

Feb. 13 Today we finished the melodic rhythem and we got it approved. We also put the notes in and decided the accompaniment. We wrote our final copy.

Portfolio Figure A-21.

Feb. 27 We practiced our piece and named it. We are using the recorder and the bass xylophone.

3-6 We performed our piece and put it on the computer. We performed it on News Channel 13.

Portfolio Figure A-22.

Portfolio Figure A-23.

Butterflies

Portfolio Figure A-24.

My Progress in Composing
and Notating Music

At the beginning of
the year, I didn't know
much about composing
or notating music. When
I started writing Butterflies,
I began to understand it
more. By looking back at
the first copy of it, I see
how much I have improved.
I even wrote a piece at
home. I am very comfortable
composing and notating
music now.

Portfolio Figure A-25.

What I Know About the Business of Music

At the beginning of the year I knew nothing about the business of music. When the project started, I thought it would be complicated and it was. The financial department had to calculate many things such as royalties, manufacturing cost, and recording cost. The art department had to design many things. The process of making a CD or tape is long and time consuming.

Portfolio Figure A-26.

Portfolio Figure A-27.

My Performances

This year, I missed the Christmas performance. I recorded my flute on the CD that our choir made. I sang and played recorder at the end of the year performance. I also played recorder and sang at the All City performance.

Portfolio Figure A-28.

My Progress in Evaluating Musical Performances

At the beginning of the year I had no idea how to evaluate musical performances. Using the method of creating criteria that Mr. Brophy taught us helped me. After doing it a couple times it got easier. Learning this process has helped me understand music better.

Portfolio Figure A-29.

My Future in Music

I plan for music to be a part of my life forever. I will try out for the youth symphony on flute. I will continue to play piano and flute. I think that my life will be fuller because I enjoy my music.

Portfolio Figure A-30.

My Progress from Fourth
to Fifth Grade in Music:
Writing, Composing and
Notating, and General
Knowledge

In fourth grade, my
writing samples were not
as complicated. They were
also more difficult to
understand. The things
I had just learned in
fourth grade were very
familar to me in fifth
grade. Writing in fifth
grade was easier because
I had experience from
fourth grade.
I have definitely improved
in composing and notating
music. I composed a
piece at home. In fourth
grade, my songs were
very short and simple.
In fifth grade they were
long, difficult, and

Portfolio Figure A-31.

interesting. I have much more confidence in composing and notating music now.

In fifth grade, music has become a much bigger part of my life. I have learned many more things on recorder. Much music terminology that I didn't understand in fourth grade I now understand. It is obvious to me that I have made much progress from fourth grade to fifth grade.

Portfolio Figure A-32.

Portfolio Figure A-33.

Portfolio Figure A-34.

Whitney

coda = conclusion ⊕

d.s. al coda ✗

tone color = timbre

AABA' = modified song form

AAB = song form

9-21 Verse-refrain ‖: A B :‖

9-28-98

ABA form = ternary form
        tripartite

10-29-98

There are three categories of
    musical forms:
① Sectional- ‖: A B :‖, AAB, AABA
② Imitative- fugues, canons
③ Developmental- motive- 3 to 5 notes,
    rhythmic values
        Sonata allegro

Portfolio Figure A-35.

	A B		11-5-98
A prime	A' B'	= prime	
A double prime	A" B"		
	A"' B"'		
	A"" B""		

2-25-99

* Harmony - a confluence of pitches that makes a specific sounds.

* Scale - a stepwise progression of tones that are used in melodies and harmonies.

* Interval - two pitches sounding simultaneously.

* Chord - three or more pitches sounding simultaneously.

Triadic Harmony

Major and minor modality: describes both scales and harmonies.

Portfolio Figure A-36.

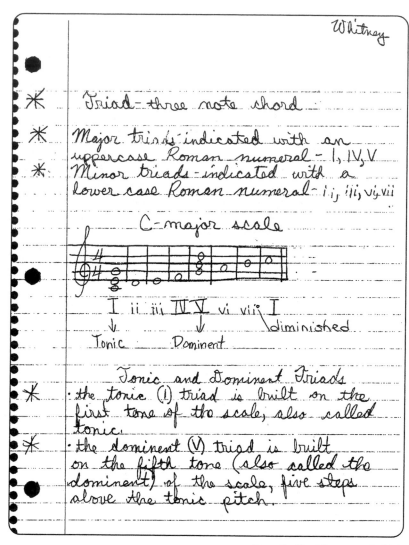

Whitney

* Triad - three note chord

* Major triads indicated with an uppercase Roman numeral - I, IV, V

* Minor triads - indicated with a lower case Roman numeral - i, ii, iii, vi, vii

C-major scale

I ii iii IV V vi vii I
↓ ↓ \diminished
Tonic Dominent

Tonic and Dominent Triads

* • the tonic (I) triad is built on the first tone of the scale, also called tonic.

* • the dominent (V) triad is built on the fifth tone (also called the dominent) of the scale, five steps above the tonic pitch.

Portfolio Figure A-37.

428

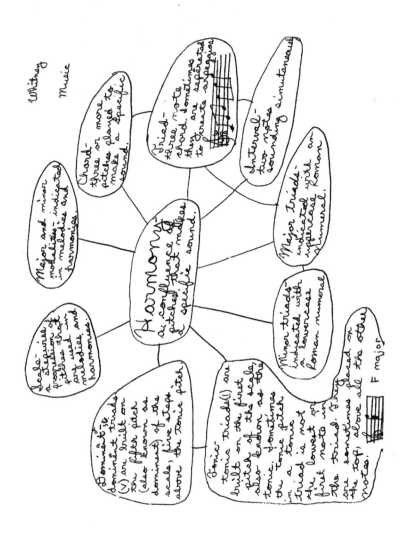

Portfolio Figure A-38.

Portfolio Figure A-39.

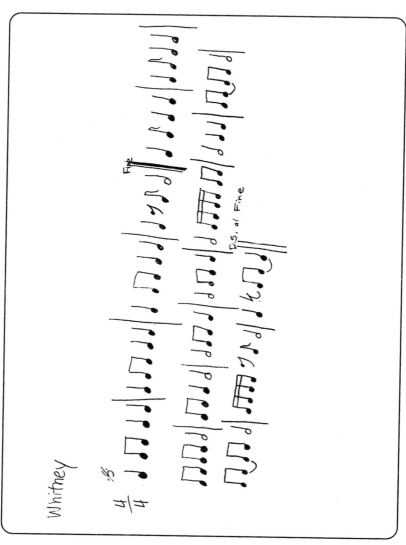

Portfolio Figure A-40.

Portfolio Figure A-41.

Portfolio Figure A-42.

Characters

Sally May..

Billy Bob..

Mary Jane..

Pa..

Friend..Whitney

Ma..

Mrs. Kay..Whitney

Portfolio Figure A-43.

Piano From the Inside Out

<Mary Jane and Sally May walk in>

<Pencil hitting string>

Sally May	What in the world are you doing, Billy Bob, with a rubber band across pencils hitting it?
Billy Bob	Well, Sally May, I was just making some music.
Sally May	Hey, Mary Jane, that's like a piano works!
Mary Jane	Yeah, it is!

<Billy Bob runs to piano and girls follow>

Billy Bob	Lemme see!

<Billy Bob opens top of piano and it slams shut>

Pa	What are 'yall kids doing in there? 'Yall woke the baby!

<Baby crying>

Mary Jane	Sorry, Pa.

Portfolio Figure A-44.

Whitney

Radio Play Self-Assessment
Piano From the Inside Out
Friend and Mrs. Kay were my
characters.
—I learned that the piano
was invented in the 1700s,
the harpsichord strings are
plucked, the dulcimer was
invented 5,000 years ago, and
the frame of a piano is
made cast iron.
—We had interesting and catchy
voices, and we had things
that made the listener laugh.
—We could have talked with
more feeling and exaggerated
our words.

Portfolio Figure A-45.

6th Grade Performances

In the 6th grade I was in Advanced Recorder, a group for talented recorder players. I was chosen to participate in All City, a concert with children from schools all over the city. I also was a part in the choir. My radio play group recorded our play at Kingsbury. I went to Ardent Recording Studio to record 2 songs with my choir. I went to a nursing home and the mall to sing with my choir. In the Christmas program, I played my flute on one of the selections. I will play my flute at the end of the year program.

Portfolio Figure A-46.

> My Progress in
> Writing About Music,
> Composing and Notating Music,
> Performing Music,
> and General Knowledge About Music
> from 4th to 6th Grade
>
> My writing has matured from 4th to 6th grade. My entries were longer in 6th grade. I wrote more complicated terms and words in 6th grade. The things I was writing about in 4th grade seemed uncomplicated in 6th grade. Since it was my third year to write about music in 6th grade, it was much easier for me.
> In 4th grade, I was not as familiar with composing and notating music. My pieces in 6th grade were much longer. They had more complex rhythms in them. My notations were neater in 6th grade. My compositions in 4th grade were simpler. I didn't write accompaniments to my pieces in 4th grade, but I did in 6th grade. I was much more comfortable composing and notating music in 6th grade.

Portfolio Figure A-46.

In 4th grade, I didn't sing at any performances. I didn't go anywhere to perform. In 6th grade, I even went to a famous recording studio, Ardent, to record two songs with my choir. I was not as confident in 4th grade when I was performing. I had more experience in 6th grade, so I was more confident. I performed more in 6th grade.

My general knowledge about music drastically increased from 4th to 6th grade. I learned all about harmony, and now I understand how it really works. The things that I was just learning in 4th grade were the basics that I built on in 6th grade. I barely knew anything about notating music in 4th grade, but in 6th grade, I knew a tremendous amount of things about it.

Portfolio Figure A-48.

Appendix B
Pooja's Portfolio, Organizing Pages

Portfolio Figure B-1.

Portfolio Figure B-2.

Portfolio Figure B-3.

Portfolio Figure B-4.

Table of Contents
Musical Composition:

Portfolio Figure B-5.

Portfolio Figure B-6.

Portfolio Figure B-7.

Portfolio Figure B-8.

Appendix C

Answers to Questions for Clarification

Chapter One

1. cognitive flexibility
2. case experience
3. situated cognition
4. assessment
5. ill-structured
6. constructivism
7. assessment
8. reflection
9. measurement
10. evaluation
11. objectivist
12. curriculum guide

Chapter Two

1. musical behaviors
2. selection of appropriate materials
3. observer
4. validity
5. reliability
6. reliability
7. variability
8. process or product
9. special needs
10. standardized music test
11. integrated project
12. single
13. rubric

Chapter Three

1. assessable component
2. task target areas

3. observation and listening
4. single-criterion scoring guide
5. plus, minus
6. concept
7. multiple

Chapter Four

1. composition, improvisation, arrangement
2. bi-level
3. melodic, rhythmic, structural, theoretical, aesthetic
4. guided composition
5. melodic
6. notation
7. multi-level, multiple-criterion
8. word cues, musical cues, free improvisation, variations
9. bi-level, multiple-criterion
10. music-based, literature-based
11. expression, instrumentation, sound association, dramatic movement
12. materials, instrumentation
13. multi-level, multiple-criterion

Chapter Five

1. critical thinking
2. procedural application, reflection, metacognition
3. plan the time
4. challenge statement
5. level of engagement
6. specific musical content
7. music specialist
8. alternative assessment
9. bi-level, single-criterion
10. in-school experts

Chapter Six

1. years
2. collection
3. file folders
4. fourth, fifth
5. serial
6. sectional
7. developmental profile progress report
8. three, four
9. standards, expectations, performance indicators, objectives
10. comment
11. self-assessment

Chapter Seven

1. scoring guide
2. responses
3. post-task adjustments
4. pilot task
5. benchmarking
6. grade-selective
7. grade-inclusive
8. objectivity

Glossary

alternative assessment — in music, an assessment technique or strategy that is situated within an authentic context other than that in which the musical learning took place

arrangement — the creation of a new presentation of a familiar piece or song, or the creation of a musical enhancement of a literary work, such as a story or poem

assessable component — a facet of any demonstration of musical knowledge or skill that can be identified and isolated for assessment

assessment — the gathering of information about a student's status relevant to one's academic and/or musical expectations

assessment context — the planned musical and environmental conditions for an assessment task, designed to facilitate the desired response mode(s)

assessment focus — the direction of the teacher's observation and judgment during an assessment task, either toward process (during performance, creating, or responding) or product (the result of the performing, creating, or responding process)

assessment model — a broad, general framework within which the music teacher can build specific assessment strategies that employ a variety of materials and approaches that suit the needs of the teacher and the curriculum

assessment response mode — the mode of assessment task response that corresponds to the artistic process(es) required to complete the task, determined by the musical behavior(s) elicited in the task; these behaviors are exhibited when the student assumes the roles of musical (a) performer (wherein the student interprets existing music), (b) creator (during which the student composes, improvises, or arranges music), and/or (c) responder (when the student behaves as an audience member)

assessment technique — a general strategy that is more specific and more limited in scope than a model, requiring the use of a specific procedure or context to obtain assessment data, but sufficiently variable to suit the teacher's assessment needs or pedagogical perspective

authentic assessment — planned assessment procedures and tasks that simulate the context in which the original learning occurred

benchmark — a response that is representative of a particular task's assessment criterion or criteria at a particular level of achievement

bi-level — when describing scoring guides, referring to two levels of achievement in relation to a given criterion

cognitive flexibility — the ability to represent knowledge from different conceptual and case perspectives, and then when the knowledge must later be used, the ability to construct from those different conceptual and case representations a knowledge ensemble tailored to the needs of the understanding or problem-solving situation at hand

complex content domain — a domain of knowledge in which a multiplicity of perspectives, gained through multiple experiences within the domain, must be obtained in order to learn in the domain

composition — the creation of new music with the intent to revise the musical product(s) to suit the composer's needs or wishes

concept map — a model for alternative verbal direct content assessment, in which a central term is first defined, then related terms and their definitions are mapped around the central term (usually each term is circled) and relationships among the terms are indicated through connecting lines

constructivism — a meta-theoretical framework that subsumes learning theories that are founded on the proposition that experience is the basis for learning and that new knowledge is constructed from previous knowledge in response to new problem-solving situations

criterion — a specific statement that describes an assessable component that is the target of a particular task

criterion-referenced — an assessment task wherein individual achievement is measured in relation to specified criteria

critical thinking in music — the ability to consciously apply cognitive processing to musical experiences, whether thinking about music (reflectively), thinking during musical performance (procedurally), or thinking about one's own personal musical growth (metacognitively)

critical thinking skill — a specific, identifiable cognitive process employed during critical thinking

data collection instrument — the format used to gather and organize assessment data

developmental profile — a type of musical progress report that profiles a student's development in music covering a variety of skills and knowledge, and designed to reflect what is expected at each grade level and to communicate to parents a student's individual progress within each expectation

enabling competencies — the basic skills that underlie and facilitate musical performance, including beat competency, imitation/echo competency, following/mirroring, and kinesthetic musical response

evaluation — the comparison of assessment data in relation to a standard or set of pre-established criteria, with the purpose of determining whether the data represents the achievement of the standard or criteria

fundamental aural discriminations — the category of aural discriminations pertaining to musical opposites (high/low, loud/soft, fast/slow, like/different, stop/start, beginning/ending, long/short) that underlie the development of musical concepts and higher-level musical understanding

guided composition — for novice composers, a process of composing music in which as many parameters are prescribed as the young composer needs to guide him/her toward the successful notation of his/her composition; also used to describe the finished composition that results from this process

ill-structured content domain — a content area where there are no rules or principles of sufficient generality to cover most of the cases, nor defining characteristics for determining the actions appropriate for a given case

improvisation — the spontaneous generation of new music without intent to revise what is created

integrated projects — assessment tasks that involve multiple learning areas, wherein selected components of each learning area are measured and evaluated

measurement — the use of a systematic methodology to observe musical behaviors in order to represent the magnitude of performance capability, task completion, and/or concept attainment

metacognition — thinking about one's own thinking, learning, and/or development

multi-level — when describing scoring guides, referring to three or more levels of achievement in relation to a given criterion

multiple criterion — when describing scoring guides, those that involve two or more criteria

musical learning area — a category of musical skill and/or content that is determined by the musical behaviors elicited during the learning and assessment of those skills and content

objectivism — a meta-theoretical framework that subsumes learning theories founded on the proposition that all knowledge is fixed fact and can be gained in a context-free environment

performance indicator — a specific statement that describes a performance that indicates the acquisition of required knowledge and/or skill

point system rubric — a type of scoring guide in which the levels of achievement for each criterion are assigned a number of points rather than a descriptor

portfolio — a collection of a student's work that he/she feels best represents his/her progress in a particular content area

procedural application — critical thinking during musical performance, updating and altering musical performance to suit the immediate musical conditions or context

process — having to do with the sequence of events and behaviors that occur during a particular musical course of action

product — the end result of the music making process

reflection — the systematic review and evaluation of one's previous achievements or accomplishments in order to respond to current needs or questions; in music, the examination of previous musical experiences in relation to one's present musical needs or questions

reliability — the extent to which a task consistently measures what it is intended to measure

rubric — another name for a type of scoring guide that expresses more than one level of achievement for one or more criteria

scoring guide — a general term that describes a specific combination of criteria and achievement levels that are used in the measurement of musical knowledge as expressed in a specific assessment task

self-assessment — the process by which metacognition and reflection are employed to review one's personal progress or achievement for the purpose of identifying one's strengths and weaknesses

single criterion — when describing scoring guides, those that involve one criterion only

situated cognition — the mode of thinking related to a particular skill or knowledge application that is available only when one is involved in an activity that is situated within the same context in which the skill or knowledge application was originally acquired; for example, in order to "think like a singer," one must be singing

task design parameter — an essential facet of a finished assessment task that is predetermined during the design of the task

task piloting — the small-scale administration of a task to test its efficacy, reliability, and/or validity

task scope — having to do with the extent of content or skill coverage within a task

task target — a specific musical behavior or skill that serves as an assessable component of a task

task target area — a category of specific musical behaviors and/or skills that are relevant to a specific assessment response mode

triangulation — the employment of assessment data from the performing, creating, and responding assessment modes to determine the degree to which a student has acquired a specific musical concept or knowledge

validity — the degree to which a task measures what it is supposed to measure; for general music, this is primarily related to the content of the task and its relationship to the purpose of the task (also called content validity)

variable — any aspect of a situation that can vary or have more than one possible outcome

weighted point system rubric — a scoring guide in which the criteria are assigned different numbers of points according to their importance to the overall task and their desired effect on the final score

well-structured content domain — a content area in which the majority of cases can be explained by general rules or principles

References

Apfelstadt, H. (1984). Effects of melodic perception on pitch discrimination and vocal accuracy in kindergarten children. *Journal of Research in Music Education 32*, 15-24.

Atterbury, B. & Silcox, L. (1993). The effect of piano accompaniment on kindergartner's developmental singing ability. *Journal for Research in Music Education 41*(1), 40-47.

Bamberger, J. (1991). *The mind behind the musical ear.* Cambridge: Harvard University Press.

Bamberger, J. (1994). Coming to hear in a new way. In R. Aiello (Ed.), *Musical perceptions* (pp. 131-151). New York: Oxford University Press.

Bartholomew, D. (1987). Problems with Piagetian conservation and musical objects. *Bulletin of the Council for Research in Music Education 93*, 27-40.

Beane, M. B. (1989). *Focus on fine arts.* Washington, D.C.: Educational Resources Information Center. (ERIC Document Reproduction no. ED 317 477).

Benson, W. (1967). *Creative projects in musicianship: CMP₄.* Washington, D.C.: Contemporary Music Project for Creativity in Music Education, Music Educators National Conference.

Bettison, G. M. (1976, March). *The relationship between the conservation of certain melodic materials and standard Piagetian tasks.* Paper presented at the meeting of the Music Educators National Conference, Atlantic City, NJ.

Biasini, A.; Thomas, R.; & Pogonowski, L. (n.d.). *MMCP Interaction* (2nd ed.). Bardonia, NY: Media Materials, Inc.

Boardman, E. (Ed.). (1989). *Dimensions of musical thinking.* Reston VA: MENC.

Botvin, G. J. (1974). Acquiring conservation of melody and cross-modal transfer through successive approximation. *Journal of Research in Music Education 22*, 226-233.

Boyle, J. D. & Radocy, R. (1987). *Measurement and evaluation of musical experiences.* New York: Schirmer Books.

Brophy, T. (1995). Critical thinking in music: A cognitive-developmental perspective. Unpublished manuscript.

Brophy, T. (1996). Concept mapping: An alternative assessment. *The Orff Echo 28*(2), 22-23.

Brophy, T. (1997). Authentic assessment of vocal pitch accuracy in first through third grade children. *Contributions to Music Education 24*(1), 57-70.

Brophy, T. (1998). Stimulus integration in alto xylophone playing experiences: A developmental perspective. *Southeastern Journal of Music Education {1995} 7*, 108-128.

Brophy, T. S. (1999). The melodic improvisations of children ages six through twelve: A developmental perspective. (Doctoral dissertation, University of Kentucky, 1998). *Dissertation Abstracts International 59*(09), A3386.

Brophy, T. S. (in press). Developing Improvisation in General Music. *Music Educators Journal.*

Brown, J. S., Collins, A. & Duguid, P. (1989). Situated cognition and the culture of learning. *Educational Researcher 18*(1), 32-42.

Cooper, N. (1993). Selected factors related to children's singing accuracy (Doctoral dissertation, Indiana University, 1992). *Dissertation Abstracts International 53*, 4244A.

Csikszentmihalyi, M. (1988). Society, culture, and person: A systems view of creativity. In R. Sternberg (Ed.) *The nature of creativity: Contemporary psychological perspectives* (pp. 325-339). New York: Cambridge University Press.

Csikszentmihalyi, M. (1996). Creativity: Flow and the psychology of discovery and invention. New York: HarperCollins Publishers.

Darling-Hammond, L. (1994). Performance-based assessment and educational equity. *Harvard Educational Review 64*(1), 30-34.

Davidson, L. (1994). Songsinging by young and old: A developmental approach to music. In R. Aiello (Ed.), *Musical perceptions* (pp. 99-130). New York: Oxford University Press.

Davidson, L. & Scripp, L. (1988). Young children's musical representations: Windows on music cognition. In J. A. Sloboda (Ed.) *Generative processes in music: The psychology of performance, improvisation, and composition* (pp. 195-230). Oxford: Clarendon Press.

DeTurk, M. (1989). Critical and creative thinking in music. In E. Boardman (Ed.) *Dimensions of Musical Thinking* (pp. 21-32). Reston, VA: MENC.

Doig, D. (1941). Creative music: I. Music composed for a given text. *Journal of Educational Research 35*(4), 262-275.

Doig, D. (1942a). Creative music: II. Music composed on a given subject. *Journal of Educational Research 35*(5), 344-355.

Doig, D. (1942b). Creative music: III. Music composed to illustrate given music problems. *Journal of Educational Research 36*(4), 241-253.

Dowling, W. J. (1988). Tonal structure and children's early learning of music. In J. A. Sloboda (Ed.) *Generative processes in music: The psychology of performance, improvisation, and composition* (pp. 113-128). Oxford: Clarendon Press.

Duffy, T. M. & Jonassen, D. H. (1991). Constructivism: new implications for instructional technology? *Educational Technology 31*(5), 7-12.

Elliott, D. J. (1995). *Music matters: A new philosophy of music education.* New York: Oxford University Press.

Erdei, P. (Ed.) (1974). *150 American folk songs to sing, read, and play.* New York: Boosey and Hawkes.

Ernst, Karl D. (1968). The nature and nurture of creativity [Subject area V committee report]. In R. Choate (Ed.), *Documentary report of the Tanglewood Symposium* (pp. 127-130).

Flohr, John W. (1979). Musical improvisation behavior of young children (Doctoral dissertation, University of Illinois at Urbana-Champaign, 1980). *Dissertation Abstracts International 40*(10), A5355.

Flohr, John W. (1984). *Young children's improvisations: A longitudinal study.* (Paper presented at the 49th meeting of the Music Educators National Conference, Chicago, IL, March, 1984). Washington, D.C.: Educational Resources Information Center. (ERIC Document Reproduction Service No. ED 255 318).

Foley, E. (1975). Effects of training in conservation of tonal and rhythmic patterns on second grade children. *Journal of Research in Music Education 23*(4), 240-248.

Gardner, H. (1983). *Frames of mind: The theory of multiple intelligences.* New York: Basic Books.

Gardner, H. (1993). *Multiple intelligences: The theory in practice.* New York: Basic Books.

Gardner, H. (1999, June). Music in the family of human intelligences. Paper presented at the Cognitive Processes of Children Engaged in Musical Activity Conference, Urbana, Illinois.

Geringer, J. (1983). The relationship of pitch-matching and pitch-discrimination abilities of preschool and fourth grade students. *Journal of Research in Music Education 31*, 91-99.

Goetze, M. (1986). Factors affecting children's singing (Doctoral dissertation, University of Colorado, 1985). *Dissertation Abstracts International 46*, 2955A.

Goetze, M. & Horii, Y. (1989). A comparison of the pitch accuracy of group and individual singing in young children. *Bulletin of the Council for Research in Music Education 99*, 57-73.

Goetze, M.; Cooper, N.; & Brown, C. (1990). Recent research on singing in the general music classroom. *Bulletin of the Council for Research in Music Education 104,* 16-37.

Gorder, W. D. (1976). An investigation of divergent production abilities as constructs of musical creativity, (Doctoral dissertation, University of Illinois, Urbana-Champaign). *Dissertation Abstracts International 37*(01), A171.

Gorder, W. D. (1980). Divergent production abilities as constructs of musical creativity. *Journal of Research in Music Education 28*(1), 34-42.

Gordon, E. E. (1965). *Music aptitude profile.* Chicago: GIA Publications.

Gordon, E. E. (1978). *Pattern sequence and learning in music.* Chicago: GIA Publications.

Gordon, E. E. (1984). *Learning sequences in music: Skill, content, and patterns.* Chicago: GIA Publications.

Gordon, E. E. (1987). *The nature, description, measurement, and evaluation of music aptitudes.* Chicago: GIA Publications.

Gould, O. (1969). Developing specialized programs in singing in the general school. *Bulletin of the Council for Research in Music Education 17,* 57-73.

Gratton, M. (1992). The effect of three vocal models on uncertain singers' ability to match and discriminate pitches (Masters thesis, McGill University, Canada, 1989). *Masters Abstracts International 30*(4), p. 986.

Green, G. (1990). The effect of vocal modeling on the pitch accuracy of general school children. *Journal of Research in Music Education 38,* 225-231.

Green, G. (1994). Unison versus individual singing in general students' vocal pitch accuracy. *Journal of Research in Music Education 42,* 105-114.

Guilford, J. P. (1967). *The nature of human intelligence.* New York: McGraw-Hill Book Company.

Hair, H. I. (1977). Discrimination of tonal direction by first grade children on verbal and nonverbal tasks. *Journal of Research in Music Education 25,* 197-210.

Hair, H. I. (1981). Verbal identification of music concepts. *Journal of Research in Music Education 29,* 11-21.

Hair, H. I. (1987). Descriptive vocabulary and visual choices: Children's responses to conceptual changes in music. *Bulletin of the Council for Research in Music Education 91,* 59-64.

Hargreaves, D. J. (1986). *The developmental psychology of music.* New York: Cambridge University Press.

Hargreaves, D. J. & Zimmerman, M. P. (1992). Developmental theories of music learning. In R. Colwell (Ed.) *Handbook of research on music teaching and learning,* pp. 377-391. Reston, Virginia: Music Educators National Conference.

Hickey, M. (1999). Assessment rubrics for music composition. *Music Educators Journal 85*(4).

Hounchell, R. F. (1986). A study of creativity and music reading as objectives of music education as contained in statements in the "Music Educators Journal" from 1914 to 1970. (Doctoral dissertation, Indiana University, 1985). *Dissertation Abstracts International 46*(12), A3643.

Inhelder, B. & Piaget, J. (1964). *The early growth of logic in the child.* The Norton Library.

Jones, R. L. (1976). The development of the child's conception of meter in music. *Journal of Research in Music Education 34,* 88-100.

Jordan-DeCarbo, J. (1982). Same/different discrimination techniques, readiness training, pattern treatment, and sex on aural discrimination and singing of tonal patterns by kindergartners. *Journal of Research in Music Education 30,* 237-246.

Kratus, J. (1985). The use of melodic and rhythmic motives in the original songs of children ages five to thirteen. *Contributions to Music Education 12*, 1-8.

Kratus, J. (1986). Rhythm, melody, motive, and phrase characteristics of original songs by children ages five to thirteen. (Doctoral dissertation, Northwestern University, 1985). *Dissertation Abstracts International 46*(11), A3281.

Kratus, J. (1989). A time analysis of the compositional processes used by children ages seven to eleven. *Journal of Research in Music Education 37*(1), 5-20.

Kratus, J. (1991b). Orientation and intentionality as components of creative musical activity. *Perspectives in Music Education 2*, 4-8. [Reprinted from C. Doane & J. W. Richmond (Eds.), *Proceedings of the 1989 Suncoast Music Education Forum* (pp. 93-104). Westport, CT: Greenwood Press.]

Kratus, J. (1994). Relationships among children's music audiation and their compositional processes and products. *Journal of Research in Music Education 42*(2), 115-130.

Kratus, J. (1995). The effect of composing tempo on the musical characteristics of children's compositions. *Contributions to Music Education 22*, 40-48.

Kratus, J. (1996). A developmental approach to teaching musical improvisation. *International Journal of Music Education 26*, 27-38.

Larsen, R. L. (1973). Levels of conceptual development melodic permutation concepts based on Piaget's theories. *Journal of Research in Music Education 21*(3), 256-263.

Larsen, R. L. & Boody, C. G. (1971). Some implications for music education in the work of Jean Piaget. *Journal of Research in Music Education 19*(1), 35-50.

Lepherd, L. (Ed.) (1995). Music education in international perspective: National systems. Toowoomba, Australia: University of Southern Queensland Press.

Levinowitz, L.; Barnes, P.; Guerrini, S.; Clement, M.; April, P. D.; & Morey, M. J. (1997). An investigation of the use of the Singing Voice Development Measure in the general music classroom. In R. Cutietta (Chair), *Symposium on Research in General Music.* Symposium conducted in Tucson, Arizona.

Lindeman, C. (1997). Frontlines. *Teaching Music 4*(6), 6-7.

Marzano, R. J.; Brandt, R. S.; Huges, C. S.; Jones, B. F.; Presseisen, B. Z.; Rankin, S. C.; & Suhor, C. (1988). *Dimensions of thinking: A framework for curriculum and instruction.* Alexandria, VA: Association for Supervision and Curriculum Development.

May, W. T. (1989). *Understanding and critical thinking in general art and music: General Subjects Center series no. 8.* Washington, D.C.: Educational Resources Information Center. (ERIC Document Reproduction Service no. ED 308 982).

Miller, B. (1999, June). *Learning through composition in elementary classroom.* Paper presented at the Cognitive Processes of Children Engaged in Musical Activity Conference, Urbana, Illinois.

Mizener, C. (1993). Attitudes of children toward singing and choir participation and assessed singing skill. *Journal of Research in Music Education 41,* 233-245.

Moore, R. (1994). Effects of age, sex, and melodic/harmonic patterns on the vocal pitch-matching skills of talented eight- through eleven-year-olds. *Journal for Research in Music Education 42,* 5-13.

Moorhead, G. E. & Pond, D. (1978). *Music of Young Children.* Pillsbury Foundation for Advancement of Music Education: Santa Barbara, CA. (original work published in 1941).

Music Educators National Conference (MENC). (1994). *What every young American should know and be able to do in the arts: National Standards for arts education.* Reston, VA: Author.

National Assessment Governing Board (NAGB). (1994). *Arts education assessment framework.* Washington, D.C.: The Council of Chief State School Officers.

Nelson, D. J. (1984). The conservation of rhythm in Suzuki violin students: A task validation study. *Journal of Research in Music Education 37*(2) 93-103.

Norton, D. (1979). Relationships of music ability and intelligence to auditory and visual conservation of the kindergarten child. *Journal of Research in Music Education 27*, 3-13.

Norton, D. (1980). Interrelationships among music aptitude, IQ, and auditory conservation. *Journal of Research in Music Education 28*, 207-217.

Novak, J. (1990a). Concept mapping: A useful tool for science education. *Journal of Research in Science Teaching 27*(10), 937-49.

Novak, J. (1990b). Concept mapping and Vee diagrams: Two metacognitive tools to facilitate meaningful learning. *Instructional Science 19*(1), 29-52.

Novak, J. (1991). Clarify with concept maps. *Science Teacher 58*(7), 44-49.

Okins, A. (1997). *Performance assessments for the general music curriculum.* Unpublished masters thesis, University of St. Thomas, Minneapolis, MN.

Paul, R. W. (1984). Critical thinking: Fundamental to education for a free society. *Educational Researcher 48*, 4-14.

Perney, J. (1976). Musical tasks related to the development of the conservation of metric time. *Journal of Research in Music Education 24*, 159-168.

Pflederer, M. (1964). The responses of children to musical tasks embodying Piaget's principle of conservation. *Journal of Research in Music Education 12*, 251-268.

Pflederer, M. (1966a). How children conceptually organize musical sounds. *Bulletin of the Council for Research in Music Education 7*, 1-12.

Pflederer, M. (1966b). A study of the conservation of tonal and rhythmic patterns in general school children. *California Journal of Educational Research 17*(2), 52-62.

Pflederer, M. (1967). Conservation laws applied to the development of musical intelligence. *Journal of Research in Music Education 15*(3), 215-223.

Pflederer, M. & Sechrest, L. (1968a). Conservation in musical experience. *Psychology in the Schools 5*(2), 99-105.

Pflederer, M. & Sechrest, L. (1968b). Conservation-type responses of children to musical stimuli. *Bulletin of the Council for Research in Music Education 13*, 19-36.

Piaget, J. (1969a). *The child's conception of the world.* Totowa, N. J.: Littlefield, Adams, & Co.

Piaget, J. (1969b). *The psychology of the child.* New York: Basic Books.

Piaget, J. (1977). *The development of thought: Equilibration of logical structures.* New York: The Viking Press.

Prével, M. (1979). Emergent patterning in children's musical improvisations. *Canadian Music Educator 15*, 13-15.

Price, H., Yarbrough, C., Jones, M. & Moore, R. (1994). Effects of male timbre, falsetto, and sine-wave models on interval matching by inaccurate singers. *Journal of Research in Music Education 42*(4), 269-284.

Reinhardt, D. A. (1990). Preschool children's use of rhythm in improvisation. *Contributions to Music Education 17*, 7-19.

Richardson, C. P. & Whitaker, N. L. (1992). Critical Thinking and Music Education. In R. Colwell (Ed.), *Handbook of Research on Music Teaching and Learning* (pp. 546-560). Reston, VA: MENC.

Robinson, M. (1995). Alternative assessment techniques for teachers. *Music Educators Journal 81*(5), 28-34.

Rutkowski, J. (1990). The measurement and evaluation of children's singing voice development. *Quarterly Journal of Music Teaching and Learning 1*(1 & 2), 81-95.

Rutkowski, J. (1996). The effectiveness of individual/small group singing activities on kindergartners' use of singing voice and developmental music aptitude. *Journal of Research in Music Education 44*(4), 353-368.

Rutkowski, J. & Miller, M. S. (1997). A longitudinal study of general students' acquisition of their singing voices. In R. Cutietta (Chair), *Symposium on Research in General Music.* Symposium conducted in Tucson, Arizona.

Saunders, T. C. (1996, April). *Authentic music performance assessment: What, why, and how?* Paper (session) presented at the meeting of the Music Educators National Conference, Kansas City, MO.

Serafine, M. L. (1979). A measure of meter conservation in music, based on Piaget's theory. *Genetic Psychology Monographs 99*, 185-229.

Serafine, M. L. (1980). Piagetian research in music. *Bulletin of the Council for Research in Music Education 62*, 1-21.

Serafine, M. L. (1988). *Music as cognition: The development of thought in sound.* New York: Columbia University Press.

Shehan-Campbell, P. & Scott-Kassner, C. (1995). *Music in childhood: From preschool through the general grades.* New York: Schirmer Books.

Sims, W.; Moore, R.; & Kuhn, T. (1982). Effects of female and male vocal stimuli, tonal pattern length, and age on vocal pitch-matching abilities in young children in England and the United States. *Psychology of Music* [Special Issue], 104-108.

Sloboda, J. A. (1985). *The musical mind: the cognitive psychology of music* (Oxford psychology series no. 5). Oxford: Clarendon Press.

Smale, M. (1988). An investigation of pitch accuracy of four- and five-year-old singers (Doctoral dissertation, University of Minnesota, 1987). *Dissertation Abstracts International 48,* 2013A.

Small, A. R. & McCachern, F. L. (1983). The effect of male and female vocal modeling on pitch-matching accuracy of first grade children. *Journal of Research in Music Education 31*(3), 227-233.

Spiro, R. J.; Feltovich, P. J.; Jacobson, M. J.; and Couulson, R. L. (1991). Cognitive flexibility, constructivism, and hypertext: Random access instruction for advanced knowledge acquisition in ill-structured domains. *Education Technology 18*(1), 24-33.

Spiro, R. J.; Vispoel, W. P.; Schmitz, J. G.; Samarapungavan, A.; & Boerger, A. E. (1987). Knowledge acquisition for application: Cognitive flexibility and transfer in complex content domains. In B. K. Britten & S. M. Glynn (Eds.). *Executive control processes in reading* (pp. 177-199). Hillsdale, NJ: Lawrence Erlbaum Associates.

Stauffer, S. (1986). An investigation of the effects of melodic and harmonic context on the development of singing ability in primary grade children (Doctoral dissertation, University of Michigan, 1985). *Dissertation Abstracts International 46,* 1862A.

Steen, A. (1992). *Exploring Orff.* Schott Music Corporation: New York.

Sterling, P. (1985). A developmental study of the effects of accompanying harmonic context on children's vocal pitch accuracy of familiar melodies (Doctoral dissertation, University of Miami, 1984). *Dissertation Abstracts International 45,* 2436A.

Swanwick, K. & Tillman, J. (1986). The sequence of musical development: A study of children's composition. *British Journal of Music Education 3*(3), 305-339.

Swanwick, K. (1988). *Music, mind and education.* Routledge: London.

Swanwick, K. (1994). *Musical knowledge: Intuition, analysis, and music education.* Routledge: London.

Swanwick, K. & Tillman, J. (1986). The sequence of musical development: A study of children's composition. *British Journal of Music Education 3*(3), 305-339.

Thomas, R. B. (n.d.) *MMCP Synthesis.* Bardonia, NY: Media Materials, Inc.

Tillman, J. (1989). Towards a model of the development of children's musical creativity. *Canadian Music Educator 30*(2), 169-174.

Upitis, R. (1989). The craft of composition: Helping children create music with computer tools. *Psychomusicology 8*(2), 151-162.

Upitis, R. (1992). *Can I play you my song? The compositions and invented notations of children.* Portsmouth, New Hampshire: Heinemann Educational Books, Inc.

Vaughan, M. M. (1971). Music as model and metaphor in the cultivation and measurement of creative behavior in children. (Doctoral dissertation, University of Georgia, Athens). *Dissertation Abstracts International 32*(10), A5833.

Vaughan, M. M. (1973). Cultivating creative behavior: Energy levels in the process of creativity. *Music Educators Journal 59*(8), 35-37.

Wang, C. & Kageff, L. (1985, March). *Effects of two modes of teaching on musical creativity of second graders.* Paper presented at the meeting of the Southern Division MENC, Mobile, Alabama.

Webster, P. R. (1977). A factor of intellect approach to creative thinking in music. (Doctoral dissertation, University of Rochester, Rochester, New York). *Dissertation Abstracts International 38*(6), A3136.

Webster, P. R. (1987a). Conceptual bases for creative thinking in music. In Peery, J. C.; Peery, I. W.; and Draper, T. W. (Eds.), *Music and child development* (pp. 158-176). New York: Springer-Verlag.

Webster, P. R. (1987b). Refinement of a measure of creative thinking in music. In C. K. Madsen and C. A. Prickett (Eds.), *Applications of research in music education* (pp. 257-271). Tuscaloosa: University of Alabama Press.

Webster, P. R. (1988). Creative thinking in music: Approaches to research. In J. T. Gates (Ed.), *Music education in the United States: Contemporary issues* (pp. 66-81). Tuscaloosa: University of Alabama Press.

Webster, P. R. (1991). Creativity as creative thinking. In D. Hamann (Ed.) *Creativity in the classroom: The best of MEJ* (pp. 25-34). Reston VA: Music Educators National Conference. (original work published in 1990).

Webster, P. R. (1992). Research on creative thinking in music: The assessment literature. In R. Colwell (Ed.), *Handbook of Research on Music Teaching and Learning* (pp. 266-280). Reston, VA: MENC.

Welch, G. (1994). The assessment of singing. *Psychology of Music 22,* 3-19.

Welch, G.; Howard, D.; Rush, C. (1989). Real-time visual feedback in the development of vocal pitch accuracy in singing. *Psychology of Music 17,* 146-157.

Wells, R. (1997). Designing curricula based on the standards. *Music Educators Journal 84*(1), 34-39.

Whitcomb, R. (1999). Writing rubrics for the music classroom. *Music Educators Journal 85*(6), 26-32.

Wilson, S. J. & Wales, R. J. (1995). An exploration of children's musical compositions. *Journal of Research in Music Education 43*(2), 94-111.

Woodford, P. (1995). Development of a theory of transfer of learning based on Dewey's conception of reflective thinking. (Doctoral dissertation, Northwestern University, 1994). *Dissertation Abstracts International 56*(3), A859.

Woodford, P. (1997). *Transfer in music as social and reconstructive inquiry.* In R. Rideout (Ed.), On the sociology of music education (pp. 43-54). Norman, OK: University of Oklahoma.

Wuytack, J. (1994). *Musica activa: An approach to music education.* New York: Schott.

Yarbrough, C.; Bowers, J.; & Benson, W. (1992). The effect of vibrato on the pitch-matching accuracy of certain and uncertain singers. *Journal of Research in Music Education 40,* 30-38.

Yarbrough, C.; Green, G.; Benson, W.; & Bowers, J. (1991). Inaccurate singers: An exploratory study of variables affecting pitch-matching. *Bulletin of the Council for Research in Music Education 107,* 23-34.

Zimmerman, M. P. (1970). Percept and concept: Implications of Piaget. *Music Educators Journal 56*(6), 49-50+.

Zimmerman, M. P. & Sechrest, L. (1970). Brief focused instruction and musical concepts. *Journal of Research in Music Education 18*(1), 25-36.

Zimmerman, M. P. & Webster, P. R. (1983). Conservation of rhythmic and tonal patterns of second through sixth grade children. *Bulletin of the Council for Research in Music Education 73,* 28-49.

Some Resources for Assessment Ideas and Research

Barrett, J.; McCoy, C.; & Veblen, K. (1997). Sound ways of knowing: Music in the interdisciplinary curriculum. Schirmer Books: New York.

Boyle, J.D. (1996). The National Standards: Some implications for assessment. In MENC (Ed.) Aiming for Excellence: The Impact of the Standards Movement on Music Education (pp. 109-116). MENC: Reston, Virginia.

Brophy, T. (1999). Orff Schulwerk in middle and late childhood. *The Orff Echo 31*(4), 7-10.

Brophy, T. (1997). Reporting progress with developmental profiles. *Music Educators Journal 84*(1), 24-27.

Brophy, T. (1997). Authentic assessment of vocal pitch accuracy in first through third grade children. *Contributions to Music Education 24*(1), 57-70.

Brophy, T. (1996). Building music literacy through guided composition. *Music Educators Journal 83*(3), 15-18.

Brophy, T. (1996). Concept mapping: an alternative assessment. *The Orff Echo 28*(2), 22-23.

Colwell, R. (1996). Why we shouldn't change the standards. In MENC (Ed.) Aiming for Excellence: The Impact of the Standards Movement on Music Education (pp. 117-124). MENC: Reston, Virginia.

Cope, C. (1996). Steps toward effective assessment. *Music Educators Journal 83*(1), 39-42.

Freedman, R. L. H. (1994). Open-ended questioning: A handbook for educators. Addison-Wesley: New York.

Hart, Diane (1994). Authentic assessment: A handbook for educators. Addison-Wesley: New York.

Hickey, M. (1999). Assessment rubrics for music composition. *Music Educators Journal 85*(4).

Lehman, P. (1998). *Grading practices in music.* Paper presented at Assessment Power Session held at the meeting of MENC— The National Association for Music Education, Phoenix, Arizona.

Marchetti, Donna, Ed. (1996, Winter). Special Issue: Assessment. *The Orff Echo 28*(2).

MENC (1996). Performance standards for music grades PreK-12: Strategies and benchmarks for assessing progress toward the National Standards. MENC: Reston, Virginia.

Persky, H. R.; Sandene, B. A.; & Askew, J.M. (1998). *The NAEP 1997 Arts Report Card* (NCES publication 1999-486). Washington, DC: Department of Education, Office of Educational Research and Improvement, National Center for Education Statistics.

Robinson, M. (1995). Alternative assessment techniques for teachers. *Music Educators Journal 81*(5), 28-34.

Shuler, S. (1996). The effects of the National Standards on assessment (and vice versa). In MENC (Ed.) Aiming for Excellence: The Impact of the Standards Movement on Music Education (pp. 81-108). MENC: Reston, Virginia.

Spaeth, J. (Ed.). (1999). Special Focus: Assessment in Music Education. *Music Educators Journal 86*(2)

Whitcomb, R. (1999). Writing rubrics for the music classroom. *Music Educators Journal 85*(6), 26-32.

Wiggins, J. (1999). Teacher control and creativity. *Music Educators Journal 85*(5), 30-35+.

Online Sources for Music Assessment Research and Ideas

The reader will find further information and assessment links at the following web sites:

MENC – the National Association for Music Education
http://www.menc.org

Music Assessment Web Site
http://www.music.utah.edu/assessment/

National Assessment of Educational Progress
http://nces.ed.gov/naepGlossary

The Educational CyberPlayground
http://www.edu-cyberpg.com

The Music Education Directory
http://www.music-ed-directory.com

Index

About the Author

Timothy S. Brophy has taught elementary general music for 16 years in Ohio, Virginia, Tennessee, and Kentucky. He holds a Bachelor of Music Education degree from the University of Cincinnati College-Conservatory of Music, a Master of Music from the University of Memphis, and Ph.D. in Music Education from the University of Kentucky.

Dr. Brophy is widely published in music education journals and is an active clinician in elementary general music teaching and assessment at the local, state, national, and international levels. His teaching and research have been recognized locally and nationally with numerous awards, and he was a 1998 Disney American Teacher Award honoree in the Performing Arts. Dr. Brophy's elementary choirs have recorded five albums. He is recognized as a national leader in classroom music assessment.